Translation in Undergraduate Degree Programmes

# Benjamins Translation Library

The Benjamins Translation Library aims to stimulate research and training in translation and interpreting studies. The Library provides a forum for a variety of approaches (which may sometimes be conflicting) in a socio-cultural, historical, theoretical, applied and pedagogical context. The Library includes scholarly works, reference works, post-graduate text books and readers in the English language.

## EST Subseries

The European Society for Translation Studies (EST) Subseries is a publication channel within the Library to optimize EST's function as a forum for the translation and interpreting research community. It promotes new trends in research, gives more visibility to young scholars' work, publicizes new research methods, makes available documents from EST, and reissues classical works in translation studies which do not exist in English or which are now out of print.

## Volume 59

Translation in Undergraduate Degree Programmes
Edited by Kirsten Malmkjær

# Translation in Undergraduate Degree Programmes

*Edited by*

Kirsten Malmkjær

Middlesex University

John Benjamins Publishing Company

Amsterdam / Philadelphia

™ The paper used in this publication meets the minimum requirements
of American National Standard for Information Sciences – Permanence
of Paper for Printed Library Materials, ANSI z39.48-1984.

Library of Congress Cataloging-in-Publication Data

Translation in Undergraduate Degree Programmes / edited by Kirsten
    Malmkjær.
        p.   cm. (Benjamins Translation Library, ISSN 0929–7316 ; v. 59)
    Includes bibliographical references and indexes.
        1. Translating and interpreting--Study and teaching (Higher) I.
    Malmkjær, Kirsten. II. McEnery, Tony, 1964- III. Benjamins translation library ;
    v. 59. IV. Benjamins translation library.

        P306.5.T728  2004
    418'.02'0711-dc22                                                      2004057454
    ISBN 90 272 1665 7 (Eur.) / 1 58811 600 X (US) (Hb; alk. paper)

John Benjamins Publishing Co. · P.O. Box 36224 · 1020 ME Amsterdam · The Netherlands
John Benjamins North America · P.O. Box 27519 · Philadelphia PA 19118-0519 · USA

# Table of contents

# Introduction*

## Translation as an academic discipline

Kirsten Malmkjær

We are privileged, in translation studies in the early part of the twenty first century, to have (largely) made the leap from discussions of how to achieve recognition for our discipline as fit for academic study into discussions of how, as an academic discipline, it can most fruitfully be shaped and pursued. Translation studies, in this century, is a buoyant field where theorists and practitioners frequently come together (often in one person), where the mutual dependencies between research and practice are well understood, and where few doubt the need to work together to improve research, teaching and practice across the board. Of course, a certain lack of awareness of the nature of the discipline and of its actual and potential modes of interacting with its fellow academic disciplines remains in some quarters, and it is still necessary, from time to time, to arm oneself with courage, confidence and some bravado to be taken seriously as a translation scholar or translation theorist ("Goodness, I didn't know there was a theory about that!!!"), but, by and large, translation is now firmly established as an academic discipline.

In the opening paper of this volume, Wolfram Wilss addresses some of the issues that arise from the position of translation within academia, warning against the pursuit of theoretical abstraction to the exclusion of empirical research and teaching designed with the practicalities of everyday translating in mind. This pursuit might have the unfortunate consequence that the profession for which we are preparing our students would lose confidence in the discipline, in which case pursuing translation as an academic subject would no longer be perceived as worthwhile, and the clear advantages of having translation studies firmly entrenched within academia would be lost. These advantages include the obvious image enhancement that accrues over time to academic disciplines: If translation is something you study at university, it must be a true profession like medicine, teaching, accountancy and law. The prospect of a job in this respectable area gives people with an interest in and talent for languages a good reason to pursue them, thereby possibly raising the level of interest in languages at school, even in countries like Britain, where, as Barbour points out, there is very little interest in learning languages other than English.

One means towards avoiding a split between a profession and its academic discipline is to ensure that teaching programmes have face validity for members of those professions in which students might seek employment. For a translation programme to achieve face validity for the translation profession, the profession needs to be convinced that graduates of the programme have acquired at least some of the knowledge and skills necessary for success in the profession. For such programmes to have face validity for students, the students need to feel reasonably confident that the programmes will equip them for a career either in the translation industry itself or in related fields involving cross cultural communication and text editing. The question then is, what kind of programme would have both types of validity, and this book offers a number of models and a number of suggestions for programme content.

Mackenzie stresses the need for programme designers to understand the world of professional translation since a number of translator competencies arise directly from the roles involved in the production of high quality translations. Clearly, one way of providing students themselves with experience of professional translation is to provide placement opportunities for students, and this has the added advantage of involving the profession directly with the students and with the university.

Yet, the position of translation programmes in universities implies a strong emphasis on education as well as on training and on research application as well as professional practice, and the intimate connections between competence and skill, and education and training in translator pedagogy is clear to see in the papers in the volume which discuss these issues directly. Wilss defines translation as 'the activation of a body of knowledge', and Beeby points out that a programme designed to produce professional translators needs to be designed on the basis of a model of translator competence. Bernardini ("The theory behind the practice"), who reserves the term "competencies" for what may otherwise be termed "skills", suggests that professional translators need three "capacities", namely, awareness, reflectiveness and resourcefulness. These, she suggests in her second contribution to this volume, can be greatly enhanced by means of what she terms "discovery learning", in her case of evidence provided by a variety of types of language corpus.

The volume addresses specifically issues that arise in connection with the teaching of translation at undergraduate level. In Britain, this practice is less common than it is in a number of countries across the world, and translator education has tended to be located at post graduate level. However, awareness is growing that a year's engagement with the theory and practice of translation, in whatever balance, is insufficient preparation for work in any branch of the profession, and that many advantages are to be gained by shaping all or part of an undergraduate degree specifically to prepare students to enter the translation profession (or other professions in which translation-related skills are required). In this volume, various models of undergraduate translation provision are described. Clearly, these are in part determined by the structures of higher education within which they are situated, so there is some international variation, and the volume introduces models from Spain (Gonzáles Davies), Slovakia (Toft and Preloznīková), Italy (Bernardini) and Britain (Schäffner). However, most undergraduate translation programmes include the following components in addition to the possible placement already mentioned and in addition to practice and input on language and culture:

–   Input on the history and theory of translation, on the assumption that any programme of education with an applied element should provide some understanding of the concepts and concerns that have entertained thinkers who are interested in the phenomenon and which underlie its practice, and of the history of the development of both the practice and the theory that informs it. It is difficult to understand the way things are unless you know something of the processes and influences that have worked to create the present state. Having such knowledge helps people to feel part of a tradition.

–   Input on the sociology of translation. It is constantly surprising to find how few people, including those who come to university to study translation, are aware of how widespread translation is and how essential a part it plays and has played in intercultural communication and in the shaping of cultures. They seem unaware of how many of the texts that surround and influence us would not have been so readily and widely available but for the mediating intervention of a translator, and this means that they have rarely, if ever, given a thought to the nature of mediated texts. For example, as Schäffner emphasises: that a mediated text is affected by the mediator's interpretation of the original; that the purpose of the mediation affects the outcome of the process (the translation); that the purpose the translation is intended to serve may differ from the purpose the original text was intended to serve; and that the audience for a translation is almost always different from the audience for the original text, which, again, affects the translation.

– Input on translation as a profession.

Interestingly, given the prominence in translating of language skills, relatively little has been written about language teaching for translators. Translation pedagogy can obviously not be equated with or subsumed under language pedagogy, but it is equally obvious that success in translation is predicated upon an ability to operate literately in more than one language; and that most people, whatever their language acquisition histories, need to be exposed to language education and training in order to become literate in *any* language. If it is possible to mold language teaching in such a way that the needs of prospective translators are catered for directly, then, as Berenguer (1996; quoted here by Beeby) remarks, time may be saved in the translation class. Beeby argues for a translation-aware language classroom for potential trainee translators, with a clear orientation towards text and discourse study and practice. She advocates a syllabus based on a model in which translation competence is broken down into six sub-competencies which can be developed on the basis of tasks derived from a number of aspects of discourse and which also relate directly to rhetorical and genre conventions. In similar vein, Bernardini ("The theory behind the practice") suggests that the idea that a prospective translator should first learn language and then learn to translate is unsound; as she puts it, 'one learns the language in order to become a translator' and language and translation learning are maximally beneficial, and most economically undertaken, when they are mutually reinforcing.

The question of whether translation learning and language learning are, in fact, mutually reinforcing is usually asked from the point of view of translation as a method of language teaching and testing. In some countries, as Schjoldager points out, translation remains in widespread use in these areas, whereas the English-speaking world has tended to shun it since the mid-twentieth century. One of the reasons often held up for this is that translation is a difficult task, and Toft and Preloznikova provide some support for this view. They suggest that student demotivation may be diminished through a dialogic approach to teaching where students come to understand that they are not alone in finding the translation task difficult or in making mistakes.

On the other hand, some language students clearly enjoy translation classes, and in her contribution, Sewell suggests that probing this enjoyment can provide clues to what may be wrong with communicative language classes, at least in the eyes of some groups of learners.

But enjoyment alone does not guarantee the efficacy of a teaching and testing methodology, and Schjoldager and Källkvist both point to the urgent need for well designed and controlled research projects aimed at establishing whether foreign language learners taught and tested (partly) through translation tasks learn and respond as efficiently as learners taught and tested without the use of translation tasks.

Although a connection would be hard to establish, it is interesting that the reluctance to introduce translation into the language classroom is most acutely felt in Britain and the United States where, also, enrolment in language classes is notoriously low in both secondary and tertiary education. In his contribution, which closes the volume, Stephen Barbour addresses a number of translation-related problems that arise from this situation.

The first problem, that much is simply not translated, so that monolinguals do not have access to it, might at first be considered a potential advantage for translators: there is plenty of work that awaits them. However, some texts, such as asides in business negotiations, which Barbour mentions, are simply not intended for translation, quite the reverse. Secondly, a monolingual may encounter problems understanding translated texts or texts written in English by non-native speakers, since they will not know how the syntax and semantics of a given source language or of the writer's native language may have influenced a given (translated) text. This puts monolingual speakers of English at a considerable disadvantage as more and more varieties of English develop: Monolinguals may in principle end up without access to a number of varieties of English – perhaps to English as an international language as such – and find themselves unable to communicate satisfactorily at international gatherings where English is used. According to Barbour, people with translator awareness constitute a body of informed people who could help to understand and explain the potential pitfalls which the use of English as an international language presents.

The future of any profession depends, like the future of a species, on many things including the environment, which, in the case of a profession means mainly markets and the public perception of the profession. In Britain, beyond a relatively small number of regular users of translation services and an even smaller number of academics, the translation profession suffers *at best* from a lack of image. In spite of the prominence the profession achieved in the early 2000s in the popular radio-soap, *The Archers*, translation remains largely overlooked among the population as a whole, except when it goes badly wrong, in which case we are all happy to enjoy the traditional howlers about ladies not having babies in the bar, and so on. *At worst*, then, the image of translation is negative.

In this, Britain compares unfavourably with northern Europe, and the British attitude is no doubt connected to the low value placed on multilingualism here. But it is quite out of step with the need for translation between English and other languages, as most of the rest of the world discovered long ago, and if the status quo remains, Britain is likely to see its translation services becoming, so to speak, "Brewed in the UK by Danes, Chinese, etc.", or perhaps imported, like cars. There is obviously nothing intrinsically wrong with importing services or with offering employment to people of many and varied nationalities, a practice which enriches a culture greatly. Nevertheless, if the trend continues, it is fairly obvious that the number of translators with English as their main language will fall, leading to the interesting scenario where English would be virtually unavailable as an L1 in translation and most translation into English would be undertaken by non-native speakers. This trend is already clear to see on the undergraduate programme on which I myself teach. At the time of writing, the first final year of this four year long undergraduate translation honours degree is about to begin. To date, the student intake has not included more than a handful of students with English as their native language and only a handful of students permanently domiciled in the UK. This situation is mirrored in staffing: only one member of the team of people regularly involved in translation teaching is a native speaker of English. I think that these patterns are not unusual in other translation programmes in Britain at both undergraduate and post graduate level.

This situation implies that the syllabus for translation students in Britain might need to differ in one or two respects from those described in this book. For example, when Berenguer (1996; referred to by Beeby this volume) mentions the need to provide exercises to develop students' expertise in the foreign culture, she means by 'foreign culture' a culture other than that in which the students live and study. Clearly, for non-British students studying in the UK, it is more likely to mean the culture in which they live while studying. The period abroad, for these students, often means a period back home with far less concentration on acculturation and language enhancement than on supplementing their learning with courses in topics not available in their British "home" institution.

These are early days, but indications are that these non-British students, who live and learn in the UK, leave us – and in the case of many, join us – with very high English skills, so that the question of directionality of translation is less of an issue for them and for us than is often implied, and joint classes on text analysis and translation enjoy the added dimension of cross linguistic comparisons and much lively discussion of cross cultural comparative text and genre analysis. In spite of the potential disadvantages of this situation for Britain, mentioned above, all this bodes very well for translation pedagogy in a world of closer educational cooperation and integration.

## Note

* The lecture that formed the basis of Stephen Barbour's contribution to this volume was one of a series know as the Sue Myles Memorial Lectures, established in memory of Susan Myles, who moved to Middlesex University (then Middlesex Polytechnic) in 1991, having been Head of German at Haberdasher's Aske's School for Girls. Susan Myles died in November 1997.

## Reference

Berenguer, Laura (1996). 'Didáctica de segundas lenguas en los estudios de traducción'. In Amparo Hurtado Albir (Ed.), *La enseñanza de la traducción* (pp. 9–30). Castelló: Publicacions de la Universitat Jaume I.

# Translation studies*
## A didactic approach

Wolfram Wilss

One lesson we may learn from modern translation studies is that an effective concern for translation shows itself not in the uttering of grand generalities with their often high-sounding verbiage, but in the specific, the concrete, and the immediate. Obviously, in discussing translation studies issues in general and translation teaching issues in particular, one should be as precise and as down-to-earth as possible.

Why is translation suitable as a subject-matter of academic study, or to raise this question in a somewhat different and perhaps more challenging form: What distinguishes everyday, intralingual communication from interlingual, "exceptional" communication? And, going on from this basically theoretically-oriented question to methodological issues: should we discuss translation at a high or very high level of abstraction, apt to make vital practical questions disappear, or should we give preference to empirical matter? I think it is the latter which the world of translation demands of the world of academic learning and which should furnish the criteria for what academic institutions should properly teach. In proceeding along this line, we can point to something real, definite, and valuable in the sense that we discover the so-called "underlying assumptions" about translation, or, less artfully expressed, about the principles which guide the translator in accomplishing more or less intricate translation tasks and understand translational task-specifications.

Of course, questions like this can also be treated – at least to some extent – outside the academic world. Hence, we have to ask ourselves: What does care for translation in the university environment amount to? What is the cash-value of academically-based translator training? What does translation mean in terms of such seemingly prosaic realities as the standards of translation-teaching, the achievement standards for undergraduates and graduates and their functioning in the academic community, the content of syllabus, the role of lectures as compared with that of seminars, the advantages and disadvantages of autonomous learning, the value of standard methods of examining?

Numerous other practical problems beset anyone involved in translation-teaching aimed at the development of translation skills and translation habits of mind. Skills and habits are bared on a "genuine body of knowledge". No one interested in translation as an academic subject-matter can fail to see how it impinges on, and interlocks with, a great many issues which have not traditionally been considered to fall within the scope of translation studies. Nevertheless, we should not be in too great a haste to define translation studies as an interdisciplinary field of study – a "composite" subject of the type that tends from time to time to achieve temporary fashionable status. One reason we should hesitate to do so is that most composite subject-matters seem to be insufficiently closely related to the needs and contours of reality.

What is desirable is that a university course in translation-teaching, in however limited and sketchy a way, should make students immune to recalcitrance towards their subject-matter, by helping them discover for themselves the manner in which the learning of translation relates to translation in the real world. To say this is only to draw out the implication of the phrase "a genuine body of knowledge". To put it in terms immediately relevant to translation teaching: translation teaching has to aim at the clarification of the relationship between the contents and patterns of translation on the one hand and the wider fields of linguistic behaviour and practical translation experience on the other.

Thus, translation teaching must in the final analysis be directed towards the day-to-day purposes of translation work, the communicative targets of translation and the systematization of translation teaching and translation learning. To deal with translation without allowing for the obstinate, the individual, the unmappable and incalculable quality of texts-to-be-translated is unacceptable in translation teaching. There is no point in basing a course in translation on some carefully selected textual highlights, e.g. exclusively on literary texts or on any other, single domain or sub-domain of specific text-type translation. What translation teachers must do is to introduce students to a plurality of related or unrelated fields to prevent premature over-specialization. Finding in their classes no self-evident principle of order, students might be debarred by the vastness of the textual material from working out a principled approach to their professional activities and from recognizing "the contours of reality".

The notion of "contours of reality" reminds us that when we translate, we deal with textual matter which is difficult to cope with because of the absence of interplay between the mind of the source text sender, the translator, and the target text reader(ship). Exceptions confirm the rule. Normally, it is impossible for the intentions of the source text sender and the expectations of the target-text client to be chalked up on a blackboard, or schematized in a textbook. Rather, what the client wants or is in need of must be grasped by individual translators themselves, however imperfectly, and with what has been called "the courage of enormous incompleteness".

Having been involved in translation teaching for more than twenty five years, I sometimes wonder if it is always possible to realize what one is committed to do in regard to pedagogical principles and the nature of the subject matter. We are often told (mostly by people who do not know the first thing about translation) that translation teaching must be improved, but do and can we always realize the full scale of the implications of such a demand? And if we do and can, should we try to reach for the impossible? No one can know or be aware of the whole problem battery we are faced with in classroom teaching. There can be no fixed canon of translation teaching methods, no series of certified and unquestionable teaching values. We may pride ourselves on being free, nowadays, from the methodological prejudice illustrated by the old-fashioned dichotomy of literal *versus* free translation which required of the student – or for that matter, the professional translator – that, faced by a specific translation task, they should do no more and no less than choose either the one or the other approach.

The perspective of translation activities is bound to change from one text situation to the next. The achievement of the right perspective is not (always) possible by an exercise of individual judgment, but by the knowledge of the context of translation, however fragmentary and imperfect this knowledge may be – fragmentary and imperfect for the reason that as a rule there is no dialogue (interaction), or not enough dialogue, between the source text sender and the translator on the one side and between the translator and the target text recipient on the other. If translators simply impose their own interpretation and evaluation on the source text, without tacitly listening to what the text-to-be-translated says, they are not *translating*; they are *teaching* the source text sender and/or the target text reader. That is why I uncompromisingly reject the frequent assertion that a given source text is inadequate for translation. One aspect of dealing with translation from an academic view-point is to pay scrupulous attention both to the message of the source text and the message of the target text – with all the linguistic and sociocultural implications involved in going from source text to target text. The source text provides the basic guidelines for the translator. The individual text, especially in the field of literary translation, has its own profile, is itself a fact of language use and history, and to assume that we have at least some access to that profile, that we are not fabricating illusions (or visions) about it, seems to be entailed by the source text, its coherence, its function, its cultural aspects which commit us to behave in a certain manner when we translate.

To speak of translation as the activation of a body of knowledge at once stirs up the controversy into which the discussion of knowledge has in the past so frequently turned. Is it more sensible to speak of a core of knowledge and peripheral layers of knowledge, or should we try, in analogy to training in two or more foreign languages, to teach a number of domains, possibly at the cost of depth of understanding of one field? In other words: Should there be a sovereign discipline and several fringe subjects, or should we spread our teaching to cover a number of domains at equal rank? And should students whose interests are primarily or exclusively scientific and technical, who are likely to be the great majority in view of professional demands, be compelled to spend part of their notoriously restricted time acquiring knowledge of what may be no more than a smattering of literature?

These are questions which, so far as translation teaching is concerned, are focussed on the techno-scientific pressure exerted on the translation profession. I see no reason to exclude literature from translation teaching as a complementary programme; but the "language for specific purposes formula", in its manifold ramifications, is today receiving more consideration than previously, a development which is due, mainly, to the arrival of the computer; and I do not see rational grounds for opposing the setting up of a strongly modern(ised), computer-oriented course in translation either, focusing not only on machine translation and machine-assisted translation, but also on artificial intelligence and cognitive psychology.

At any rate, the continuation of completely parochial courses is of no help to translation teaching institutes, because it would render them strangely remote from practical professional work. This itself is an indication of the degree to which translation teaching and translator training have developed and, as a result, travelled away from the shadow of traditional "hard-copy" teaching targets and moved to new targets which have become known as "desktop publishing"' and "human/machine interaction", requiring a would-be translator to be equipped with all the knowledge and skills necessary for combining speed ("Fast is smart") and the maintenance of an acceptable degree of quality. Student translators must feel that the impact of the "new age" is reflected in their programmes.

These are, of course, grand aims, and we must ask ourselves whether we can be confident of reaching them. What we can say is that translation teaching has found, or is *en route* towards finding, its own characteristics, in the sense in which history or philology or other traditional academic disciplines have established theirs. Any academic field must have its own characteristic features, and one of the marks of a body of knowledge genuinely related to translation teaching is that it makes it incumbent on us to offer some paramount coordinating effort which will give translation teaching its own unmistakably academic profile.

One of the characteristic features of translation teaching is the combination of knowledge and skills. A discipline such as translation teaching shows that translational information processing in the long run should offer a way of turning the notorious "black box" of the translator into a "white box", more amenable to systematized translation teaching than the analytically almost impenetrable black box. It is interlingual and intercultural information-processing which is the typical, the identifying centre of translation teaching.

The proposition that translation is based on a genuine body of knowledge and skills and that the appropriate discipline for its study is translation teaching seems to be coupled and to move together. It is the nature of translation which determines what translation teaching should be. Translation teaching is a multifarious subject-matter. Take, e.g., the well- known fact that it is difficult, indeed almost impossible to draw a hard-and-fast line around the domain of translation. One has only to mention some great names in translation studies – say Luther, Schleiermacher, Benjamin, Nida, Mounin, the representatives of *Stylistique Comparée* – to remember how many and how various are the interests into which the student translator, in pursuing the relevant study of any of these and many other authors, is likely to be led. Those who remind us of this – whether they know it or not – are in fact strengthening the case for translation teaching as the umbrella discipline of translation studies. This must be a discipline which is flexible enough, of sufficiently general application, and sensitive enough in its touch, its impact and appeal, to be able to take into account, and set in some sort of order, everything that may turn out to be relevant to the study of translation, thereby providing principles for translator behaviour which are spacious enough to accommodate them all.

As said before, there may well be no *single* approach to translation teaching which is, even theoretically, capable of organizing this vast plurality of concerns and specializations. There are simply too many problem areas. To add to the difficulties already noted, the problems are interlocking, so that to dwell on one or two of them, to the exclusion of others, is artificial, and distorts them.

There is the danger of such a multiplication of misconceptions that no amount of dialogical simplification can guarantee the possibility of a dialogue between the various "schools" of translation studies.

The most salient misconception is, as should be clear by now, the belief that there is a royal way in translation teaching methodology. As a reference to creative problem-solving or routine aspects of translation shows, there is no such thing. We must be wary of the danger of translation studies becoming a world of undisciplined and subjective whims and fancies, where every researcher does what is right in his or her own eyes, and where order is imposed not by the strongest arguments, but by the loudest voice. Either/or dichotomies have done translation studies a great deal of harm. What we should strive for is a body of established results which the next generation of researchers and students can build on.

The next stage in translation teaching is probably a concerted effort at the evaluation of translations (not "translation criticism" which seems for the most part to be wayward and largely undisciplined). Common sense takes it for granted that evaluations must be personal. There may be some truth in this, but all the same it is surprising how easily – e.g. in the evaluation of the German translation of Lemprière's dictionary by Lawrence Norfolk – people can say, in a rather dogmatic way, that they agree or disagree with the translation. Agreement and disagreement are presumably no longer appropriate terms. I think there is a good deal of evidence at this juncture that translation studies – and in its wake translation teaching – will have to be more flexible than has been the case in the past.

## Note

* This article touches on a selection of issues which I have dealt with extensively in the following books:

## References

Wilss, W. (1992). *Übersetzungsfertgkeit. Annäherungen an einen komplexen übersetzungspraktischen Begriff.* Tübingen: Narr.
Wilss, W. (1996a). *Übersetzungsunterricht. Eine Einführung.* Tübingen: Narr.
Wilss, W. (1996b). *Knowledge and Skills in Translator Behavior.* Amsterdam and Philadelphia: John Benjamins.

Wilss, W. (1999). *Translation and Interpreting in the 20th Century. Focus on German.* Amsterdam and Philadelphia: John Benjamins.

# The theory behind the practice
## Translator training or translator education?

Silvia Bernardini

> Un sous-titreur et un traducteur médical sont aujourd'hui aussi différents
> qu'un ambulancier et un vendeur de glaces, même si tous les deux utilisent
> une voiture comme outil de travail.
>
> Yves Gambier (2000)

## 1. Introduction: Ambulance drivers and ice-cream sellers

In order to address the topic of this paper, namely the relationship between
different degree courses for language professionals, we could do worse than
consider what the translation profession appears to be like in today's world, or,
more precisely, what the current attitude to, and perception of, the profession
is. And in these regards, I think that Gambier's claim that "A subtitler and a
medical translator are as different from each other as an ambulance driver and
an ice-cream seller, despite the fact that both use a car as an instrument in
their job" is quite revealing of a very common attitude towards the translating
profession, and consequently towards the education of future translators.

The main implication of this statement is not, I would suggest, that medical
translators and subtitlers face very different tasks in their daily work. Few
would deny this. Rather, here general translation skills are compared to an
instrument, a car. What this statement is implicitly saying is that translating
skills can be learnt and automatised, in the same way as one learns to drive a car.
They must be swiftly mastered and set aside (with the further implication that
they *can* be swiftly mastered, that they are cognitively "easy", but I'll leave this
for the moment), in order to start acquiring the real, specific skills of the job, be
it subtitling, medical translation etc. The professional profile of a translator, in

other words, is only minimally to do with general translating skills: the subject matter and situational constraints of her job have a more important role to play in her profession than the general ability to translate. The conclusion to be drawn by institutions concerned with the education of language professionals is obvious: specialisation at all costs.

I do not intend this summary discussion as a critique of Gambier, whose views on the subject are not, I believe, in contrast with those expressed here. This statement, however, summarises a view of translation that seems to underpin, at various levels, current translation-related policies and attitudes, in Europe at least. Consider for instance the position taken by the EU and especially by the European Commission translating services. In a booklet titled *Multilinguismo e traduzione – Il Servizio di traduzione della Commissione europea* (*Multilingualism and translation: The translation service of the European Commission*), published by the European Communities, it is stated that candidates for training periods and permanent jobs alike need not have an educational background in translation: would-be translators need only have a University degree, perfect knowledge of the mother tongue, and in-depth knowledge of two other official languages of the Union, including either English or French (pp. 9–11). No mention is made either of a linguistics-oriented background, or of translation theory and/or practice. Professional expertise as language mediators is given the same recognition as a background in economics, finance, law etc.. If we look at in-house training (p. 17), we find a similar picture: area knowledge, computer skills, and language knowledge are virtually the only aspects focused upon.

If this is the case at what is probably one of the largest and most prestigious (translation) institutions in Europe, we should not be surprised to find the same picture at the other end of the scale, the very local level. A questionnaire distributed to Italian business people during a survey of the translation market in Emilia Romagna, an economically thriving region of Italy (Chiaro & Nocella 1999: 365), shows a similar lack of concern with translation-specific skills. The authors report that a) a mere quarter of their interviewees claimed that they employ personnel with some sort of linguistic background for translation related jobs, and b) that over 54% of those they employ have in fact had no formal linguistic/translational instruction. When asked whether they agreed or disagreed with the statement that "translation is easy if you know two languages", 51% of interviewees agreed/strongly agreed, whereas only 27% disagreed/strongly disagreed. On a more comforting note, over three quarters of the interviewees claimed that knowledge of the language of their sector is crucial. The authors wonder, however, whether cultural differences may not be equally important, especially in marketing products: the business people taking part in this survey appear to be utterly unaware of such a possibility.

Potential employers are asking for specialised professionals, with a good command of one or more foreign languages and of the mother tongue, possibly with some knowledge of the technical language of their field, good area knowledge and computer skills. These sound undoubtedly like sensible requests. And yet one might wonder whether the only, or main aim of educators is that of passing on to their students a number of competencies and specific skills in order to satisfy the market requirements. In what follows I shall claim that in so doing they might in fact do a bad service to the students and to their prospective employers: *training* someone through a transfer of knowledge is relatively easy and fast, but hardly a generative process. On the other hand, *educating* a student takes time and effort, but one can trust that she can then go out and learn the rest for herself.

I have just surreptitiously introduced two central notions of this paper, namely *training* and *education*. I shall now move on to explain my understanding of these notions, particularly as they relate to the priorities of undergraduate and postgraduate degree courses for translators.

## 2.    Translator training or translator education?

According to Widdowson (1984: 201–212), a fundamental distinction should be drawn in language pedagogy (and I think in pedagogy in general) between training and education. The aim of the former is to prepare learners to solve problems that can be identified in advance through the application of pre-set, or "acquired" procedures. Learning through training is a cumulative process, in which the learner is required to put together as large an inventory of pieces of knowledge as possible in the field in which she is being trained. This approach is suitable for teaching *e.g.* Language for Specific Purposes, particularly when the short-term objectives of the course and the long-term aims of instruction coincide to a large extent. One extreme, and therefore clear, example provided by Widdowson of a good training situation is "language for air traffic control purposes".

On the other hand, the core aim of education is to favour the growth of the individual, developing her cognitive capacities, and those attitudes and predispositions that will put her in a position to cope with the most varying (professional) situations. Learning in an educational framework is viewed as a generative rather than cumulative process, whose aim is to develop the ability to employ available knowledge to solve new problems, and to gain new knowledge as the need arises. In other words, the ability to use finite resources indefinitely is a result of education, not training. This approach is suitable for teaching Language for General Purposes, in which the short-term objectives of the course do not coincide with its long-term aims, the former being to give the learners the instruments to achieve the latter.

The distinction between training and education can help us shed light on the priorities of translation teaching, and on the differences distinguishing undergraduate from postgraduate courses. In the remainder we shall consider what the (long-term) aims and the (short-term) objectives of each course may be, and whether they can be made to coincide. In order to do this, we clearly need to determine what it is that would-be professional translators need, and what they can achieve, at each stage of their instruction.

### 3.  The educational priority of translation pedagogy: Prepare aware, resourceful and reflective professionals

For reasons that I have discussed at length elsewhere (Bernardini 2000), and that I am obliged to summarise here, I believe that professional translators need awareness, reflectiveness and resourcefulness, by which I mean:

1. (Awareness) that a translator must develop the critical ability "not simply to look through language to the content of the message, but rather to see through language to the ways in which messages are mediated and shaped" (Carter 1993: 142). She must go beyond the single words and texts, and see language as a network of connected choices, which are influenced by the culture they express, which in their turn they influence. This awareness is the first step towards a professional and ethical attitude towards their job, as learners realise that they are not simply "trans-coders", substituting word for word, but constructors of meaning, mediators of culture.

2. (Reflectiveness) that it is important for a translator to develop the capacity to practice, store and use more or less specific strategies and procedures involved in translation. My impression is that there is no agreement yet as to what these may be. At the very basic level, text analysis, reading and writing procedures and strategies may be relevant. Project management and group work also have their supporters, and there is quite a large and varied literature

on local translation strategies (cf. e.g. Chesterman 1998; Kussmaul 1995, and the literature on process-oriented translation research in general).

3. (Resourcefulness) that attention should be devoted to fostering the ability to exploit finite resources indefinitely (competencies and capacities) to cope with new and unexpected challenges, and to acquire new resources autonomously, as the need arises.

This list is probably not exhaustive, and certainly not operational, i.e. it makes no claim of applicability in actual curricula. However, I believe it does have a merit: it stresses the fundamental point I would like to make in this paper, namely that the priorities of translation courses should be dealt with by focusing on capacities to be fostered rather than competencies to be gained. If we agree that, in very loose terms, the main long-term aims we should have in mind when we plan university level courses to form translators should be defined in terms of awareness, reflectiveness and resourcefulness, then it follows that long-term aims and short-term objectives, by definition, do not coincide, or, in other words, that we are dealing with an educationally-oriented type of instruction.

This kind of instruction takes time and cannot be short-cut. It involves making a future translator aware of the ways in which languages and texts work, with their stratified and often hidden meanings and uses, so that she learns to be on the lookout for such meanings in any task she is faced with, and knows, in case her knowledge or skills are not sufficient, how to acquire them quickly and efficiently.

The role of technology in this scenario is crucial, yet not as straightforward as is often believed. Practice in the use of the latest electronic tool or translation aid should not be considered only or mainly in competence-oriented terms (i.e. how to learn to use that specific tool or aid), but as a means toward the educational goals just mentioned (i.e. developing strategies that can be adapted in learning to use any other tool in the future). The rationale behind such practice is banal: the latest generation of technological tools have the advantage of being, in general, easy to master, and the disadvantage of quickly becoming obsolete, thus making a large investment of classroom time and energy on a single programme doubly unwise. It is unlikely that any translating tool will take longer than a month to master if one is motivated and "resourceful" enough. Knowing when to use it, how, for what purpose and to what effects, and what to use if technology cannot help, on the other hand, is hard, and clearly cannot be learnt in a month.

This view seems to be shared by Brian Mossop (1999) of the Canadian Government Translation Bureau and York University Translation School, who has poignantly made the following claim during the online forum on translator education organised by A. Pym in the Spring of 2000:

> So what are the general abilities to be taught at school? They are the abilities which take a long time to learn: text interpretation, composition of a coherent, readable and audience-tailored draft translation, research and checking, correcting. But nowadays one constantly hears that what students really need are skills in document management, software localization, desktop publishing and the like. I say nonsense. If you cannot translate with pencil and paper, then you can't translate with the latest information technology.

I will not labour this point further. I hope that the above discussion has brought to the fore some reasons for looking with suspicion at the European Commission trainee admission policy and translator recruitment, according to which translation graduates have no priority status with respect to other graduates. Such a policy is both educationally and theoretically questionable. First, because it implies that the ground that translation graduates have covered in their three or four years of studies in terms of increased awareness, resourcefulness and reflectiveness can be replaced by practice and professional (technical) training without substantial effects on the quality of the translators' work. Second, because this procedure appears to hide a low conception of translation and of the translator profession, implying as it does that one can be "trained" to translate as one is trained to drive a car, through a short introduction to the tools of the trade, plus some practice. This position perpetuates a view of translation as a mechanical activity of substitution of words in one language for words in another, on which the discussions of the last ten or twenty years among translator theorists and educators seem to have had precious little effect.

## 4.  Pursuing educational aims: Some pitfalls

The discussion of the (educational) priorities of translation teaching has led us somewhat astray from our main line of argument, to which I would now like to return. The core of the argument so far has been that translation is an activity that requires educated rather than trained professionals. Since education is a constitutive feature of translation professionalism, and since it takes time and effort, it clearly cannot be relegated to short accessory courses. Rather, long undergraduate translation degree courses should be centred around educational aims, focusing on the acquisition of awareness, resourcefulness and reflectiveness.

The possible ways of achieving these aims must be given serious reflection. Translation pedagogy is still in its infancy, and is in need of substantial theorisation. Without going through an extensive discussion, I think it is important to point out one danger that appears to be linked to the above discussion. There seems to be a tendency among practitioners to assume that the best way to teach undergraduates to translate is to replicate a potential professional situation. This is probably a reaction against accusations coming from the job market of University courses being too rigid, detached from the real world, academic and unprofessionalising. I believe this to be the wrong reaction and, once more, to hide a reductive view of translation. As I have claimed elsewhere (Bernardini 2000), so called "replication activities", that is activities that replicate in the classroom real world situations in which learners are likely to take part once they graduate, have a dubious status because any learning environment has its own conventions, interests, priorities and motivations, as well as its intellectual, spatial and temporal limitations. A number of applied linguists have convincingly argued against this wide-spread attitude within the communicative language teaching approach (among them Widdowson 1984 and 2000; Breen 1985). According to Breen (1985), an authentic learning activity is one that exploits the social potential of the classroom and the current concerns of learners rather than their potential future problems. Therefore, in his view, "one of the main authentic activities within a language classroom is communication about how best to learn to communicate". One should be careful not to confuse means with ends, or to assume that in order for learners to achieve a certain goal, or to become able to carry out a certain activity, it is enough to practice such a goal-oriented activity. This assumption is wrong both in a product-oriented and in a process-oriented perspective: first, it may not produce the desired effects since the ultimate aim is not to memorise fossilised procedures, but rather to develope flexible strategies; and, second, it disregards developmental and environmental factors: learners are not (yet) professionals, they do not have the same age nor the same experience, therefore they may fail to be engaged by such unusual tasks and/or not be able to carry them out and draw the lesson(s) that the teacher expects them to draw.

Rather than attempting the impossible, asking learners to play the role of professional translators, using the class as a stage, it might be better to treat them as learners, giving them a chance to develop those skills and competencies they will not have time for during their professional training, through classroom-specific activities whose currency in the professional arena may be limited, yet are designed to be pedagogically and situationally appropriate. As the name suggests, role-playing activities are like scripts that learners are asked to rehearse, in preparation for the play. But a script is not something actors are able or allowed to adapt much, and this is exactly what (good) future translators will be required to do in their professions. They will be playwrights, not actors.

It is now clear, I think, why I believe that replication activities belong to training rather than education, and as such inherently endorse a reductive view of the profession and should be given limited space within undergraduate translation courses.


## 5.    Translator education: An Italian example

The above discussion should not be taken to imply that training, technology and real-life assignments are useless. I would merely argue that they should not be uncritically adopted on the basis of pedagogically unmotivated market pressures, especially in undergraduate translation courses (my objection does not apply, for instance, to Kiraly's (2000) adoption of "authentic" translation assignments in his translation courses, which is fully motivated by the social constructivist pedagogical approach in which they are set). In order to raise the learners' awareness, resourcefulness and reflectiveness, some information technology will certainly be necessary, but it should be introduced as a means to an end, rather than an end in itself. Awareness of current professional trends should not be hindered, insofar as it may help learners feel more confident of their own capabilities and make the passage from an educational to a professional environment smoother. But it should not become a priority.

Once learners have gone through a solid translator education (i.e. long and demanding, both cognitively and culturally), they are ready to start their training. I think that postgraduate degrees can very well take care of this aspect, whilst pursuing further the educational aims discussed so far. But this implies that only translation graduates should have access to postgraduate translation courses and this is not the reality, except where undergraduate and postgraduate courses are organised around independent yet closely integrated modules. The Italian university system seems to be heading in the direction of this type of integration, following reforms at the end of the twentieth century.

Traditionally, Italian undergraduate courses lasted four years, ending with a Masters-like dissertation. Very little existed in the way of specialisation or postgraduate courses. Undergraduate translation and interpreting courses have followed a similar model, the so-called "Y model": the first two years are common to all students, then the course forks, and students specialise in either translation or interpreting. Unfortunately, as Pym claims in his survey of translator training institutions, this model has often suffered from "rigidity and inability to adapt to some of the more specialised modes of translation".

The reform meant change throughout the Italian university system. Instead of a monolithic block, each degree course is subdivided into two successive components. At the end of the first three years students are awarded a general, BA type of degree, and can subsequently proceed to take a specialised, or MA-like type of degree, which involves the production of an independent piece of research. Furthermore, the rigid exam-based system criticised by Pym has been replaced with a credit-based system in which the students, the faculty and the Ministry all have their share of choice. And choice applies not only to the courses offered, but also to alternative credit-providing experiences such as practical training, international exchange programmes and so on.

As far as translation and interpreting degrees are concerned, the general 3-year degree in "Disciplines of Linguistic Mediation" aims at providing:

- solid linguistic and cultural, written and spoken competencies in at least two languages
- a general background in economics, law, history, politics, literature and social anthropology
- a good understanding of the fields in which students will be likely to operate (depending on the socio-economic situation of each institution and its specialised interests)
- a good command of communication and information technology tools
- the development of the socio-cultural skills required for international relationships and for every aspect of linguistic support for businesses
- the capacity to work autonomously and to adapt easily to variable working situations

The degree in "Disciplines of Linguistic Mediation" constitutes the prerequisite to access a degree in "Conference Interpreting", "Literary/Technical Translation", or "Applied Foreign Languages". These prepare graduates for the professions of interpreter (conference and consecutive, but with options, for instance, for community and court-interpreting), literary or technical translator (involving competencies, respectively, in desk-top publishing, literature/history/culture, and terminology management, specialised languages etc) and language expert (with an in-depth understanding of two or more languages and cultures, international relations, resource management, social and political science, information technology and so on). In all cases, there is a requirement for courses to foster the development of the ability to co-operate with peers towards a goal, and to adopt a professionally correct attitude towards work. Teaching and research skills are also focused upon, since these degrees will prepare not only the professional interpreters, translators and language experts of tomorrow, but also the interpreting, translation and language *teachers* of tomorrow.

## 6. A lesson to be drawn?

The preference for short postgraduate Master-level programmes hides a truly training-oriented view. The implication is that once language skills have been mastered (this is to be achieved at BA level), the translation-specific value added can be acquired in one or two years at most. As we have seen, this is unlikely to be the case. Furthermore, I would object to the view that language skills and translation skills can be treated as two independent variables: first learn the language, then learn to translate. Rather, one learns the language in order to become a translator, not an economist or a politician: language knowledge and skills must necessarily be consistent with translation skills, so that the two strengthen each other. This consistency of intents between language teaching, translation teaching and other relevant knowledge area teaching appears to be a fundamental requirement of translator education, and one that cannot be achieved in a system that relies on a relatively long general language learning programme followed by a short and specialised translator training programme. The Italian system constitutes an effort to understand and answer the needs of the market for specialisation and flexibility, whilst at the same time resisting its unreasonable pressures, not relinquishing the ethical obligation to educate future translators to become sensitive, self-aware, intelligent and consequently successful professionals and individuals. Whether the system will be successful in practice is a different matter.

## 7.  Conclusion: Education, training, and ice-cream cones

Summarising the views expressed in this paper, I would suggest that translators be formed through a reasoned, timely and thought-out balance of education and training. This long and effortful instructional period is a necessary requirement if we are to form competent professionals, and should be organised around two study periods.

Undergraduate courses should focus decidedly on education, adopting curricula and methodologies which take into account the specific professional requirements of language mediators and cater for these by providing learners with the awareness, resourcefulness and reflectiveness that they will certainly require, no matter what their specific professional niche will be. The pedagogic approach adopted in the various courses, be they translation theory and practice, linguistics and language, or law and economics courses, should be consistent and oriented towards the goal of developing (translation-related) capacity, in the widest possible sense of the notion. The whole approach, as well as the success of an undergraduate course for translators, should be judged not so much on the basis of **products** but of **processes**: how the learners read the texts, question their first impressions, are or are not logical in their renderings and stubborn in searching for solutions, are more or less able to assess the reliability of their reference materials, know their limits and know where to look for help, are able to collaborate with others and so on. The accuracy of products (the translated texts) should be viewed as an indirect measure of these processes, rather than an end in itself (Kiraly 2000).

The aims of postgraduate translation courses should be coherent with those just described, yet different. If undergraduate courses have been successful, students have gone through a period of at least two or three years devoted to thought-stimulating, awareness-raising, autonomising activities, during which they have familiarised themselves with the various skills involved in translating, revising, researching *etc.* and acquired a broad understanding of culture. They are now ready to deepen these capacities and competencies, effectively gaining professional specialisation as well as the research and teaching skills that can place them at the forefront of the discipline. Postgraduate courses can thus afford to be shorter (lasting one or two years) because they are building on fertile soil and are concerned with skills and competencies whose learning burden is arguably less intense, and more selective, because they are producing an elite of language professionals.

In conclusion, I think that translators can do without training but not without education. They can do without a postgraduate translation course, but should be discouraged from doing without an undergraduate translation course. This is because training may come with experience, but education is unlikely to follow the same course. Therefore I would suggest we stop looking at the two as alternative ways of getting a translation qualification, as is nowadays often the case, and start to see them as integrated, sequential wholes, one part of which is necessary, and comes first, and the other accessory.

Going back to the subtitler and medical translator we began with, I hope I have made clear why I believe that they are not as different from each other as an ambulance driver from an ice-cream seller, and that they share more than a mere "instrument". Subtitling devices, technical glossaries and cars are instruments. Translation skills are the very essence of the translation and translating professions: They are what the professions have in common and what, first and foremost, we should teach the translators of tomorrow.

## References

Bernardini, S. (2000). *Competence, Capacity, Corpora – A Study in Corpus-Aided Language Learning*. Bologna: Clueb.

Breen, M. P. (1985). "Authenticity in the language classroom". *Applied Linguistics, 6* (1), 60–70.

Carter, R. (1993). "Language awareness and language learning". In M. Hoey (Ed.) *Data, Description, Discourse*. London: Harper Collins.

Chesterman, A. (1998). "Communication strategies, learning strategies and translation strategies". In K. Malmkjær (Ed.) *Translation and Language Teaching, Language Teaching and Translation*. Manchester: St.Jerome.

Chiaro, D. & G. Nocella (1999). "Language management in Italy". In S. Bassnett, R. M. Bollettieri Bosinelli, & M. Ulrych (Eds.), *Translation Studies Revisited* [Special issue of *Textus*], *12* (2), 351–368.

European Commission (2000). *Multilinguismo e traduzione – Il servizio di traduzione della Commissione europea*. Luxembourg: Ufficio delle pubblicazioni ufficiali delle Comunità europee.

Gambier, Y. (2000). "Les défis de la formation: Attentes et réalités". Paper presented at the *translation theory and practice seminars*. Luxembourg and Brussels: EC Commission translation service. Online: http://europa.eu.int/comm/translation/theory/lectures/2000_tp_gambier.pdf [visited 23.09.04]

Kiraly, D. (2000). *A Social Constructivist Approach to Translator Education*. Manchester: St. Jerome.

Kussmaul, P. (1995). *Training the Translator*. Amsterdam and Philadelphia: John Benjamins

Mossop, B. (1999). "What should be taught at translation school?" In A. Pym (Ed.), *Innovation in Translator and Interpreter Training – An online symposium*. Online: http://www.fut.es/~apym/symp/mossop.html [visited 23.09.04]

Pym, A. *List of Training Institutions by Country*. Based on M. Caminade & A. Pym (1995). *Les formations en traduction et interprétation. Essai de recensement mondial*. Paris: Société Française des Traducteurs. Online: http://isg.urv.es/tti/tti.htm [visited 23.09.04]

Widdowson, H. G. (1984). "English in training and education". In *Explorations in Applied Linguistics 2*. Oxford: Oxford University Press.

Widdowson, H. G. (2000). "On the limitations of linguistics applied". *Applied Linguistics, 21* (1), 3–25.

# The competencies required by the translator's roles as a professional

Rosemary Mackenzie

## Introduction

The view of translation as a professional service allows analogies to be drawn between the translator's task and that of the architect. It has been said that the architect's job is "to prevent the client from building his or her dream house", but to look at it in a more positive light, we might say that the architect helps the client to come as close as possible, in the given circumstances, to realising their dream. Similarly, the professional translator's client needs a text to function in a given situation, and it is one of the translator's tasks to advise them on how to achieve the best possible result in that particular situation. An architect is seldom if ever given a free hand to build a house for a client: the client will have needs, and in addition to these, the house will at least have to suit the plot and the client's purse. Decisions have to be made on factors such as size, materials, time frame, degree of finishedness – clients might want to do some of the finishing work themselves – and many others. The architect designs the house but is not usually involved in actually building it, whereas the translator usually produces the text he or she has designed. This simply goes to show that there is a higher degree of differentiation between trades and tasks in the construction industry than there is in the translation industry, which is still relatively young. Nevertheless there is a growing need for translation consultants whose role is to oversee but not necessarily to perform the actual translation work.

Justa Holz-Mänttäri was among the first to talk about translators as experts and to analyse translation as a professional activity taking place in a world where specialisation and differentiation of roles is the trend. In her dissertation she introduced what she called the basic situation for translational action (the role model), in which the translator's role is presented in relation to those of the other actors in the same situation (Holz-Mänttäri 1984: 106). She divides the translation process into four stages, each of which corresponds to one of the professional translator's roles: product specification, research, text production and text evaluation. Juan Sager has also written about the translation process in the context of the language industry, using a very similar model to analyse the translation task (Sager 1993: 166). Traditionally these tasks have been performed by one and the same person, i.e. the translator.

Generally speaking, as an expert or specialist in translation, the translator produces texts for a client on the basis of an order, or advises the client on how to go about having the needed text produced. More specifically the professional translator specifies what is required by analysing the translation situation (asking the relevant questions), which may require direct dealings with the client, and also advising the client about what it is they need. Secondly the translator searches and researches information in order to solve any problems that may arise from lack of knowledge, information, terminological or linguistic competence, or from deficiencies in the source text. Thirdly the translator acts as text producer, and finally as the evaluator of his or her own text or those of other translators.

If these roles are differentiated, they give rise to such professional roles as those of the terminologist, the information specialist, the project co-ordinator, the account manager, the reviser and the quality manager in addition to that of the translator. In large translation companies, these roles are usually separate. However, in order to prepare student translators for working life in the translation industry today, it seems reasonable to give them the opportunity to practise all of these roles in the course of their training.

## Competencies required by the translator's roles

From the above it is evident that in the translation industry today, the translator's roles require not only linguistic-cultural skills, but also interpersonal skills, since translation is becoming more and more of a team effort. Other skills required, particularly in the context of research and text production, are IT skills. These skills, which are now assumed to a degree not even imaginable in the 1970's or early 80's, include word processing skills, competence in using the tools available to assist the translation process such as translation memory tools, terminology software and the Internet. A further aspect of the translator's task that is often neglected is marketing ability. Without marketing that brings the translation supplier to the notice of the client, the twain may never meet. It may be argued that all of the skills listed above cannot possibly be taught in an undergraduate degree, but it makes sense to prepare students for working life by giving them at least an introduction to these realities.

All the roles described above correspond to the competencies required of a translator working in a small or medium sized translation company, but they are no less important for a translator working as free-lance or in a large organisation. The roles are also compatible with the quality loop of a service-oriented company working according to a quality system, which involves marketing, service design, delivery, evaluation and feedback into design for continuous improvement (see Mackenzie & Nieminen 1997:344). One can also categorise the translators' skills in terms of management skills, since quality in translation requires management of the whole translation process, which in turn implies management of all its phases: client management, time management, resources management, information management.

## How can these competencies be developed?

Learning by doing, knowing-how rather than knowing-that: these are almost clichés in pedagogical theory today. What they mean in practice is using skills in real or simulated situations that have been arranged by the teacher. Donald Kiraly describes an experiment in which he has put students in a real situation, giving them a real assignment as group work and letting them work out for themselves what they need to know and how to acquire the necessary resources, with the teacher acting in the role of consultant (1995:72ff.). However, such authentic situations may be difficult to arrange without the co-operation of an understanding and patient client. I would therefore prefer to create simulated situations and later operate in real, but controlled situations.

Practice in translation skills is not enough to a make a professional. Professionals need to have a background in the history, theory and methodology of the subject in order to give them insight into their role and thus to strengthen their self-image as professionals. By reading the history and theory of translation students can, for example, be made to realise the significance of their role for society and how it has changed and developed over the ages, from that of a mere servant, to that of a rhetorician, an evangeliser, a scholar, a communicator and finally that of a professional supplying a service in the translation industry (see e.g. Chesterman 1997:Chapter 2). Translation is placed in a wider historical framework. Sager places it in a wider social framework – that of the language industry – when he classifies translation as a type of text modification, parallel, for example, to abstracting (Sager 1993: 106–113).

## Target text specification and planning

Product specification involves analysing the situation and the text-in-situation to decide whether it is usable as a source text as such or whether it needs some form of modification to be suitable for its purpose. In order to do this the translator needs knowledge of text types and of their uses in the respective cultures.

Situation analysis means analysing all the factors involved in the situation, using e.g. the rhetorical formula "Who is saying what to whom, why, how, by what means, for what purpose?" as proposed by Christiane Nord (1991), and deciding whether the target text has to meet the same criteria as the source text. At least the audience will have changed and as a rule the purpose (function) of the target text has changed, too.

The second phase is to analyse the text (what is being said), decide whether the information is sufficient or redundant and plan the what and the how (suit text type to culture, register to audience and function etc.) of the target text. At this stage the translator should also decide whether he or she is competent or able to translate the text under the conditions provided by the client. This is where time, resource and client management skills are needed, i.e. the ability to manage one's own time, to evaluate one's own skills and if necessary to negotiate new terms with the client.

## Text research

During the first phases of situation and text analysis problems have probably been noted – a source text is seldom suited as such for literal translation. The problems may be due to inadequacies in the source text that need to be remedied, to lack of information, or to the translator's lack of terminological or linguistic knowledge. Solving such problems usually requires research and the use of tools for research. Consultation with the author of the source text may help to remedy its deficiencies. Consultation of dictionaries, or with colleagues or subject or language experts, and the use of terminology databases or the Internet may solve problems arising from the translator's own deficient knowledge. Knowing where to look for information, whom to consult, and how to classify and systematise information sources, i.e. information management, is part and parcel of this competence.

## Text production

Once the target text has been planned (the what and the how), the next stage is to produce it. Here the student needs text composition skills. Basic skills include mastery of the rules of coherence and cohesion, and the ability to recognise and write in different registers. Information search and research is part of this competence, especially when translating into the non-mother tongue, as students will need to find parallel texts and be able to evaluate and utilise them. This is also true when translating source texts on unfamiliar subject matter, even into the mother tongue. Practice is needed in the management and use of textual material (parallel texts) to produce a target text that meets the relevant quality criteria, i.e. a text that meets the initial product specification.

Text processing skills are nowadays taken for granted. Although the ability to touch type is no longer necessarily stressed, this skill is still regarded as important for a professional translator, for example, by Geoffrey Samuelsson-Brown (1998:6). Nowadays, knowledge of translation memory tools and their applicability to various tasks is a definite advantage for an aspiring translator, and will probably soon become a prerequisite. Although skill in using these tools can probably only be acquired on the job, or through a post-graduate course, an introduction to their principles and uses would be recommendable at undergraduate level.

## Text evaluation

How to assess the quality of one's own or another's translation? Apart from the basic knowledge of texts and text norms in the respective cultures, quality management skills are needed. We must know the criteria against which to measure the result. We need to know the function of the text in order to judge its quality. Does the situation require a highly polished translation, a rough or gist translation, or even just a summary of the source text? Sometimes a linguistically less than perfect text is acceptable when speed is the main criterion. Deciding how much and what kind of revision is required is a necessary part of this phase. Client management also comes into the picture in the form of eliciting and evaluating feedback, as well as justifying one's own translational decisions to the client, whose satisfaction is, in practice, the single most important criterion of quality in translation, as in any other service industry.

## Teaching translation according to the co-operative model

The translation methodology presented here has been developed from the co-operative model proposed by Holz-Mänttäri, which is directly applicable to the translation industry as it is today. In order to prepare students for their future roles as translators, the trainer needs to know the world he or she is training students for, in order to be able to create situations in which the students can practise the above listed roles and the competencies they involve. Role-playing is one way of doing this. Medical students are nowadays taught how to deal with patients very early in their training by putting them into real situations – under supervision, of course, and naturally in situations where they can do no real harm to anyone!

The situations in which student translators are placed should also be firmly controlled at first. Using texts that have been translated in a real situation the teacher can take the role of client, expert consultant, or language reviser (teaching translation into the non-mother tongue the trainer very often plays that role anyway). The students, working in groups of three, can alternate as terminologists, translators or revisers, or they may work on longer texts where co-ordination of terminology, register, layout etc. is needed. They may even act as clients themselves. This might be done by asking students to write a text e.g. a speech to be given in another language or to find a text that they for some reason want translated – say a paragraph from a textbook in another language. They can be asked to consider why they want it translated and what kind of text they expect to receive.

It makes sense to practise different situations and different text types, starting with familiar, clearly definable texts types for which models are easily found (simple instructions, travel brochures) and going on to more complex situations, involving journalistic texts, articles, legal documents, technical documentation and longer projects. Real projects are ideal if the client is willing to co-operate and give sufficient time for realising the pedagogical purposes of the project. The projects ideally involve teamwork between several translators working on the same text, possibly also into different languages. The advantage of working on real projects is that the students are better motivated when they feel responsibility to a real client. They will also have the opportunity to deal with the client in reality (see Mackenzie & Nieminen 1997).

## Multilingual project

To close I should like to describe briefly, as an example of how students can be given practice in the required competencies, a project implemented in 2000 at the University of Turku. The project was set up by three teachers of translation into the non-mother tongue and involved a real translation assignment - the translation of a brochure needed by the Centre for Translation and Interpreting to inform foreign applicants about its course for conference interpreters. The leaflet was translated into four languages: English, German, French and Spanish. The project was planned, explained to the students and a timetable drawn up. The students were divided into groups of four with one student acting as a co-ordinator. The project involved not only actual translation work, but also making an offer for the translation and terminology work (calculating the length of the text, the time needed and the cost), invoicing and requesting feedback from the client. Three groups worked on terminology alone, producing as a result of their work a small five-language glossary, giving sources and contexts for the terms, with the help of a terminology management system (Multiterm).

The translating teams were expected to work as autonomously as possible, dividing the work internally as they saw fit regarding translation and revision, co-ordinating their efforts with the other language teams and adhering to the timetable. One condition of the commission was that the leaflets should not differ significantly in layout or in content. Sessions were scheduled for consultation with the other groups, for consulting the client on problems relating to the text and for consulting the trainer on linguistic problems. Finally the leaflets were revised and edited and a feedback session was held. The feedback from students was analysed and will be used in setting up further multilingual projects.

## Conclusion

It may seem an overwhelming task to prepare students in the course of an undergraduate degree for all the challenges they will be meet as professionals working in the translation industry. One essential prerequisite for success is that the students are highly motivated. One of the translator trainer's main tasks and roles is to inspire motivation by arranging conditions in which students can practise skills they see as relevant for their future.

## References

Chesterman, A. (1977). *Memes of Translation: The Spread of Ideas in Translation Theory.* Amsterdam and Philadelphia: John Benjamins Publishing Co.

Holz-Mänttäri, J. (1984). *Translatorisches Handeln.* Annales Academiae Scientarium Fennicae.

Kiraly, D. (1995). *Pathways to Translation.* Kent, Ohio and London: Kent State University Press.

Mackenzie, R. (1995). "Quality through contextualisation of translation teaching". In P. Mayorcas & G. Dennet (Eds.), *ITI Conference 8 Proceedings.* London: Institute of Translation and Interpreting.

Mackenzie, R. & Nieminen, E. (1997). "Motivating Students to Achieve Quality in Translation". In K. Klaudy & J. Klohn (Eds.), *Transferre Necesse Est, Proceedings of the 2nd International Conference on Current Trends in Studies of Translation and Interpreting.* Budapest: Scholastica.

Nord, C. (1991). *Text Analysis in Translation Theory: Methodology and Didactic Application of a Model for Translation-Oriented Text Analysis.* Amsterdam and Atlanta: Rodopi.

Sager, J. C. (1993). *Language Engineering and Translation: Consequences of Automation.* Amsterdam and Philadelphia: John Benjamins Publishing Co.

Samuelsson-Brown, G. (1998). *A Practical Guide for Translators: Third Revised Edition.* Clevedon: Multilingual Matters Ltd.

# Language learning for translators
## Designing a syllabus

Allison Beeby

## Introduction

The general context of the proposal presented in this chapter is language learning as a part of an undergraduate degree designed to train professional translators. The emphasis here is on undergraduate degrees; foreign language proficiency is often, rightly or wrongly, taken for granted in postgraduate degrees. Basic guidelines for teaching language for translators can be established within this general context, but in practice, each teaching situation presents a different set of priorities and restrictions which vary according to country, institution, other subjects in the degree programme, entry requirements for students, the language being taught and the final skills required. The author is most familiar with the teaching situation in Spain, where translation has been taught as an undergraduate degree since 1972.[1]

Research and experience in the field of translation, translation training and language acquisition are pre-requisites to establishing the declarative and procedural knowledge needed by the trainee translator. In the first stage of syllabus design, the teacher draws up a pre-syllabus that includes these general learning objectives for trainee translators, based on this research and experience. The pre-syllabus provides a check list of all those elements that intervene in the acquisition of language for translators. At a later stage, these elements will be tailored to fit the needs of a specific learning situation and a syllabus is drawn up with specific objectives. The syllabus design proposed here has three stages. The first one is to identify the elements of a translation-based, student-oriented pre-syllabus. The second stage is to identify the elements of a discourse-based, translation-oriented pre-syllabus. The third stage is to design a genre and task-based syllabus that integrates the elements of the first two stages, with very specific objectives for each task.

The examples from a genre and task-based syllabus given at the end of this chapter are designed for a first year English B language course for undergraduate translation students at the Facultad de Traducción e Intérpretación of the Universidad Autónoma de Barcelona (FTI/UAB). The languages taught in the FTI/UAB can be studied as A, B or C languages. The A languages (mother tongue languages) are Spanish or/and Catalan. The B languages (first or active foreign languages) are English, French and German. The C languages (second foreign languages) are Arabic, Chinese, Japanese, English, French, German, Italian, Portuguese and Russian. Students that study English as a B language use English in direct translation (English ⇒ Spanish/Catalan), inverse translation (Spanish/Catalan ⇒ English) and consecutive and simultaneous interpreting (English ⇒ Spanish/Catalan). They have studied English at school and have passed an entrance exam and English language for translators is only taught in the first two years of the four-year degree course. On the other hand, Chinese is taught as a C language, which means that the students start as beginners, study Chinese intensively throughout the four years and only start direct translation (Chinese ⇒ Spanish) in the third year. They know they will have to spend a couple of years in a Chinese speaking country if they are to use their Chinese professionally. Obviously, the priorities and restrictions for designing a syllabus for these two languages are very different.

Very little has been written about language learning for translators. Berenguer's pioneer proposal (1996) is based on the skills she considered to be important for a translator in the context of German as a C language. She proposed exercises to develop five main skills: (1) Reading comprehension exercises based on 'deverbalisation' (Delisle 1980) and translation-oriented discourse analysis (Nord 1991; Elena 1990). (2) Exercises to separate the two languages in contact that focus on differences in: writing conventions, vocabulary, grammar and text types. (3) Exercises to develop documentation techniques. (4) Exercises to develop cultural expertise in the foreign culture. (5) Exercises to develop translation awareness. Berenguer's proposal is important because it clearly situates language for translators as a language for special purposes within the applied branch of translation studies (Holmes 1972).

Other publications on language learning for translator training tend to concentrate on one aspect of the learning process. Brehm (1997) focuses on reading for translators and incorporates useful insights from studies in reading acquisition in first and second languages. Nord (1999) recommends a textual competence approach for language learning in A, B, and C languages. She proposes a progression from text-analytical competence and text-production competence in lingua-culture A to text-analytical competence and text-production competence in lingua-cultures B and C. Noting textual differences and similarities between the lingua-cultures is an important part of this progression. Séguinot (1994) points out the usefulness of teaching technical writing to trainee translators and Koltay (1998) defends including technical and academic writing in translation curricula. Both authors stress the learning of genres and documentation needed for technical writing as being important for translators. The idea that language learning should be situated in a general framework of translation training is implicit in all these publications.

The syllabus (that is, specific objectives, progression and teaching methodology) proposed in this chapter incorporates aspects of the genre-based approach to teaching languages which has emerged from Halliday's systemic functional linguistics (Cope & Kalantzis 1993) and contrastive rhetoric (Connor 1994). This approach seems to provide a methodology that is appropriate for teaching language for translation, and indeed for teaching translation, particularly inverse translation. Genre literacy and contrastive rhetoric are essential components of translation competence (Beeby 2003). However, before we can reach this final stage in syllabus design, we have to establish the course content through (1) a translation-based, student-oriented pre-syllabus and (2) a discourse-based, translation-oriented pre-syllabus (see Appendix).

## Stage 1: A translation-based, student-oriented pre-syllabus

If the purpose of a degree programme is to train professional translators, then learning objectives should be based on a concept of professional translator competence: what we can know, or discover, about professional translators. There are at least two ways of finding out more about professional translators. The first is to study the translation market to see who translates what and how. A few surveys have been carried out (see for example Grindrod 1986; Mackenzie 2000; McAlister 1992, etc.) and they show that conditions vary greatly from country to country. For example, inverse translation, translation into the foreign language, is very rare in the UK, very common in Finland and quite common in Spain (Beeby 1998). Furthermore, the profession is in a state of constant change and these surveys need to be brought up to date periodically.

New technologies have revolutionised the way translators work and agencies may only hire translators who know how to use the latest model of a certain translation memory. However, when establishing degree programmes, a balance has to be kept between teaching the latest technology (which may be obsolete the following year) and learning to become expert bilingual, bicultural readers, writers and translators. Mossop (2000) takes a rather extreme view on this:

> In my view, the function of a translation school is not to train students for specific existing slots in the language industry, but to give them certain general abilities that they will then be able to apply to whatever slots may exist 5, 10, 15 or 25 years from now, In other words, I think university-based translation schools must uphold the distinction between education and training. They must resist the insistent demands of industry for graduates ready to produce top-notch translations in this or that specialised field at high speed using the latest computer tools.

While sympathising with this point of view, it does seem that the technological changes in the last twenty years have been so great that not only the process but also the product may be qualitatively different.

The second way to find out about how translators work is through process studies of translators at work,[2] such as the PACTE (*Proceso de Aprendizaje en la Competencia Traductora y Evaluación*)[3] project. PACTE works with a translation competence model that is divided into six sub-competencies: communicative competence in two languages, extra-linguistic competence, transfer competence, instrumental and professional competence, psycho-physiological competence and strategic competence. The model allows for and expects that the importance of different competencies will vary in different translation situations. For example, declarative and procedural knowledge of new technology is part of the professional/instrumental sub-competence and the importance given to this aspect of training will depend on contextual variables. However, all questions related to the translation brief, which is another aspect of this sub-competence, will always be central to any professional translation or professional translation training.

In order to decide which sub-competencies should be given priority in the foreign language class, the language teacher should know what the students are learning or are going to learn in other classes and what the objectives of the translation and interpreting classes are at different levels. Taking a professional translation competence model does not mean that an expert level should be an objective even in the final year of the degree. Acquiring translation competence is best described in terms of a continuum from *novice* to *expert* (PACTE 2000: 103–105). The degree of expertise aimed at in the language class will depend on the final objective for a particular language at a particular time and place in the whole degree programme. This knowledge will help us to provide progression in the language class.

The teacher needs to be aware of what kind of knowledge the students should be acquiring at each stage of training. Is it theoretical or practical, conscious or automatic, *declarative* or *procedural* knowledge? One type of knowledge does not exclude the other, they may co-exist in a learning situation, or, as novice becomes expert, declarative knowledge may give way to procedural knowledge. The PACTE hypothesis about the kind of knowledge that makes up expert translation competence is that it is essentially procedural knowledge in which the strategic component is primordial. Dreyfus and Dreyfus (1986) characterise expert knowledge as non-reflective or automatic. In introspective translation studies, the automatic nature of expert, procedural knowledge is illustrated by the difficulties expert translators have in verbalising their mental processes (Kiraly 1995). Therefore, declarative knowledge about contrastive rhetoric may be acquired in the first and second years, but may not become fully procedural until the translator has been working for several years.

For example, an Egyptian student who is writing his thesis on legal genres in Spanish and Arabic at the FTI/UAB is very knowledgeable about genre differences in Spain and Egypt (declarative knowledge). However, he still finds it very difficult to avoid using rhetorical patterns that are popular in Arabic when writing his thesis for a Spanish university (procedural knowledge). He finds it difficult to avoid starting a chapter by quoting all the 'experts' who have written anything on the subject to show that he is in good company, rather than presenting his own individual argument and supporting it when necessary with a quote from an expert. When this is pointed out, he can see it immediately and recognises that this is an Arabic rhetorical device that would begin, 'Behold! . . .' Equally, despite my interest in contrastive rhetoric, I still tend toward an 'English' rhetorical style, even when writing in Spanish. Therefore, we will have to apply conscious declarative knowledge for his thesis to be recognisable as a Spanish academic genre.

The PACTE translation competence model, like any other theoretical model, is one way of segmenting reality, and we are already thinking of adjusting it in the light of our experimental results. Exploratory tests have raised interesting questions. For example, the difference in the translation process between a young translator who works for a translation agency and was using translation tools throughout the whole process, and an older freelance translator who only used the Internet as a source of documentation at the end of the process; the fact that the Spanish-English translators found the inverse translation into English easier than the direct translation into Spanish and that one translator explained this in terms of the genres used: the inverse translation was a standardised genre and the direct translation a hybrid genre. The PACTE model (still a site under construction) allows for and expects that different sub-competencies will vary in different translation situations and it provides a useful checklist for designing any translation-related syllabus. Priorities can be established in relation to which competencies are going to be worked on in other classes, and in relation to the students' position on the novice-expert continuum at different stages of the degree programme. The sub-components of translation competence as defined by PACTE (2000: 101–102) are as follows:

1. Communicative Competence in two languages can be defined in general terms as the system of underlying knowledge and skills necessary for linguistic communication. Following Canale (1983), we distinguish linguistic, discourse and socio-linguistic components. Of course, for translators, this competence should be separated into understanding in the SL and production in the TL.

2. Extra-linguistic Competence is composed of general world knowledge and specialist knowledge that can be activated according to the needs of each translation situation. The sub-components may include explicit or implicit knowledge about translation, bicultural, encyclopaedic and subject knowledge.

3. Instrumental-Professional Competence is composed of knowledge and skills related both to the tools of the trade and the profession. The sub-components may be very diverse: knowledge and use of all kinds of documentation sources and new technologies, knowledge of the work market (translation briefs, etc.) and how to behave as a professional translator, especially in relation to professional ethics.

4. Psycho-physiological Competence can be defined as the ability to use all kinds of psychomotor, cognitive and attitudinal resources. The most important of these may be psychomotor skills for reading and writing; cognitive skills (e.g. memory, attention span, creativity and logical reasoning); psychological attitudes (e.g. intellectual curiosity, perseverance, rigour, a critical spirit, and self-confidence).

5. Transfer Competence is the central competence that integrates all the others. It is the ability to complete the transfer process from the ST to the TT, that is to understand the ST and re-express it in the TL, taking into account the translation's function and the characteristics of the receptor. The sub-components include (1) comprehension competence

(the ability to analyse, synthesise and activate extra-linguistic knowledge so as to capture the sense of a text), (2) the ability to "deverbalise" and to maintain the SL and the TL in separate compartments (that is to control interference), (3) re-expression competence (textual organisation, creativity in the TL), (4) competence in carrying out the translation project (the choice of the most adequate method).

6. Strategic Competence includes all the individual procedures, conscious and unconscious, verbal and non-verbal, used to solve the problems found during the translation process. The problem-solving process can be described as a series of acts or recursive, complex acts that lead from an initial state to an objective. There are several stages in this process, the first of which is recognising there is a problem (Sternberg 1996). Examples of strategies are: distinguishing between main and secondary ideas, establishing conceptual relationships, searching for information, paraphrasing, back translating, translating out loud, establishing an order for documentation.

It seems obvious that language-for-translation teachers should have experience as translators, should understand the language skills needed by a translator, should be aware of what translation is, not only from reading about translation competence research models, but also from their own experience. Unfortunately, in my experience, the language teachers in translation faculties are not usually translators, and this may be one reason why there has been so little research in language for this special purpose.

Attempts to define this awareness of what translation is, that translators translate texts/cultures for a purpose, always seem too obvious, too simple. Nevertheless, in practice, every time I teach first year students, or talk with people who have no translation experience, I realise that it's not so obvious or simple. For many people, understanding translation requires a totally new way of looking at words, language and the world and it takes time to introduce new schemata and change existing ones. Mariana Orozco (2000) has carried out an interesting survey of the development of translation awareness amongst translation students over a period of five years, in five faculties in Spain. Although the principal purpose of her research was to test the validity of her measuring instruments, her results suggest that the development of this awareness does take time and is related to the methodology used in translation classes. As Berenguer (1996:10) suggests, if language teaching is translation-oriented, much precious time can be saved in the translation class.

## Stage 2: A discourse-based, translation-oriented pre-syllabus

Of course, the apparent simplicity of translation awareness is deceptive, because there are so many aspects of translation that the 'ordinary' reader/writer is not conscious of. Experienced translators who have not 'studied' translation, may incorporate all these elements without being conscious of them. Procedural knowledge may be developed without passing through a declarative stage. Nevertheless, all these elements should be made explicit to trainee translators so as to speed up the process of acquiring this procedural knowledge. The problem for the teacher is how to highlight the parts of what is really a holistic process, that is, to define very specific learning objectives (see Delisle 1993; Beeby 1996a; Hurtado 1996, 1999). When teaching language for translation we should be working towards a genre and task-based syllabus that integrates objectives from translation and discourse-based pre-syllabuses.

Hameline (1976) establishes the characteristics of learning through tasks, what he calls 'rational' versus 'traditional' teaching. The following Table 1 is my translation of the chart used by Martínez Melis (2001: 188–189) to illustrate his approach. The characteristics provide a second useful checklist for teachers designing a task-based syllabus that requires evaluation criteria.

The change caused by applying translation awareness to language teaching for trainee translators can be compared to the revolution caused in linguistics by discourse analysis, 'The moment one starts thinking of language as discourse, the entire landscape changes, usually for ever' (McCarthy & Carter 1994: vii). Discourse approaches to second language teaching face the same problem of integrating top-down and bottom-up elements of discourse analysis. Fortunately for us, a great deal of research has been put into finding solutions to this problem in second language acquisition. Our first priority general objective is obviously going to be communicative competence in the foreign language and we can draw on this research.

Recent research into textual genres for second language learners seems to suggest very useful ways for integrating specific objectives and real language in use. Most of the research is based on English, so English language teachers still have a great advantage over teachers of other languages. Hoey (2001) is particularly useful for language-for translation teachers because it incorporates insights from contrastive rhetoric (see also Connor 1996 and Simpson 2000).

It is difficult to select and classify discourse elements for a translation-oriented pre-syllabus without reference to a specific learning situation, therefore the classification proposed in this section has been based on English as a B language for Spanish trainee translators, that is, for first year students who

Table 1.

| | TRADITIONAL | RATIONAL |
|---|---|---|
| LEARNING SITUATION | Focused on the teacher's performance and content | Focused on the student's performance and learning |
| THE TEACHER'S ROLE | The teacher dispenses information | The teacher diagnoses, organises, motivates and provides resources |
| OBJECTIVES | Normally, objectives are not clearly defined | Objectives are formulated in terms of the student's behaviour and are presented at the beginning |
| ACTIVITIES | Lectures | Varied activities aimed at helping learning |
| PARTICIPATION | Sporadic | Active |
| EVALUATION | Usually one type at the end of the course | Frequent tasks applied soon after a teaching unit |
| TESTS | The student attends the course and then takes an exam for which a single grade is given | Tests are prepared to measure the acquisition of the objectives established at the beginning of the course |
| INTERPRETATION OF RESULTS | The tests are normative (following a normative graph in relation to the rest of the class to give a grade) | The tests are based on objective criteria and a student's success is not related to the rest of the class |
| MASTERING OBJECTIVES | The teacher assumes one third of the class will be good, one third average and one third will fail | The teacher assumes that with time all the students will be able to master the objectives |
| THE SUCCESS OF THE COURSE | Usually the success of the course is evaluated subjectively by the teacher | The objectives and the evaluation help the teacher to improve teaching materials and to know if the students have mastered the objectives |

need their English for direct translation in the first and second years and inverse translation in the second year. Thus, the emphasis is on written texts. The second-year syllabus designed to cover the oral discourse skills needed for interpreting classes in the third and fourth years is not included here. Writing is not often taught explicitly in Spanish schools, but most students reach university with a few fixed ideas about "style". One of these is that more is better than less, so quantity may be seen as making up for quality. Another is that variation is better than repetition, so they may use synonyms in English texts where clear reference through repetition is more important than using an 'elegant' style. Finally, they tend to use 'long' words with a Latin origin that are similar to a Spanish word and avoid 'four-letter' words. Therefore, one objective in the language class is recognition of which English genres prefer brevity, clarity and clear reference. Another objective is to realise that the use of too many words of Latin origin can distort the tenor of a text. Simpson (2000) reviews studies of Spanish-English rhetorical contrasts that confirm these features. Her own study is a comparative analysis of the topical structure of academic paragraphs in English and Spanish. The results of this study confirm other differences between Spanish and English writing, particularly questions of coherence and cohesion, that I found in studying parallel texts (Spanish and English originals of the same genre) for inverse translation classes (Beeby 1996a: 215–230).

The pre-syllabus discourse elements have been classified into four sections: (1) textual interaction, (2) textual organisation, (3) contrastive rhetoric and (4) genres. I have incorporated ideas from many different sources, principally, Connor (1996) Hoey (2001), McCarthy and Carter (1994) and Beeby (1996a),[4] however, I have tried to avoid using their specific terminology because few authors tend to agree on the meta-language needed for discussing these subjects. Furthermore, some of the teachers who might want to follow this syllabus may not have much background in discourse, rhetoric and translation theory and, even more important, the students certainly will not.

In the following two charts, the left-hand column lists the selected discourse elements and the right-hand column lists the translation sub-competencies that could be developed by working creatively with these aspects of discourse. Obviously, all the discourse elements should contribute to the students' communicative competence in the foreign language. The problem-solving aspect of learning by tasks, particularly tasks that require analysis and synthesis, should help develop some aspects of the elusive but essential strategic competence. Therefore, these two competencies should be developed in every task.

## 1. Textual interaction

| ASPECTS OF DISCOURSE | TRANSLATION COMPETENCE |
| --- | --- |
| Texts say different things to different people in the same culture: different versions of the same event (matrix). | People in different cultures *Communicative, Strategic, Extra-linguistic, Transfer.* |
| The communicative situation: signals from writer to reader | Translator/TT reader *Communicative, Strategic, Transfer* |
| Text as a site for interaction amongst writer and reader | Translator/TT reader *Communicative, Strategic, Extra-linguistic* |
| Purposes of interactions amongst writer and reader | Translation brief *Instrumental-professional* |
| Inferring information about the situation from the text | Reasoning, creativity *Psycho-physiological* |
| Forming hypotheses about texts, predicting | World views *Communicative, Strategic Extra-linguistic* |

A text that could be used to introduce textual interaction is the following extract from *Bridget Jones' Diary* by Helen Fielding. This gives us a good example of genres within genres, each with its own linguistic features:

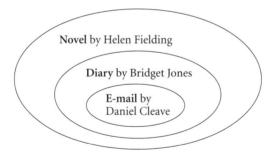

Thursday 5 January

9st 3 (excellent progress – 2lb of fat spontaneously combusted through joy and sexual promise), alcohol units 6 (v.g. for party), cigarettes 12 (continuing good work), calories 1258 (love has eliminated need to pig out)

**11 a.m. Office.** Oh my God. Daniel Cleaver just sent me a message. Was trying to work on CV without Perpetua noticing (in preparation for improving career) when Message Pending suddenly flashed on top

of screen. Delighted by, well, anything – as always am if is not work – I
quickly pressed RMS Execute and nearly jumped out of my skin when I
saw Cleave at the bottom of the message. I instantly thought he had been
able to tap into the computer and see that I was not getting on with my
work. But then I read the message:

> Message Jones
> You appear to have forgotten your skirt. As I think is made perfectly
> clear in your contract of employment, staff are expected to be fully
> dressed at all times.
> Cleave

The first part of the text is particularly useful for inferring information about
the situation from the text, forming hypotheses and predicting. Students are
asked to infer implicit information from what is explicit.

| EXPLICIT INFORMATION | IMPLICIT INFORMATION |
|---|---|
| 9st 3 (excellent progress – 2lb of fat spontaneously combusted through joy and sexual promise) | This morning I weigh 9 stones 3lbs, which is very good because I have lost 2lbs since yesterday morning when I weighed 9 stones 5lbs. I probably burnt up those 2lbs thinking about having an affair with Daniel Cleve. |
| alcohol units 6 (v.g. for party) | I only drank 6 glasses of wine, which is very good, considering that I went to a party last night and I usually drink much more. |
| cigarettes 12 (continuing good work) | I only smoked 12 cigarettes, which is less than I usually smoke, so I can be considered to be in the process of giving it up. |
| calories 1,258 (love has eliminated need to pig out) | I only ate 1,258 calories, which is very good. I've probably lost my appetite because I'm in love. |

The use of abbreviations and omissions continue in the second part of the diary
and these can be exploited to consider the language features of a diary as well
as a straightforward language exercise, centred on tenses and articles.

> Daniel Cleaver (has) just sent me a message. (I) Was trying to work on
> (my) CV without Perpetua noticing (in preparation for improving (my)
> career) when Message Pending suddenly flashed on (the) top of (the)
> screen.

The third part of the text, Daniel Cleaver's E-mail leads to discussion about the language features of electronic correspondence in general and the new genres that have emerged as a result of the Internet. Finally, this is a good example to illustrate the fact that genres develop from an institutional setting, that the formal register (the tenor) is used because Daniel is Bridget's boss, but that the humour makes it a hybrid genre. If possible, it is always useful to compare the Spanish and Catalan published translations of the texts, to compare genres and discuss foreignising and domesticating strategies.

## 2. Textual organisation

| ASPECTS OF DISCOURSE | TRANSLATION COMPETENCE |
| --- | --- |
| Culturally popular patterns of text organisation (mapping) | *Communicative, Transfer,* |
| Signals of text patterns | *Extra-linguistic,* |
| Coherence | *Instrumental-professional,* |
| Cohesion | *Psycho-physiological* |

As an introduction to text structures, mapping and writing summaries, the following examples of genres produced by Australian junior school children[5] illustrate very basic aspects of text organisation. One broad distinction between Text 1 and Text 2 is that the first is organised non-chronologically and the second chronologically. Text 2 is in the past tense and Text 1 in the present. Text 2 is more personal and individualised (*a kangaroo* is unique, whereas in Text 1, *the shark*, or *sharks* serve to generalise. As they include common mistakes made by children, they can also be used for punctuation, spelling and grammar exercises.

> **Text 1**: "Sharks!" When people think of sharks they think of harsh, savage fish that attack at sight as a matter of fact they are completely wrong. Although there has been reports of shark attacks these are very rare. Most sharks won't even come near the shore so people swimming near the shore can consider themselves almost guaranteed safe.
>
> Sharks have special sense organs that can sense things up to one mile away. The shark uses fins to balance itself and it has to keep swimming or else it will sink. The shark's teeth are razor blade sharp and although you can only see two layers of teeth there are many in the jaw. Usually smaller fish follow the sharks around in hope of gathering up scraps that the shark may leave.

Text 2: A long time ago there was a kangaroo who did not have a tail and all the animals laughed at him and that made him sad. How did he get it back? He got it back by dipping his tail into lolly-pop syrup. The animals started to like him and then thay played with him. Would you like it? I would not because it wold be most annoing.
The End.
Decide which characteristics are true for each text and justify your choice:
1.  Organisation: Chronological/Non-chronological?
2.  Time: Specific/unspecific?
3.  Actors: individual/generic?

Text 3: The blood [in the egg] is full of food from the yolk. The tiny chick begins to grow. It is called an embryo. All animals are called embryos when they first begin to grow.
The following linguistic features are characteristic of scientific genres. Can you find examples of any of these characteristics in the above text?
1.  The universal present tense
2.  The impersonal passive
3.  The verbs identify experiential processes
4.  The sentences are asserted (rather than framed as questions) and contain verifiable propositions

Are these characteristics limited to scientific discourse?
Are these characteristics present in similar Catalan or Spanish genres?

## 3. Contrastive rhetoric

CONTRASTIVE RHETORIC

Contrasting cultures
Contrasting genres
Contrasting language systems

Several authors have pointed out the ideological pitfalls related to using contrastive rhetoric and genres in second language learning and learning to write at school. The problems, related to globalisation, social exclusion, multiculturalism and ethnocentricity are very clearly laid out in Cope and Kalantzis (1993: 1–21, 38–89). However, their arguments in favour of a genre-based approach to teaching language are even more convincing and they claim that,

"Lending consciousness does not require cultural and linguistic assimilation" (Ibid.: 18). Only by unlocking the secrets of the seemingly transparent and democratic discourse of globalisation, can outsiders learn to use the system and become insiders, or reject the system and fight against it.

Therefore, it is useful for students to understand the origins of Kaplan's expository (or informative) essay, known in US schools as the five-paragraph essay. Paragraph 1: Tell the reader what you are going to write about – develop the topic with one point in the following three paragraphs – Final paragraph: Tell the reader what you have written. Spanish readers often find US/UK writing incredibly obvious and simple. It is enlightening on this point simply to compare the layout of US/UK/Spanish textbooks.

The ideological questions are interesting, but in language for translators, whether or not to learn about standardised genres and contrastive rhetoric is not really at issue. This information is essential for their professional practice. Certainly, it is also important for them to realise that even standardised genres are dynamic and develop as the institutional practices they represent change. The business letter in Latin America and the Eastern European countries illustrates this point well, as changing business practices bring about changes in commercial correspondence (Beeby 2002). Some stereotypes still function even among European cultures. Knowing the norms will help students to interact with English texts for translation oriented discourse analysis for direct translation and to produce pragmatic English texts of the kind in demand in the inverse translation market.

## 4. Genres

The choice of genres for the language class will again depend on many factors, both pedagogical and professional. If we were designing a syllabus for inverse translation for third and fourth year students, the conditions of the work market would be essential in choosing genres to work with. As was mentioned above and in earlier publications (McAlister 1992; Beeby 1998) conditions of the inverse work market vary greatly from country to country, for example, it is very rare in the UK, very common in Finland and quite common in Catalonia. A recent survey of 29 translation agencies in Barcelona "Estudio sobre el mercado de la traducción de/al inglés/francés en las agencias de Barcelona"[6] indicated that the most common language combination requested by clients was Spanish-English and that the most common genres were: technical, commercial, publicity, legal, computer manuals and tourism (in that order). Furthermore, new technologies, such as the Internet, are 'redesigning'

English and Spanish, creating new genres, new texts and new identities. Predicting the effects of globalisation on language use is an uncertain business, nevertheless, some stereotypes still function. Knowing the 'norms' will help students to produce 'pragmatic' English text that will be acceptable in the US and the UK. However, increasingly, much inverse translation into English in Barcelona is translation into English as an international language. The language of the translation may be English but the multiple contexts of the TT may be very far from an English cultural context.

However, in designing a first year English language programme, it is not necessary to restrict class material to the most commonly translated genres. There are other criteria that are just as important. Which genres are most useful for illustrating textual interaction and organisation? Which genres are most useful for illustrating cultural, textual and language contrasts? Which genres best illustrate the use of specific macro-structures, registers, discourse markers, grammatical, lexical and formal features of English? Which genres are most useful for translation classes? Which genres are most useful for developing documentation skills and are most commonly translated? Which genres are likely to motivate the students and develop the cognitive skills and psychological attitudes that they are going to need as translators?

The following is a list of genres that might be suitably exploited in the first year language class for reading, writing and analysis. Genre studies are still at an early stage in classifying and describing genres and a lot of work still has to be done to write a comprehensive discourse-based grammar for different genres. Therefore, the features are in many cases intuitive and the list is provisional and only intended to provide yet another checklist to help teachers to find the right texts and tasks for class.

> **Academic abstracts:** Textual organisation: non-chronological SPRE[7] patterns. Language systems: tenses, modality, linking words +/− initial position, reference and repetition, articles.
> **Advertisements:** Textual interaction: intertextuality, hybrid genres, changing genres. Textual organisation: SPRE.
> **Agony columns:** Language systems: tenor, modality, degrees of probability.
> **Business letters:** Textual interaction: politeness systems. business cultures and changing genres, different stages in the negotiation (US/UK/Spain). Textual organisation: Layout, formulas. Language systems: pronouns, modality. Terminology and documentation.
> **CVs:** Textual interaction: Writing for a purpose (US/UK/Spain). Textual

organisation: Layout. Language systems: nominalisation.

**Editorials:** Textual organisation: opinion, argumentation, paragraph and sentence coherence, topic statement +/– initial position. Language systems: tenses, modality, position of linking words, cohesion, style-guides.

**Film and book reviews:** Language systems: tenses, modality, probability, hedging and asserting.

**Horoscopes:** Language systems: tenor, modality, degrees of probability.

**Instruction Leaflets:** Textual organisation: chronological and non-chronological SPRE patterns. Language systems: tenses, modality, linking words +/– initial position, reference and repetition. Terminology and documentation.

**Job applications:** Textual interaction: Writing for a purpose (US/UK/Spain).

**Jokes:** Textual interaction: culture and humour. Textual organisation: SPRE, parallel structures, repetition, change of deictic centre.

**Letters to the Editor:** Textual organisation: opinion, argumentation, counter-argumentation, paragraph and sentence coherence. Language systems: tenses, modality, linking words +/– initial position, cohesion.

**News articles:** Textual interaction: different versions of the same event in different newspapers, ideology. Textual organisation: SPRE patterns, paragraph and sentence coherence. Language systems: tenses, modality, linking words (time place adverbials) +/– initial position.

Newspaper headlines: Textual interaction: inferring information about the context, function (UK/US/Spain). Language systems: nominalisation, agent, metaphor, alliteration, rhyme.

**Public administration documents:** Textual interaction: Writing for a public for a purpose, politeness systems, Plain Language Movement (US/UK/Spain). Textual organisation: layout, coherence. Language systems: tenor (pronouns), modality, cohesion. Terminology and documentation.

**Scientific articles:** Textual interaction: adapting to different levels of specialisation (register). Textual organisation: non-chronological SPRE patterns. Language systems: tenses, modality, linking words +/– initial position. Terminology and documentation.

**Stories:** Textual interaction: adapting to readers from different cultures (US/UK); inferring information about the context from the text, ideology. Textual organisation: chronological narrative. Language systems: tenses, phrasal verbs, nominalisation and verbalisation.

## Stage 3: A genre and task-based syllabus integrating Stages 1 and 2

Experience in using parallel texts of original genres in both languages for translation classes has shown the usefulness of starting with genres to teach features
of language and strategies used in different genres in different cultures. Recent
research in discourse analysis, genre studies and contrastive rhetoric suggests
that we are beginning to be able to list discourse and language features in
standardised genres. Although it is true that we are still far from a comprehensive discourse-based description of any language, it seems to be the most
fruitful line of research for teaching writing, second language acquisition and
in particular, language for translators. Halliday (1978) suggests a three-part
division of emphasis for learning languages: (1) Learning language: the acquisition of the appropriate rules and conventions for using that language; (2)
Learning through language about culture and civilisation; (3) Learning about
language: conscious reflection and understanding of the way language works. I
have adapted this division to design a genre and task-based syllabus integrating
the translation and discourse elements defined in the pre-syllabuses.

1.  Learning language for translation: interacting with texts, translation ori-
    ented reading and writing for a purpose (procedural knowledge).
2.  Learning through language about translation, culture and civilisation
    (declarative knowledge).
3.  Learning about language for translation: conscious reflection and under-
    standing about the way language works for translation through contrasting
    cultures, rhetoric, genres and language systems (declarative knowledge).

In the past, we have worked with large, content-based language modules, using
a process-based communicative methodology. This approach can work with
small groups and unlimited time, but the pressures of numbers and limited
time have shown us that it is an inefficient use of the students' time. Practical
skills have to be learnt by doing, but if the doing is not focused, it will take a very
long time. It is essential to make a reasoned choice of priorities. Furthermore, if
students with intermediate-to-advanced language skills do not have very clearly
defined learning objectives, it is very difficult for them to realise that they are
making progress. Therefore, they are in danger of losing motivation, which
is the most precious of all the elements in a learning situation. The syllabus
proposed here is based on short, genre-based modules with task sheets to work
on the three-level division described above.

## Sample tasks

An introductory text could be an extract from a best seller that has been published in the UK and the US and translated into many different languages. A good choice for a first year class could be *Harry Potter and the Philosopher's Stone* that was published in the US as *Harry Potter and the Sorcerer's Stone*, in Spanish as *Harry Potter y la piedra filosofal* and in Catalan as *Harry Potter i la pedra filosofal*. It is a good choice because it can be worked on at all three levels and can be used to develop all the translation sub-competencies. It is:

- Student-oriented: Many students will have read or know about the Harry Potter phenomenon. The coherence, cohesion, syntax and word order are standard.
- Translation-oriented: The differences between the English and the American versions illustrate cultural transfer; the UK cultural markers are pronounced and the book provides a wide variety of challenges to the translator.
- Genre-oriented: The book includes a variety of genres that are recognisable as standardised English genres.

The following three task sheets (1ª, 2ª, and 3ª) are based on the first chapter of the four versions.

**Task Sheet 1ª**
**Learning language for translation**
*Harry Potter and the Philosopher's Stone* Chapter 1: 'The boy who lived'
Pre-reading activity: (Group work)
1. What do you know about the Harry Potter series, J. K. Rowling and who she was writing for?
2. What do you expect the first chapter is going to be about from the title?

Reading activities: (Individual work)
1. Read the text once and then skim pages 7–11 looking for vocabulary that describes what it means to be a Dursley and what it means to be 'as unDurleyish as it was possible to be'. Make two contrasting lists and give a title to each that sums up the main characteristics.
2. Identify the different genres in the text. Identify two linguistic clues that helped you to identify the genres. Which tenses are used most frequently in the different types of writing?

GENRE
CLUES
TENSES

3. Compare the verbs used to report speech in the Dursley and the unDursley dialogues.[8]
4. Is the 'normal' English SVO word order maintained in all the sentences on page 7? List the subjects of all the sentences and identify the cohesive strategies used by the author.[9]

<u>Writing activities:</u> (Pair and individual work)
Think of a recent event that was strange or mysterious:

1. Tell your neighbour about it.
2. Together, write about the event in the form of a brief news bulletin (100 words) for the BBC six o'clock news.
3. As homework, write about the event in a paragraph that is going to be the introductory paragraph for <u>one</u> of the following: a romantic story in a woman's magazine, a science fiction novel, a detective novel, an article in a scientific journal, an article on the first page of the *Sun*, an article in the *Sunday Times* Colour Supplement.

Task Sheet 2[a]
**Learning through language about translation, culture and civilisation**
*Harry Potter and the Philosopher's Stone* Chapter 1: 'The boy who lived'
<u>Cultural and translation awareness:</u> (Group work)

1. Identify cultural differences:
   – Where do you think the Dursley's live?
   – What is their house like?
   – What and when do they eat?
2. Which translation method would you choose if you were asked to translate *Harry Potter and the Philosopher's Stone* into Catalan or Spanish for a Barcelona publishing house?

METHOD:

3. Identify five culturally bound references in the text: objects or activities that have no obvious equivalent in Catalan or Spanish. Which strategies would you follow to choose an appropriate translation technique for each one?

REFERENCE
STRATEGIES
TECHNIQUES

Task Sheet 3ª
Learning about language for translation
Read this extract from Harry Potter in the four versions: UK, US, Spanish, Catalan

1. Identify and try to explain <u>any</u> differences between the UK and the US versions (format, punctuation, vocabulary, etc.).
2. Compare the Spanish and the Catalan translations and identify different translation techniques (format, punctuation, vocabulary, etc).
3. Do you think the translators followed the same translation method?
4. Do you think that they would have the same effect on the readers?
5. Do you think that they are representative of the norms of translating children's literature into Spanish and Catalan?[10]

**UK:**

**HARRY POTTER**

*and the Philospher's Stone*

J.K.ROWLING
Triple Smarties Gold Award Winner

**US:**

**Harry Potter**

AND THE SORCERER'S STONE

J.K.ROWLING

**SPANISH:**

J.K. ROWLING

**Harry Potter**

**y la piedra filosofal**

salamandra

**CATALAN:**

**Harry Potter**

*i la pedra filosofal*

J.K. ROWLING

EMPÚRIES

| HOGWARTS SCHOOL OF WITCHCRAFT AND WIZARDRY | HOGWARTS SCHOOL of WITCHCRAFT and WIZARDRY |
|---|---|
| Uniform | UNIFORM |
| *First-year students will require:* | First year students will require: |
| *1. Three sets of plain work robes (black)* | 1. Three sets of plain work robes (black) |
| *2. One plain pointed hat (black) for day wear* | 2. One plain pointed hat (black) for day wear |
| *3. One pair of protective gloves (dragon hide or similar)* | 3. One pair of protective gloves (dragon hide or similar) |
| *4. One winter cloak (black, silver fastenings)* | 4. One winter cloak (black, silver fastenings) |
| *Please note that all pupil's clothes should carry name tags* | Please note that all pupil's clothes should carry name tags |
| Set Books | COURSE BOOKS |
| *All students should have a copy of each of the following:* | All students should have a copy of each of the following: |
| The Standard Book of Spells (Grade 1) *by Miranda Goshawk* | *The Standard Book of Spells (Grade 1)* by Miranda Goshawk |
| A History of Magic *by Bathilda Bagshot* | *A History of Magic* by Bathilda Bagshot |
| Magical Theory by *Adalbert Waffling* | *Magical Theory* by Adalbert Waffling |
| A Beginnners' Guide to Transfiguration *by Emeric Switch* | *A Beginnners' Guide to Transfiguation* by Emeric Switch |
| One Thousand Magical Herbs and Fungi *by Phyllida Spore* | *One Thousand Magical Herbs and Fungi* by Phyllida Spore |
| Magical Drafts and Potions *by Arsenius Jigger* | *Magical Drafts and Potions* by Arsenius Jigger |
| Fantastic Beasts and Where to Find Them *by Newt Scamander* | *Fantastic Beasts and Where to Find Them* by Newt Scamander |
| The Dark Forces: A Guide to Self-Protection *by Quentin Trimble* | *The Dark Forces: A Guide to Self-Protection* by Quentin Trimble |
| Other Equipment | OTHER EQUIPMENT |
| *1 wand* | 1 wand |
| *1 cauldron (pewter, standard size 2)* | 1 cauldron (pewter, standard size 2) |
| *1 set glass or crystal phials* | 1 set glass or crystal phials |
| *1 telescope* | 1 telescope |
| *1 set brass scales* | 1 set brass scales |
| *Students may also bring an owl OR a cat OR a toad.* | Students may also bring an owl OR a cat OR a toad. |
| PARENTS ARE REMINDED THAT FIRST-YEARS ARE NOT ALLOWED THEIR OWN BROOMSTICKS | PARENTS ARE REMINDED THAT FIRST YEARS ARE NOT ALLOWED THEIR OWN BROOMSTICKS |

| COLEGIO HOGWARTS DE MAGIA | ESCOLA DE BRUIXERIEA HOGWARTS |
|---|---|
| UNIFORME | *Uniforme* |
| Los alumnos de primer año necesitarán: | *Els alumnes de primer necessitaran:* |
| – Tres túnicas sencillas de trabajo (negras). | *– Tres conjunts de roba de treball sense guarniments (negra)* |
| – Un sombrero puntiagudo (negro) para uso diario. | *– Un barret punxegut sense guarniments (negre) per a ús diari* |
| – Un par de guantes protectores (piel de dragón o semejante) | *– Un parell de guants protectors (antidrac o similars)* |
| – Una capa de invierno (negra, con broches plateados) | *– Una capa d'hivern (negra, amb cremallera platejada)* |
| (*Todas las prendas de los alumnos deben llevar etiquetas con su nombre.*) | *Recordeu que totes les peces de roba han d'anar marcades amb el nom de l'alumne/a.* |

LIBROS
Todos los alumnos deben tener un ejemplar de los siguientes libros:
*El libro reglamentario de hechizos* (clase 1), Miranda Goshawk.
*Una historia de la magia*, Bathilda Bagshot.
*Teoría mágica*, Adalbert Waffling.
*Guía de transformación para principiantes*, Emeric Switch.
*Mil hierbas mágicas y hongos*, Phyllida Spore.
*Filtros y pociones mágicas*, Arsenius Jigger.
*Animales fantásticas y dónde encontrarlos*, Newt Scamander.
*Las Fuerzas Oscuras. Una guía para la autoprotección*, Quentin Trimble.

*Llibres*
*Tots els alumnes han de tenir un exemplar dels llibres següents:*
*Llibre d'encanteris(nivell1)*, de Marina Fetillera
*Història de la màgia*, de Dolors Plorós
*Teoria de la màgia*, d'Albert Xarramecu
*Introducció a la transfiguració*, de Xavier Mudancer
*Mil i una herbes i bolets màgics*, de Rosa Rosae
*Pocions i beuratges màgics*, d'Arsènic Calze
*Bèsties fantàstiques i on trobar-les*, d'Ernest Salamàndric
*Les forces del mal: guia per a l'autodefensa*, de Pere de Tramolar

RESTO DEL EQUIPO
1 varita
1 caldero (peltre, medida 2)
1 juego de redomas de vidrio o cristal
1 telescopio
1 balanza de latón

*Material divers:*
*Una vareta màgica*
*Una marmita (de peltre del número 2)*
*Un joc de flascons de vidre*
*Un telescopi*
*Un joc de pesos de llautó*

Los alumnos también pueden traer una lechuza, un gato o un sapo.

*Els alumnes poden portar un mussol o un gat o un gripau.*

SE RECUERDA A LOS PADRES QUE A LOS DE PRIMER AÑO NO SE LES PERMITE TENER ESCOBAS PROPIAS

*US RECORDEM QUE ALS ALUMNES DE PRIMER NO ELS ESTÀ PERMÈS TENIR ESCOBRA VOLADORA*

## Notes

1. The Escuela Universitaria de Traductores e Intérpretes at the Universidad Autónoma de Barcelona was founded in 1972 and became the Facultad de Traductores e Intérpretes in 1992.

2. For bibliographical references to empirical research in the translation process, see Fraser (1996) and PACTE (2000).

3. The PACTE group is led by A. Hurtado and includes A. Beeby, M. Fernández, O. Fox, N. Martínez, W. Neunzig, M. Orozco, M. Presas, P. Rodríguez. For a description of the PACTE project, see PACTE (2000) and Beeby (2000).

4. In *Teaching Translation from Spanish to English*, the meta-language for talking about translation is based on Hatim and Mason (1990).

5. Texts used by Cope and Kalantzis (1993).

6. This survey was coordinated by Nicole Martínez (1999–2000) and was carried out by Ariadna Teixidó and Virginia Menguy.

7. Situation, Problem, Response, Evaluation.

8. This is a useful exercise for the students to recognise and start to use the great variety of 'verbs of saying' that are so characteristic of this genre in English: *chuckled, muttered, faltered, hissed, sobbed, murmured, chortled, grunted, mumbled, snapped*.

9. This is a 'textbook' example of English cohesive devices and simple co-ordination. The S-V-O word order is maintained throughout and the sentences are linked by conjunctions such as *and, then, but*. It is an excellent 'model' for students to follow.

10. In general, the Spanish translation method is foreignising (or adequate) whereas the Catalan is domesticating (or acceptable). The Catalan version is more concerned with preserving the humour than staying close to the original. This does seem to be a norm in Catalan translations of children's literature and television programmes that may be explained in terms of policies designed to promote and standardize Catalan as a minority language (Izard 2000).

## References

Beeby, Allison (1996a). *Worlds beyond Words: Teaching Translation from Spanish to English*. Ottawa: Ottawa University Press.

Beeby, Allison (1996b). "Course Profile: Licenciatura en traducción e interpretación". *The Translator, 2* (1), 113–126.

Beeby, Allison (1998). "Directionality". In Mona Baker (Ed.), *Encyclopedia of Translation* (pp. 63–67). London and New York: Routledge.

Beeby, Allison (2000). "Choosing an Empirical-Experimental Model for Investigating Translation Competence: The PACTE model". In Maeve Olohan (Ed.), *Intercultural Faultlines: Research Models in Translation Studies I: Textual and Cognitive Aspects* (pp. 43–56). Manchester: St. Jerome Publishing.

Beeby, Allison (2002). "Contrastive Rhetoric in Translator Training: Awareness of Hybrid Genres in the Global Village". In Luis Iglesias Rábade & Susana M. Doval (Eds.), *Studies in Contrastive Linguistics* (pp. 179–188). Santiago de Compostela: Universidad de Santiago de Compostela Publicación.

Beeby, Allison (2003). "Genre literacy and contrastive rhetoric in teaching inverse translation". In Dorothy Kelly et al. (Eds.), *La direccionalidad en traducción e interpretación: Perspectivas teóricas, profesionales y didácticas* (pp. 155–166). Granada: Editorial Atrio, S.L.

Berenguer, Laura (1996). "Didáctica de segundas lenguas en los estudios de traducción". In Amparo Hurtado Albir (Ed.), *La enseñanza de la traducción* (pp. 9–30). Castelló: Publicacions de la Universitat Jaume I.

Brehm, Justine (1997). Developing Foreign Language Reading Skill in Translator Trainees. Unpublished PhD. Universitat Jaume I.

Canale, M. (1983). "From Communicative Competence to Communicative Language Pedagogy". In J. C. Richards & R. W. Schmidt (Eds.), *Language and Communication*. London: Longman.

Connor, Ulla (1996). *Contrastive Rhetoric*. Cambridge and New York: Cambridge University Press.

Cope, William & Kalantzis, Mary (Eds.). (1993). *The Powers of Literacy: a Genre Approach to Teaching Writing*. London: The Falmer Press

Delisle, Jean (1980). *L'Analyse du discours comme méthode de traduction*. Ottawa: Ottawa University Press.

Delisle, Jean (1993). *La traduction raisonnée. Manuel d'initiation à la traduction profession-elle de l'anglais vers le francais*. Ottawa: Ottawa University Press.

Dreyfus, H. L. & Dreyfus, S. E. (1986). *Mind over Machine*. Oxford: Blackwell.

Elena García, Pilar (1990). *Aspectos teóricos y prácticos de la traducción*. Salamanca: Publicaciones de la Universidad de Salamanca.

Fraser, Janet (1996). "The Translator Investigated. Learning from Translation Process Analysis". *The Translator, 2* (1), 65–79.

Grindrod, M. (1986). "Portrait of a Profession: The Language Monthly Survey of Trans-lators". *Language Monthly, 29.*

Halliday, M. A. K. (1978). *Language as Social Semiotic*. London: Edward Arnold.

Hameline D. (1976). *Les objectifs pédagogiques en formation initiale et en formation continue*. Paris: Editions ESF.

Hatim, Basil & Mason, Ian (1990). *Discourse and the Translator. London:* Longmans.

Hoey, Michael (2001). *Textual Interaction: An Introduction to Written Discourse Analysis*. London and New York: Routledge.

Holmes, James (1972). "The Name and Nature of Translation Studies". Unpublished manuscript. Reprinted in 1988, *Translated! Papers on Literary Translation and Translation Studies*, 66–80. Amsterdam: Rodopi.

Hurtado Albir, Amparo (Ed.). (1996). *La enseñanza de la traducción*. Castellón: Universitat Jaume I.

Hurtado Albir, Amparo (Ed.). (1999). *Enseñar a traducir*. Madrid: Edelsa.

Izard, Natalia (2000). "Dubbing for Catalan Television". In Allison Beeby, Doris Ensinger, & Marisa Presas (Eds.), *Investigating Translation*. Amsterdam and Philadelphia: John Benjamins Publishing Company.

Kiraly, D. C. (1995). *Pathways to Translation. Pedagogy and Process*. Kent: The Kent State University Press.

Koltay, Tibor (1998). "Including Technical and Academic Writing in Translation Curricula". *Translation Journal, 3* (2). wysiwyg://44/http://accurapid.com/journal/04educ.htm

Leki, Ilona (1991). "Twenty-five years of contrastive rhetoric: Text analysis and Writing Pedagogies". *TESOL Quarterly, 25* (1), 123–144.

Mackenzie, Rosemary (2000). "POSitive Thinking about Quality in Translator Training in Finland". In Allison Beeby, Doris Ensinger, & Marisa Presas (Eds.), *Investigating Translation* (pp. 213–222). Amsterdam and Philadelphia: John Benjamins Publishing Company.

McAlister, G. (1992). "Teaching Translation into a Foreign Language – Status, Scope and Aims". In Cay Dollerup & Anne Loddegaard (Eds.), *Teaching Translation and Interpreting: Training Talent and Experience*. Amsterdam and Philadelphia: John Benjamins Publishing Company.

McCarthy, Michael & Carter, Ronald (1994). *Language as Discourse: Perspectives for Language Teaching*, London and New York: Longman.

Martínez Melis, Nicole (2001). Évaluation et Didactique de la Traduction: les cas de la traduction dans la langue étrangère. Unpublished PhD Thesis, Universitat Autònoma de Barcelona.

Mossop, Brian (2000). "What should be taught at translation school?" *Innovation in Translator and Interpreter Training*. http://www.fut.es/~apym/symp/mossop.html

Nord, Christiane (1991). *Text Analysis in Translation. Theory, Methodology and Didactic Applications for a Translation-Oriented Text Analysis*. Amsterdam and Atalanta: Rodopi.

Nord, Christiane (1999). "Translating as a Text-Production Activity". *Innovation in Translator and Interpreter Training*, http://www.fut.es/~apym/symp/nord.html

Orozco, Mariana (2000). Instrumentos de medida de la adquisición de la competencia traductora: construcción y validación. Unpublished PhD Thesis, Universitat Autònoma de Barcelona.

PACTE (2000). "Acquiring Translation Competence: Hypotheses and Methodological Problems of a Research Project". In Allison Beeby, Doris Ensinger, & Marisa Presas (Eds.), *Investigating Translation* (pp. 99–116). Amsterdam and Philadelphia: John Benjamins Publishing Company.

Scollon, Ron & Scollon, Suzanne Wong (1995). *Intercultural Communication*. Oxford UK and Cambridge USA: Basil Blackwell.

Séguinot, Candace (1994). "Technical Writing and Translation: Changing with the Times". *Technical Writing and Communication, 24* (3), 285–292.

Simpson, Jo Ellen (2000). "Topical Structure Analysis of Academic Paragraphs in English and Spanish". *Journal of Second Language Writing, 9* (3), 293–309.

Sternberg, R. J. (1996). *Cognitive Psychology*. Fort Worth: Harcourt Brace.

## Appendix

### Stage 1: A translation-based pre-syllabus

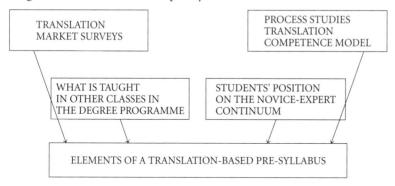

TRANSLATION
MARKET SURVEYS

PROCESS STUDIES
TRANSLATION
COMPETENCE MODEL

WHAT IS TAUGHT
IN OTHER CLASSES IN
THE DEGREE PROGRAMME

STUDENTS' POSITION
ON THE NOVICE-EXPERT
CONTINUUM

ELEMENTS OF A TRANSLATION-BASED PRE-SYLLABUS

### Stage 2: Discourse based translation-oriented pre-syllabus

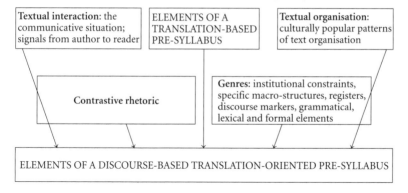

Textual interaction: the
communicative situation;
signals from author to reader

ELEMENTS OF A
TRANSLATION-BASED
PRE-SYLLABUS

Textual organisation:
culturally popular patterns
of text organisation

Contrastive rhetoric

Genres: institutional constraints,
specific macro-structures, registers,
discourse markers, grammatical,
lexical and formal elements

ELEMENTS OF A DISCOURSE-BASED TRANSLATION-ORIENTED PRE-SYLLABUS

### Stage 3: Context and task-based syllabus integrating Stages 1 and 2

| | |
|---|---|
| **LEARNING LANGUAGE FOR TRANSLATION:** Interacting with texts, translation-oriented reading and writing for a purpose | TASK 1A TASK 2A TASK 3A |
| **LEARNING THROUGH LANGUAGE ABOUT TRANSLATION, CULTURE AND CIVILISATION** | TASK 1B TASK 2B TASK 3B |
| **LEARNING ABOUT LANGUAGE FOR TRANSLATION (CONSCIOUS REFLECTION AND UNDERSTANDING):** contrasting cultures, rhetorics, genres and language systems | TASK 1C TASK 2C TASK 3C |

# Undergraduate and postgraduate translation degrees

## Aims and expectations

María González Davies

## Introduction

> Globally, this is the age of mass communications, of multi-media experiences and a world where audiences demand to share the latest text, be it film, song or book simultaneously across cultures. Nor has the development of English as a world language slowed down the process of translation; it has, on the contrary served to emphasize the significance of translation, as questions of cultural practice appear on the agenda.
> Susan Bassnett (1996: 20–21)

A number of operative questions come to mind when trying to relate undergraduate and postgraduate studies of translation. For example:

- What do we expect from an undergraduate student?
- What do we expect from a postgraduate student?
- What are these students' interests and needs?
- How are we going to organise their studies to cater for their needs?
- What do the students expect from us?

and, depending on the answers to the above,

- How and when can practice be offered considering the – mainly – professional orientation of Translation Studies?
- Should training be similar for undergraduates and for postgraduates?

It is unlikely that one set of answers to these questions will have universal validity, given the differences between different societies' concepts of university studies, their organisation, pedagogical approaches and generally accepted practices of translation. Nevertheless, there is surely something we can learn from one another, and in this paper, I would like to describe developments in Spain during the last decade of the twentieth century. Here, undergraduate and postgraduate "Translation and Interpreting" programmes are very popular and during the decade in question, they became very widespread. This rapid growth has, of course, both advantages and disadvantages and I will touch upon problems that have arisen and, in some cases, remained unsolved.

## Setting up an undergraduate degree

The educational system in Spain is highly centralised, each level depending to a great extent on the decrees, rules and regulations issued by the *Ministerio de Educación* in Madrid. These rules are published in the *Boletín Oficial del Estado* (*B.O.E*) and are prescriptive. In Catalonia, this system is taken a step further with the publication of the *Document Oficial de la Generalitat de Catalunya* (DOGC), which regulates Catalan affairs.[1]

In all autonomous communities, translation has to be offered in both official languages. This, of course, increases the number of hours, subjects and teachers required and raises the cost of the programmes.

At university level, there are four kinds of subject: (i) *troncales* (core), which are set by the *Ministerio* and are compulsory throughout Spain, (ii) *obligatorias de universidad* (obligatory for the university) compulsory subjects set by each faculty and approved by their university, (iii) *optativas* (optional), which are proposed by each department and have to be approved by the faculty and the university, and *de libre elección* (free choice), which can be chosen from other studies at the university. As from 1987, to obtain a degree, at least 300 credits must be completed.[2] This usually takes four years divided into two cycles. Most subjects are four-monthly with a minimum of 4,5 credits and some are yearly with a minimum of 9 credits, as decreed by the *B.O.E.*. Before 1987, to obtain a degree, students had to complete programmes lasting five or six years and centred on subjects as opposed to credits.[3]

In the 1970s and 80s Translation Studies was taught in three Spanish universities: the Autònoma in Barcelona, Las Palmas in the Canary Islands, and Granada. These programmes, however, were not full degrees (*licenciatura*), but three-year *diplomaturas*. This situation has changed dramatically since 1991 when Translation Studies became *licenciaturas*. There are now nineteen Translation degrees, as well as eleven postgraduate and nine doctoral programmes. Directly related to this, an Association of Spanish University Centres and Departments of Translation and Interpreting (*Conferencia de Centros y De-*

*partamentos Universitarios de Traducción e Interpretación del Estado Español* – www.confetrad.org) was set up in 1993 to promote and co-ordinate all these centres and academic translation activities. The association, which is independent of the Ministerio, meets once a year (more often if necessary) to deal with specific issues such as the design of new programmes. The success of the faculties has also favoured the creation of a professional association or *Colegio* – a concept deeply ingrained in the Spanish tradition. For the moment, there are strong associations in Catalonia, Granada and Las Palmas that will probably set up a *Colegio* in the next two years.

Translation started as an option within philology, the only *licenciatura* that involved a foreign language. However, different factors contributed to the greater popularity of translation studies, mainly the access it offered to a broader range of languages, its professional orientation, the wider choice of jobs it might lead to compared to philology and, last but not least, the fact that Spain is one of the countries with the highest output of translations per year, not only into Spanish but also into the other languages spoken in the country. In 2003[4] about 26% of all publications in Spain were translations, a percentage that had not changed substantially from 1994. These translations also include translations between the languages spoken in Spain, an expanding market. English, Spanish, French and German are the most translated languages. Seventeen per cent of these publications are literary. In English-speaking countries percentages of translations are usually between 3% and 5% of total publications a year and are mostly literary (Venuti 1995; Bellos 1999).

The most published subjects in Spain are social sciences and the humanities, followed by literature, and then teaching and education, including text books and, finally, science and technology.[5] These preferences have informed the choice of specialised translation subjects offered at the faculties of translation as market output is usually considered when setting them up. However, the choice is often limited by the profiles of the available teaching staff who, at universities, are usually contracted according to a given professional and academic specialisation. Departments and curricula are usually divided according to languages and centred around language combinations as in most universities in the world. Proposals to change this structure have been put forward by, for instance, Robinson (1999), who suggests a move from territorial cultures to professional or discipline cultures which would call upon translators to act as intermediaries. In such a structure, in translation schools, there would be departments of legal, commercial, or scientific translation, for instance, instead of the traditional focus on country-to-country translation.

At the POSI[6] meeting held in London in 1998, it became clear that different countries favour different approaches to translation training. In some, it is conceived as an undergraduate degree and in others, especially in mainly English-speaking countries, it exists mainly as a postgraduate degree. In Spain, the 1991 decree transforming translation *diplomaturas* into *licenciaturas* only came into existence as a result of, as Beeby puts it (1996: 119), "arduous negotiations between Barcelona, Granada, Las Palmas and the Ministry of Education". Against it stood academic and political considerations: the prevalent view of translation and interpreting as "non-academic" studies, not suitable for a university framework, and the fierce opposition of philology departments which foresaw a drop-off in student numbers. Perhaps not surprisingly, established professional associations of translators and interpreters were also opposed, viewing the *licenciaturas* as potential sources of market competitors.

On the other hand, extending *diplomatura* studies by a year would not only amount to an admission that translation and interpreting were subjects suitable for academic studies; the move also paved the way for new teaching jobs. In addition, a whole new area of research opened before non-tenured university teachers. The university reforms provided the opportunity to adjust to a world more and more dependent on technology, and to young people used to communicative ways of learning. Ironically, though, professional translators did not qualify for the new teaching posts, because university teachers in Spain need both a PhD qualification and to pass a public exam and there were no translation and interpreting graduates until 1995.

One solution to this problem was to contract, on the one hand, translators with a university degree as associate teachers and, mainly, philology PhD holders who were also part-time translators. This mix of staff is the norm in translation departments in Spain, which can place translation students and their teachers at cross purposes, because their expectations as to what university studies imply are different. Philology-oriented teachers wish to see more linguistics and literature in the curriculum, whereas the more professionally oriented students wish for more practice and not too much theory.

Foreign language teachers in secondary schools have traditionally taught as if philology was the direct destination of their best students and have not included translation activities in their classes. However, since the introduction of translation and interpreting as a full university degree, there are signs of change: the number of talks and workshops on translation in foreign language learning has increased at foreign language teaching conferences in Spain.

## Teaching undergraduates

Those of us who teach undergraduates can see mirrored some of the most traditional views of the non-specialist in their opinions and approach to translation, especially, of course, in their first year. That is why, when setting up an undergraduate programme, two questions are crucial: what do we expect from an undergraduate student? and, what do they expect of us? Students with little experience of translation have specific needs that do not correspond to those of postgraduate students who are usually older, more mature and have professional experience. On the other hand, we have observed that students who enrol for a postgraduate course who have not followed a degree in translation lack skills – such as resourcing or more cognitive skills such as the application of translation strategies – which are familiar to translation graduates. Students with a translation degree have received training in knowledge management of different disciplines and in problem-spotting and problem-solving skills which they can apply to most text types and disciplines, an advantage in a professional world where translation is considered more as a business than an art and where multidisciplinary translators are in high demand (see, for instance, Bajo et al. 2001; González Davies & Scott-Tennent 2001; González Davies & Scott-Tennent 2005; Kussmaul 1995; Lörscher 1991, 1992; Orozco 2000; Scott-Tennent & González Davies 2000; Séguinot 1991; Tirkkonen-Condit 2001). Students with a degree who later follow a postgraduate course in translation have a greater command of the terminology and concepts of a given field but lack the flexibility and translating skills of someone who has been practising and reflecting on the subject for four years.

An added difficulty for teachers of translation and interpreting as academic subjects is that, owing to the scant tradition in translation training, there are very few publications directed at the undergraduate. Most articles and books on training are addressed to teachers of postgraduate courses or to experienced translators. However, translation training does seem to be moving away gradually from traditional teacher and text-centred instruction based on the "read and translate" directive and is drawing from more updated pedagogical approaches such as the communicative, the humanistic or the social constructivist (Kiraly 1995, 2000; González Davies 2004) and from methods such as task-based learning that favour a systematic approach to training, learner autonomy and team work (Hurtado (Dir.) 2000; González Davies (Ed.) 2003).

Finally, we are still looking for answers to the question of what translation competence consists in; what basic tools our students need to cope reasonably with a translation; what the characteristics of undergraduate translation students are; which activities will

- motivate them
- make them more autonomous problem solvers
- help them with problem-spotting and solving
- encourage them to identify and respect text types, conventions of presentation and styles
- make them understand the full importance of the translation assignment and reader

and to the still much debated question of the amount of translation theory a programme should include. For instance, recent research seems to point to the fact that students who follow a course on Translation Theories in their first year perform better sooner than those who do not do the course until later (Orozco 2000).

The aims of an undergraduate degree in translation studies published by most universities are close to the following, taken from the *Facultat de Ciències Humanes, Traducció i Documentació* at the University of Vic:

a.    To produce translators and interpreters in, at least, two foreign languages and prepare them to become part of a competitive market with high intellectual, professional and technical skills.
b.    To produce native language editors and style correctors who can work in publishing.
c.    To create the basis for graduates to work in journalism, television and cinema (dubbing and subtitling),[7] radio, public relations, tourism, companies with international relations, etc.
d.    To prepare students for teaching jobs in the foreign and native languages.[8]
e.    To prepare students for postgraduate studies and research.


## The learning process: Translation

Variables such as age, maturity, world knowledge, and opinions about translation are crucial in the first stages of translation training. The student intake consists of foreign language learners who still think that translation has basically to do with comparing languages and with dictionaries (González Davies & Cotoner 1999). In most parts of Spain, students are accustomed to the communicative approach to language learning, which forbids any use of translation in the classroom except, sometimes, for exams. Therefore, students' attitude towards translation is, at the least, ambiguous: they either think it is "easy" or, quite the contrary, in Alan Duff's words "a painful experience" (1993:17) probably precisely because they have never really dealt with it in context, but only in relation to exams or to corrections where the emphasis is on what is wrong. As Lörscher says (1992:111)

> In my corpus of translations produced by foreign language learners, a large number of indicators of sign-oriented translation can be detected. In sign- or form-oriented translating, subjects transfer source-language text segments by focusing on their form and by replacing them with target language forms. This transfer of forms/signs is brought about without recourse to the sense of the two segments involved.

Students are often confused and strive for a "correctness/equivalence" which they believe the dictionary can give them. A first step, then, seems to be to help the students become aware of two main points:

a.  in translation, the process is as important as the product
b.  different factors such as the translation assignment will situate the transla-
    tion on a cline of degrees of fidelity between literal and free translation

In their second year, all this can be dealt with in further detail to take the students to a stage where they are aware of the problems – or at least wary!

The subjects taught in these first two years are traditionally divided into the following groups:

a.  *Language A,* native languages, which in the autonomous regions are two. The students have to choose into which Language A they want to take their main translation subjects although they can study the other Language A in optional subjects (210 hours).
b.  *Language B or C,* foreign languages. B indicates excellent skills, C, a lower level of expertise. (240 / 285 hours).
c.  Translation from B languages into their chosen A language (210 hours).
d.  Background subjects such as an introduction to theories of translation or computer skills applied to translation.

Most faculties in Spain are revising these divisions and wish to increase the number of hours dedicated to studying C Languages, reverse translation and the students' native languages, because experience has shown that an unexpected poor performance can often be traced to an inadequate command of a Language A.

In their third year different modalities of specialised translation are introduced, such as dubbing and subtitling, scientific, legal, commercial, or literary texts. It is at this point that students start translation from their C language and follow subjects on resourcing for specialised terminology.

It is also in the third year that students have to decide whether they wish to specialise as translators or as interpreters and follow one pathway or the other. This is not always easy and levels may vary since not all faculties offer the same number of credits in interpreting owing to the high cost of the equipment, the difficulty in finding teachers and the low number of students who choose this pathway.[9]

The students' attitude and approach to translation in the third and fourth years change positively in general, and specifically in aspects such as increased self-confidence and awareness of different ways to solve problems (improved resourcing skills, justification of translation choices, etc.). This is a time for consolidation after which students can proceed to a third cycle and/or professional practice.

We can say, then, that the undergraduate degree as it stands sets the foundations and lays emphasis on the following points:

a.  instrumentalisation, i.e. familiarisation with available tools and resources, especially new technologies
b.  pre-specialisation, i.e. an introduction to different fields to encourage flexibility – an openness to face any specialisation later on
c.  transferable skills that can be applied to most language combinations, i.e., strategy choice, decision-making based on motivated choices, awareness of conventions and cultural markers
d.  ability to move away from an exclusively mechanical practice of translation towards reflective practice and constant updating.

These areas can be taught in a programme that tries to redress the balance between professional and academic issues by including subjects related to the following:

1.  Language work: continual acquisition and improvement of the source language(s) and target language(s), awareness of the existence and pitfalls of cross-linguistic transfer.
2.  Subject matter: introduction to encyclopaedic knowledge related to different disciplines, awareness of conventions of presentation in both the source and the target languages, introduction to terminology management.

3. Translation skills: problem-spotting and problem-solving, encouragement of creativity and self-confidence as translators, awareness and use of strategies, ability to decide on degrees of fidelity according to translation assignment and text function, learning to meet client's expectations, ability to produce quality translations at speed, overcoming constraints, practising direct *and* reverse translation to meet real market demands, self and peer evaluation skills.
4. Resourcing skills: paper, electronic, and human.
5. Computer skills: familiarisation with a translator's workbench, computer-assisted translation, human assisted automatic translation, acquisition of electronic resourcing skills: databases and access to digital sources, unidirectional (e.g. WEB pages) and bi-directional (e.g. e-mail) distance communication.
6. Professional skills: awareness of translator's rights, contracts, payment, familiarisation with different editing processes and as much real life practice as possible at least in their last two years.

These points reflect a realistic perspective on what can be achieved and on the conclusions drawn up at the POSI meeting in Belgium in 1997, where the participants tried to reach an agreement about the basic components needed to set up translator training courses. The published conclusions (no author specified 1997) were that a model course should be professionally oriented and include an entrance examination and classes on methodology of translation and translation theory – all this bearing in mind the effects of globalisation which require high quality translation into many languages (not only into the native tongue), inclusion of courses on language technology and computerisation, modularization of courses to meet growing specialisation, documentation and terminology, and internships.

At the meeting of the *Conferencia de Centros y Departamentos Universitarios de traducción e Interpretación del Estado Español* in 1998, the faculties agreed to distribute a questionnaire to follow their graduates' activities and, thus, carry out an assessment of the appropriateness of their courses. At the 1999 meeting, three had done so and the others were in the process. The results were similar for all three and have not varied substantially in the last four years: about 20% of graduates who replied had continued studying, 40% were working in jobs which deal directly with translating or interpreting, and 20% were working in jobs related to their knowledge of languages but not necessarily to translating or interpreting.

## Postgraduate studies

The third university cycle includes postgraduate, master and doctoral degrees. In Spain, postgraduate and master programmes are not subject to official regulation,[10] whereas doctoral programmes are tightly controlled by the regulations in *B.O.E.* 30.4.98. The latter include two periods, the first focused on classes and lectures (20 credits) and the second on the completion of a tutored dissertation (12 credits). In an effort to make doctoral studies – traditionally considered as very academic and only suitable for students who wish to become academics themselves – valid for jobs outside the academic sphere, they are gradually being tailored to resemble postgraduate or master studies and a certificate is offered after the completion of each of the mentioned periods.[11] This has meant that, in some centres, doctoral programmes also function as master degrees, especially in professionally oriented studies such as law, medicine or translation. That is, with the new focus, the student's aim when starting a doctoral programme is not necessarily to become a Doctor. Another clear indication are the *Doctoralia* courses, organised by French universities. These are addressed to doctoral students and aim at helping them to establish contact and become familiar with the business world. This immediately raises the question of where the line between research and professional training should be drawn, if it should be drawn at all, or whether specific degrees have different requirements.

The aims of doctoral courses according to the *B.O.E.* (1998) are mainly four:

a.   to train new researchers,
b.   to encourage research teams,
c.   to train new teachers and,
d.   to ensure professional, scientific, technical and artistic development.

However, probably because changes are still recent, students who enrol in these programmes are more interested in research than in a professional orientation. As Rusiecki (1999:9) suggests, two kinds of research can be distinguished: what he calls "original research, type A" which covers "research leading to new discoveries, new generalisations, new theories; that is, enlarging the frontiers of human knowledge", and "original research, type B" which is more modest and covers "the ability to marshal well-known facts in a new way, to present generally accepted theories from a new angle, to look at well-researched social or literary phenomena with the eye of an observer coming from another culture...". Both types can be observed in Spanish doctoral theses where the emphasis is on analysing and interpreting one or more of the issues to which the students were introduced in their undergraduate studies.

There are doctoral programmes in translation in Spain at universities that do not offer an undergraduate degree in translation, and there is a clear distinction between the contents of programmes organised by philology departments and those offered by translation faculties: the former are more centred around literature and the history of translation, the latter more around a combination of academic subjects and professional skills.

There are two kinds of non-doctoral postgraduate courses: *posgrados*, which usually take a year and involve around 200 contact hours and lectures, and *másters* which cover two years and involve at least 300 contact hours to which must be added 100 hours dedicated to writing a dissertation or following an internship. Their main aim is invariably professional: to give the students the skills and knowledge to find their place in the market.

From the university standpoint, these programmes promote greater collaboration between universities and companies as far as programme contents are concerned and also because of the higher number of professional translators that are involved in the teaching. The great majority deal with non-literary subjects and even those that are centred around literature, if organised by a faculty of translation, are mostly oriented towards publishing practices as exemplified in the following quotation from a description of a postgraduate course on Literary Translation (2000–2001) whose aim is "to enable the students to participate in the different stages of the publishing process of literary translation". This is done by combining subjects about literary translation with others such as "Professional alternatives in the field of literary translation".

In 1991 a meeting of 28 universities was held at the University of Valencia[12] to deal with what was in those days the dawning of postgraduate courses, almost unknown in Spain and regarded as an importation from the USA. The conditions of registration for a postgraduate course were to hold a degree and... to be rich! Indeed, this is still the case, since postgraduate courses are much more expensive that any other course at universities. In the early 1990s, it was standard practice for a postgraduate course to offer a minimum of 50 credits. Private institutions have also offered postgraduate courses in the past, but recently they find they need to be affiliated to a university for prestige and credibility. Often, these courses are designed by companies that later take on the students so that the high price is "justified" by guaranteeing a job later on.

## Teaching postgraduates

In postgraduate courses the students' aims are clear: they register for further specialisation in one or more subjects that they have followed as undergraduates, to cover formative voids left by the first degree, to cater for new professional needs, to update their knowledge in the field, to reorient their careers or, simply, to extend their student life. In all cases, the overall final aim is entry into a profession. Therefore, a postgraduate course centres around fine tuning and further enhancement of understanding of the contents suggested for an undergraduate degree: Language work, subject matter, translation skills, resourcing skills, computer skills, and a special emphasis on professional skills. Real life practice is easier with postgraduate students because, as graduates, there are no legal impediments for them to work.[13] Also, many participants in postgraduate courses already work as translators.

Here, it may be worth mentioning that postgraduate translation programmes also differ depending on whether they are set up for philology students or translation graduates. This means that the subjects and topics will have to be different to cater for the students' needs depending on their academic background.

The general aims for postgraduates, then, could be summarised as follows:

a.  specialisation and knowledge management
b.  refining of transferable skills
c.  adaptability to a productivity market with clients and companies with different expectations and standards.

## Conclusions

What then can a university Translation programme offer at any level? Neurological research seems to indicate that the sooner a skill is developed, the more receptive and tuned the brain will be towards it. If our students learn to understand the process of translating, to evaluate products after reflective learning, they can talk about their work and move away from intuitive explanations by developing their critical skills. And they will probably do all this much sooner and with a more solid grounding than most translators who have not been through this experience. So, in a first stage they can acquire general skills with emphasis on procedural knowledge (knowing *how*). This will enable them to opt for a professional postgraduate programme or a research-based doctoral programme where they will specialise by moving onto the appropriate declarative knowledge (knowing *what*) and expanding the procedural knowledge dealt with in their undergraduate years.

New challenges include improving what we already have and offering our students training in translation quality evaluation, in localising and globalising, and in computer skills which must move from being part of specialised subjects to being practised in all subjects in one way or another – with regular in-service training for teachers. Optimising teaching skills is another challenge in a discipline with scant tradition in the area: Translation classes should adapt to the students and encompass a variety of pedagogical approaches, laying the emphasis on pedagogic or on professional activities depending on whether the sessions are aimed at undergraduates, postgraduates, or professional translators. As to the teaching method perhaps we should lean towards meaningful learning and favour learner autonomy at all levels. Most researchers agree that we now live in a Post-Method Condition (Block 2000): research in Foreign and Second Language Acquisition seems to show that there is no one-and-only best method but that the key is adaptability of the teacher to the group and the subject, to use the most appropriate method for each teaching context, and to establish real communication between teachers and students.

As to the teachers and researchers, we need more empirical and experimental studies on the academic and the professional fronts to bridge the gap between the theory, the practice and the social and professional recognition of our students and our centres.

Certainly, an underlying question in our field and indeed in any other professionally oriented programme of university studies is: practice *versus* academe or practice *plus* academe? We can offer an introduction to both at a first stage and then let the students themselves opt for one or the other once they have graduated.

## Notes

1. For instance, the requirements, as regards undergraduate studies, for authorisation as a court translator are slightly different for translating into Spanish (*B.O.E.* 23.2.96 and 2.4.97) or into Catalan (DOGC 30.3.00).

2. Each credit corresponds to 10 contact hours.

3. All this may change with the integration of Spanish Universities in the European Credit System in 2010.

4. These are the latest available official numbers at the time of writing, published by the *Ministerio de Educación* in September 2003.

5. Statistics taken from *Estadísticas: Libros, Archivos y Bibliotecas*, 2003. Ministerio de Cultura.

6. POSI stands for *Praxis-orienterte Studieninhalte / Practice-oriented study content for the training of translators*. It is a European project whose main aim is to promote quality and uniformity in translator training programmes.

7. Again, a much wider market than in English-speaking countries owing to the great amount of English-speaking films and media products that are imported into Spain.

8. Here we could add the teaching of translation.

9. All faculties have to offer the 16 credits stipulated by the *B.O.E.*

10. Permission for the universities to offer these courses was published in the 1983, 1987 and 1998 *B.O.E.* where it simply says that "Universities... can offer courses for graduates... especially oriented towards professional issues" (art. 17).

11. The headlines in most Spanish newspapers following the diffusion of the decree (30.4.98) were similar to these: *El Ministerio de Educación crea un título de especialización entre la licenciatura y el doctorado* (The Ministry of Education creates a specialised qualification between an undergraduate degree and a doctorate) (*La Vanguardia*, 1st May 1998) or *Fer un doctorat també ajudarà a trobar feina* (Taking a doctorate will help you find a job) (*Gaceta Universitària*, 3rd May 1998).

12. Information given by Francisco García Manrique, vicerrector of postgraduate studies at the Universidad de La Laguna, Tenerife (1991).

13. In Spain at least, it is difficult to set up internships with undergraduates because of established practitioners' fear of interference. This has been compensated for by setting up a professional environment either in the traditional classroom or, more imaginatively in some faculties, in a specially organised space.

## References

Bajo, T., Padilla, P., Muñoz, R., Padilla, F., Gómez, C., Puerta, C., Gonzalvo, P., & Macizo, P. (2001). "Comprehension and memory processes in translation and interpreting". *Quaderns. Revista de Traducció, 6,* 27–31.

Bassnett, S. (1996). "The Meek or the Mighty: Reappraising the Role of the Translator". In R. Álvarez & C. A. Vidal (Eds.), *Translation, Power, Subversion* (Topics in Translation, 8). Clevedon: Multilingual Matters.

Beeby, A. (1996). "Barcelona: Licenciatura en traducción e interpretación". *The Translator, 2* (1), 113–126.

Bellos, D. (1999). "Nuestra lengua propia y ajena. El panorama de la traducción literaria en Gran Bretaña en los años noventa". *Vasos Comunicantes, 13,* 26–34. Translation by Celia Filipetto.

Block, D. (2000). "Is Method Really Dead?". *A.P.A.C. of News, 34* (June), 5–10.

García Manrique, F. In the radio programme "De par en par", RNE-1 (Radio Nacional de España), 12.4.91.

Duff, A. (1993). "Our Interviews: Alan Duff". In Davies M. González (Ed.), *A.P.A.C. of News, 19*, 17–19.

*Estadísticas: Libros, archivos y Bibliotecas* (2003). Ministerio de Cultura. www.mcu.es/libro

González Davies, M. & Cotoner, L. (1999). "Aproximación a una metodología activa en las clases de traducción". *Traducción, Interpretación, Lenguaje*, Madrid: Actilibre.

González Davies, M., Scott-Tennent, C., & Rodríguez, F. (2001). "Training in the Application of Translation Strategies for Undergraduate Scientific Translation Students". *Meta, 46* (4), 737–744.

González Davies, M. (Ed.). (2003). *Secuencias. Tareas para el Aprendizaje Interactivo de la Traducción Especializada*. Barcelona: Octaedro.

González Davies, M. & Scott-Tennent, C. (2005). "A problem-solving and student-centred approach to the translation of cultural references". *Meta, 50* (1). Special Issue: *Enseignement de la traduction dans le monde*.

González Davies, M. (2004). *Multiple Voices in the Translation Classroom. Activities, Tasks and Projects*. Amsterdam and Philadelphia: John Benjamins.

Hurtado, A. (Dir.). (2000). *Enseñar a traducir. Metodología en la formación de traductores e intérpretes*. Madrid: EDELSA.

Kiraly, D. (1995). *Pathways to Translation*. Kent, Ohio and London: The Kent State University Press.

Kiraly, D. (2000). *A Social Constructivist Approach to Translator Education. Empowerment from Theory to Practice*. Manchester: St. Jerome.

Kussmaul, P. (1995). *Training the Translator*. Amsterdam & Philadelphia: John Benjamins.

Lörscher, W. (1991). *Translation Performance, Translation Process, and Translation Strategies. A Psycholinguistic Investigation*. Tübingen: Narr.

Lörscher, W. (1992). "Process-oriented research into translation and its implications for translation teaching". *Interface, Journal for Applied Linguistics, 6* (2), 105–117.

Orozco, M. (2000). *Instrumentos de medida de la adquisición de la competencia traductora: construcción y validación*, unpublished PhD, Universitat Autònoma de Barcelona.

POSI (1997). "Making Translator Training More Practical", *Language Today*, December, 4–5.

Robinson, D. (1999). "La formació de traductors al nou milleni. Globalització i localització". Round Table organised by the *Facultat de Ciències Humanes, Traducció i Documentació*, University of Vic, Spain. 21.10.99.

Rusiecki, J. (1999). "Postgraduate Study of English in Europe". *The European English Messenger, VIII* (2), 7–12.

Scott-Tennent, C. & Gonzalez Davies, M. (2000). "Translation Strategies and Translation Solutions: Design of a didactic prototype and empirical study of results". In A. Beeby, D. Ensinger, & M. Presas (Eds.), *Investigating Translation* (pp. 107–117). Amsterdam and Philadelphia: John Benjamins.

Séguinot, C. (1991). "A Study of Student Translation Strategies". In S. Tirkkonen-Condit (Ed.), *Empirical Research in Translation and Intercultural Studies* (pp. 79–88). Tübingen: Gunter Narr.

Tirkkonen-Condit, S. (2001). "Metaphors in Translation Processes and Products", *Quaderns. Revista de Traducció, 6*, 11–15.

Venuti, L. (1995). *The Translator's Invisibility*. London and New York: Routledge.

# The role of translation studies within the framework of linguistic and literary studies

Soňa Preložníková and Conrad Toft

Generally accepted opinion states that translation studies *per se* should only be offered as a full undergraduate or alternatively, and perhaps preferably, as a postgraduate programme; that this is the only way in which professional translators can be prepared for entry onto the market. Our aim here is not to challenge that assumption as the ideal, but to demonstrate that this ideal is not always available under local conditions and to suggest the best approach to translation studies for environments in which compromises have to be made. We will show that whilst we cannot expect to produce professional translators in such a study, it can be a worthwhile component of linguistic and literary studies.

## Background

Many of the examples below come from our own experience teaching at Department of English and American Studies in the University of Constantine the Philosopher in Nitra, Slovakia. The national language of Slovakia, Slovak, is spoken by less than six million people worldwide, most of these people living within the country itself. When we consider the situation within Europe where at least 35 majority languages are used (BBC 2001), we can see that Slovak is not in a unique position as a "small" language. The phenomena we describe here are equally true for many other languages, and the environment is common to many of the countries in Central and Eastern Europe. However, not all the languages with small numbers of speakers within Europe suffer from the same difficulties. When we consider languages such as Slovene or Welsh, local geographical or political conditions make these languages more attractive to translation institutes and more translators are produced to satisfy the needs of local markets.

Now that Slovakia and its neighbours are integrated with the European Union, graduates from translation institutes which provide professional training in translation and interpreting are being employed within governmental organisations and the European Union itself. The current European Union policy is that all majority languages (defined as those which are national languages of the member states) are official languages of the European Union. Slovakia's accession to the European Union, requires the services of Slovak translators and interpreters for all the other EU majority languages. Until recently, the only Slovak Translation Institute with a long tradition was in the capital, Bratislava (one of only two in former Czechoslovakia, together with the Institute of Translation Studies at Charles University, Prague). It would not have been able to produce enough trained translators for the market (even if it covered all of those languages), and so other universities across Slovakia have recently opened translation studies of their own. However, the results of these newer institutes will not be seen for some time to come. The situation in Slovakia is better, however, than in some of the European Union's other new Member States. When the European Commission held a concourse for translators and interpreters in 2003, it found that a great many people applied, but very few of them were trained translators, who had the skills necessary for the work. The EU needed 135 assistant translators from each of the new Member States but less than half the required number passed the entry tests for Lithuania, and only 37 for Malta. More than double the required number were successful in Slovakia (SME 2004).

There is also an increasing demand for translators locally. At the same time, the general lack of language graduates and increasing internationalisation of local business interests mean that those who are trained for the translation profession may find themselves attracted by inflated salaries for work other than translation within the business sector (but not as translators) and increased opportunities abroad. The situation is not helped by the fact that as in many other countries translation is not widely viewed as a profession – translators here are underpaid and have low status. With the collapse of many traditional industries after the collapse of Communism at the end of the nineteen eighties, the governments in these countries are trying to promote the tourist industry (with varying degrees of success). The result of all these changes is a widening gap between the demand for and supply of professional translators.

Until this gap is narrowed we are faced with a situation in which the shortfall of professional translations is filled with translations performed by untrained translators with often amusing but potentially serious results. With the exception of sworn translators for official documents there is no regulation of translators and anyone can set up as a translator. We can see already that government bodies are employing graduates of other disciplines, such as language and literature graduates, to fulfil translation roles (relying on in-house training) despite their lack of adequate training and the importance of such work. Whilst our own university is primarily a teacher-training institute, many of our graduates translate part-time (perhaps not surprisingly given the low level of secondary school teachers' wages).

Universities have already responded to the need for more translation institutes to be opened to satisfy the demand. That is clearly a good long-term solution but requires teacher-training and help from other European institutions to achieve. In 2002, the University of Constantine the Philosopher in Nitra opened its undergraduate translation and interpreting degree, but the first graduates from this programme, for example, will not emerge until 2007.

Meanwhile the demand continues to grow. One solution offered in Slovakia has been a part-time postgraduate translation studies programme. This programme was first opened in 1999 at four universities with combinations of French, English, and German. However, even this programme produced fewer than 100 graduates during its first four years. Another solution to the problem is that which is described here – that translation is included within language studies to make up the shortfall, as a temporary measure to ensure that translations produced by our graduates will meet at least basic requirements. Even when the market matures, the need to give language graduates at least an introduction to translation will continue, as graduates are likely to translate on an *ad hoc* basis to supplement their primary income, or as a supplementary part of other work. Including optional translation classes within a language and literature degree provides a solution that can be used successfully as long as the limitations of such a programme are recognised and the course is carefully planned. If graduates of the programme wish to become full-time translators in the future, then the postgraduate programme mentioned above, or other forms of in-service training could achieve that goal.

## General aims

While there is a need to pass on the fruits of tradition and past experience through the educational process, there is also increasingly a need to prepare future professionals for lifelong learning; empower them to adapt existing

> tools to meet new demands; and construct new tools as novel challenges arise
> in the future.                                                   (Kiraly 2000a: 26)

We know that we cannot produce professional translators, instead we aim to produce *competent* translators – our graduates should know how to approach a text and how to evaluate their work once it is complete with the aim of improving future translations. It is also important that they are given enough know-how to recognise their own limitations, including knowing when to refuse a translation task. We expect our graduates to be involved only on the periphery of the translation industry, that they would either be involved in translation of business letters and internal company documents[1] within their general work or that they would take on translations for individuals to supplement their incomes. With that in mind we try to give the students as much exposure as possible to the process of translation in the limited time available and introduce them to the different kinds of text they are likely to encounter.

There is no attempt to include interpretation into the programme, despite the need for more interpreters in the market. The skills of interpreters require more time to develop than we could possibly devote to them within the already condensed programme. Interpreter training should be left to full-time degrees, where sufficient time and attention can be devoted to them.

The courses are not aimed at improving L2, although we recognise that some improvement naturally takes place as many of the in-class discussions are held in L2 and, indeed, some students take the course with the false belief that that is our intention. The responsibility for such improvement is partially covered by linguistics courses within the programme and partially the responsibility of the individual student if there are significant deficiencies.

Before we go on to discuss the contents of such study, we must deal with the issue of translation into L2. Once again, the ideal is that students should not translate out of L1. As Mackenzie states when describing the situation for Finnish, this ideal is achieved only in a limited number of countries where "major world languages are spoken and which have access to an almost unlimited supply of native speakers of other languages who are willing and able to translate" (1998: 17). Even in Spain, where L1 is a major language, "more than half of many professional translators' work is done into their L2" (Weatherby 1998: 21). For languages where there are only a limited number of native speakers of the second language (and possibly no professional translators amongst them) translation into L2 is an unfortunate necessity and therefore we should equip our students with the necessary tools for tackling this difficult task.

## Curriculum constraints

The attempt to include translation within language and literature studies has many inherent problems. The greatest of these problems are time and motivation.

Within a Translation Institute there may be as many as 300 semestral hours available over five years of study. In contrast when we look at a language and literature degree with a similar number of hours available for all subjects, we can only expect a very limited time to be devoted to translation. We can also discount the initial year of study as the students' general level of L2 is such that the number of binary errors made within their translations causes difficulties. Whilst Pym states that it is possible "to teach translation when students are making numerous binary errors" (1992:285), in practice the time taken to deal with these errors means that insufficient time is left to focus on non-binary errors below a certain language level. In our own institution the students have a total of 82 semestral hours available for each of their two majors (plus additional hours for general pedagogy), from which only 24 hours are available specifically for translation studies (although there are other relevant courses within the linguistics and cultural studies disciplines).

The lack of time means that the study has to be highly focussed, concentrating on the main text types which our graduates are likely to encounter. We concentrate more on the translation process, linguistic accuracy and function of the text than on style. We do not spend much time discussing the translation industry itself in depth; this is something best left to a study which would prepare students for direct entry to that industry, such as the postgraduate translation programmes.

We must further consider whether translation should be included as compulsory or optional within the main study. We have stated that our students will probably translate in some capacity after they graduate, which would suggest a compulsory course core to their studies. However, this would be difficult to justify as part of a study (such as our own) that aims to produce teachers, and would add a certain legitimacy to graduates working as full-time translators which would be unfounded. As a series of optional courses, we should benefit from a greater level of interest from the participants – students who have chosen to take the course. In theory this would reduce the number of motivation problems. The courses are popular amongst students as many of them recognise that they have a need for the skills involved and that this will be relevant to their future careers. As an optional course, though, the courses have low priority within the students' workload. The initial enthusiasm upon entering a course can soon wane as the difficulty of the subject and the relatively high workload become apparent. Many of the students give up the idea of translating after their initial introduction to the subject, whereas those who find an aptitude for the subject continue through optional subjects and perhaps go on to take the postgraduate route.

## The general framework of study

Within the linguistics and literature study students have some compulsory courses that are relevant to translation study including Morphology, Syntax, Lexicology, and Stylistics (of L2). In addition students can take various optional courses that will help them such as Close Reading, Text Analysis, Contrastive Linguistics, Semiotics, Functional Sentence Perspectives, Business Language and various Cultural Studies courses.

The translation study itself is divided into two parts, as is university study itself since recent legislative changes (into bachelors and masters degrees). Only students who have successfully completed the basic study (achieved top grades in both courses) can go on to the advanced study. Students who pass the advanced study and a state exam have 'with Translation Studies' added to their degree title.

The first two courses the students complete are practical courses. The first course is an atomistic, exercise-based introduction to the basic problems of translation, and in the second course students begin to work with real texts, covering the full range of texts they are likely to encounter as *ad hoc* translators. After that the practical seminars divide to concentrate on particular types of text – currently courses available include Journalistic Translation, Literary Translation, Specialised Translation and Translation into L2. The texts chosen for the Specialised Translation course reflect those texts common in the marketplace for occasional translation that are terminologically rich, technical documents. It does not attempt to deal with texts requiring a more thorough knowledge of a sub-language, such as law, or those normally translated by in-house agencies, such as government texts. The inclusion of Literary Translation within these subjects is partially a historical hangover from before the creation of the full-time translation and interpreting study (the current students are not expected to be future literary translators), although it also allows the students to become aware of the considerable difference between literary texts and other kinds of texts in translation. In addition, the students have many literary courses, and can apply the knowledge gained in those courses.

We do not cover the theory of translation until after these courses have been completed. By this time the students have enough practical experience to put the theory into context. These theoretical courses include Introduction to Translation Studies, History of Translation, Methodology of Translation, and Literary Interpretation.

Specific L1 courses include Morphology, Syntax, Stylistics, and Lexicology.

Further information on the study programme can be found in Gromová and Müglová (2001) or on our university web site (http://www.ff.ukf.sk/kaaa).

## Changing assumptions

In the first part of the study we aim to change students' basic assumptions about translation. As a post-Communist country, we have one advantage in this research which is that most languages have only been widely taught at secondary school level in recent years (with the notable exceptions of Russian and German). As such, communicative methods are widely used in the classroom and fewer students have been exposed to the grammar-translation method. Therefore, students have fewer fixed ideas about translation although we, of course, still face the usual presuppositions about translation.

Our first major hurdle is for students to recognise that the task of the translator is not simply substituting words but expressing ideas for another readership (with a different language and culture). The students must learn that they are not the author of the text and must express the meaning faithfully according to the target audience. The students also need to become aware that translation is an art and not a science – that there is not a single 'correct' translation.

The reliance on bilingual dictionaries is also challenged at this level. When students enter the study most see these as the first and last resort for finding equivalent terms. We need to show them the need to work with other reference books (monolingual dictionaries and encyclopaedias) and parallel texts, especially given the low quality of available Slovak bilingual dictionaries. However, when doing so it is vital that we do not allow students to become too focussed on the words themselves rather than the message of the text.

Whilst the students are aware of their limitations with L2, they do not have the same awareness regarding their mother tongue. We have to lead them to the realisation that they have deficiencies in their knowledge of L1 as well – both in comprehension and production. This is particularly relevant for Slovak, which has a complex grammar system. Students must appreciate that identifying and correcting these errors is an important part of the translation process. An additional problem within our own institution is that some of our students come from a Hungarian linguistic minority, and our courses only deal with Slovak, which is their second language.

## Strategies and techniques

The courses need to concentrate on the process of translation rather than the product in order to maintain the motivation of the students (discussed below) and also because, quite simply, *it is the process that we are trying to teach.* According to Gile (1995: 11),

> the process-oriented approach is suited to the beginning of a course or to a program aiming at increasing awareness of Translation issues, but it is not sufficient as the sole tool for raising students to a high level of professional Translation expertise.

We do not attempt to take our students to the high level mentioned and so the process-oriented approach is suitable for our programme.

As with the assumptions, it is not simply enough to introduce the strategies. We must constantly remind the students of them to help these to become internalised.

## Choice of texts

The lack of time for the studies means that the choice of texts for working with is vital. These texts must be long enough that the students can have experience with a variety of translation problems but at the same time short enough so that the teacher can deal with those problems with the students. The solution we generally use is to provide students with a full text but only ask them to translate a particular section. One problem we have encountered doing this is that not all the students read the full text before tackling the translation;

Table 1.

|  | Into L1 | Into L2 |
|---|---|---|
| Instructions for Use | ✓ | |
| Journalistic texts | ✓ | |
| Simple specialised texts | ✓ | |
| Literary texts | ✓ | |
| Business Letters | ✓ | ✓ |
| Tourist texts | | ✓ |
| Menus | | ✓ |

in order to reduce this problem, the section of text to be translated is not mentioned until after the initial text analysis has been completed.

As has been said many times before, the use of authentic and up-to-date texts is important. In addition we must select texts of an appropriate difficulty level and based on the market conditions. The texts that are likely to be translated by our graduates are not the same as those to be translated by professional translators and our choices should reflect that – there is little reason to translate ministerial papers when full-time government translators translate these in the local market. We also include some texts (such as literary texts) to allow students to find their preferences for the future, should they choose to study further to become professional translators. As a result, we deal with the text types in Table 1.

The appearance of tourist texts and menus within the list is of particular importance to our local environment. The high costs of translation and lack of available translators locally mean that many small businesses in the tourist and leisure industries rely on non-professional translators.

## Motivating the students

One of the serious difficulties affecting us is retaining student motivation. Perhaps part of the reason for this is that we are taking something that they believe is a simple task and showing them just how difficult and complex the task is. Surprisingly we found that one of the best ways to motivate the students was to show them that they were not the only ones who found the task difficult. Whilst students are demotivated by mistakes in their own work, they are motivated by finding mistakes in previous students' work and even more so, by those in official translations.

We have found that it is very important not to be viewed as the 'fountain of all knowledge' and that students learn from seeing how we solve problems in the class rather than simply supplying an equivalent word or phrase. Kiraly also discusses this when describing the transmission perspective (knowledge flowing from the teacher to the students) and transformation perspective (where the student is constructing their own knowledge) (Kiraly 2000a: 22). Our own use of reference materials and parallel texts in class helps the students to see the advantages and limitations of these materials and gives them confidence when they realise that the teachers are not infallible. There is a temptation to simply give an answer when you have discussed the same problem with three or four other classes but it is vital that this does not happen as it can have a seriously demotivating effect and the students would also learn just the words without the techniques for dealing with similar words.

## Classroom approach

We try to maintain a variety of different teaching styles within the classroom, and ensure that we tackle the problems of each stage of the translation process – starting with general text analysis, moving through analysing specific texts for translation, the translations themselves and revision. Folowing Nord's (1998) translation-relevant text analysis a lot of emphasis is placed on the function of the source and the target texts. The four categories of translation problems (culture-specific, language pair-specific, text-specific and pragmatic) are discussed, too.

Most of the lessons are conducted as dialogues, either between students in group-work or whole classroom discussion. These discussions encourage the students to learn from each other. However, in order for this to work effectively we need to create a sympathetic environment where the students are unafraid of giving opinions.

One well-known exercise we also use in class is that students bring in trans- lations they have done as homework and use them to build a compromise translation in small groups. During the student discussions leading to the con- sensus (it is very rare that these discussions do not lead to consensus), we find that students defend their own particular choices through descriptions of the methods they used to come to their own decisions. However, there is a poten- tial problem with compromise translations as the final choice is more often a result of the strength of personalities of individual students within the group, rather than the most appropriate solution. As mentioned in an online discussion on collaboration, teamwork and groupwork in translator training, "the group dynamics [determine] the final version: the more confident students getting 'their' bits in rather than the shyer ones" (Kiraly 2000b). This means that all compromise translations should also be discussed thoroughly in class.

The questions asked after the students have completed their draft translations are not aimed at just reaching high-quality translations, but at establishing:

- the difficulties that students found whilst preparing the translation;
- how those problems were solved or need to be solved;
- what implications they have for dealing with future texts.

By way of example, we had a text dealing with air travel for translation from English into Slovak. In each of the classes, students reported that they had a problem dealing with the term 'hub airport'[2] which appeared in the text. We elicited suggestions for the translation of this term from the students and then discussed where these suggestions had come from and how this affected their reliability. From this exercise the students constructed their own model for researching difficult terminology. The students were asked in a later lesson to summarise the procedure of finding an unknown term based on this model.

Within the translation classes themselves we encourage students to differentiate between the styles of texts. For example, the students compare the differences in style between tourist brochures in C1 (cultures using L1) and C2 before approaching a tourist translation.

We also address the question of different readers through practical exercises – we ask the students who are the potential readers of a text and how it would be written in a different way for a different reader. Students are asked to summarise a newspaper article for a reader of their choice (the article chosen has political and economic implications which could be stressed and includes specific information which would be already known to some of the potential readers of the summary). During all of their translations they are asked to specify the readership of the source text and the target text. Normally, they chose an appropriate readership for the target text themselves to allow them to develop the skills to identify this in the future.

## Two native speakers

Whilst most of this paper has discussed the disadvantages we face in our own form of study and how we overcome them, there is one area in which we feel very fortunate. We are able to have two teachers present for some of the courses, one a native speaker of the students' L1, the other a native speaker of their L2.

This gives us wider opportunities for discussing cultural differences between the two language groups and both teachers are involved in all stages of the translation (from text analysis to revision).

It is also an opportunity for having a language consultant in the classroom (not only for students but also for each other). The students quickly see situations in which a quick question can resolve a problem or eliminate the need for lengthy research. The students see how much we rely on each other for specific information (such as secondary connotations and cultural implications) and this helps them to overcome their assumption that translation is only a linguistic substitution.

## Student evaluation

We try to use our evaluation process as a way of extending the learning time available for the students through the use of translation diaries. The students are asked to produce final versions of each of the translations that we have worked on during the semester, together with commentaries. This revision is a helpful lesson for the future and the commentaries are an opportunity for the students to reflect on their experiences working with individual texts and allow us to attempt to mark process as well as product. In addition, the students write a commentary on the course as a whole, which allows us to see what they think they have learned and gives us valuable insights into how to improve the courses in the future. After marking the diaries, there is a consultation with the student and the final mark is given (based on the diary, class participation and attendance).

The idea of the diaries is that the students complete the work throughout the term, but in reality this is often not the case. Many of the students simply forget about each translation as soon as it is finished and then try to write the whole diary at the end when their time is stretched between the many other subjects they study, leading to incomplete commentaries which lack in detail. Whilst students should have the self-discipline to work throughout the term, we have to ensure that this is the case in reality.

## Conclusion

The programme of study needs to be carefully designed to make the best use of the limited time available. Where translation into L2 is needed in the market place, this should also be included in such study. The texts used should reflect the local market for non-professional translators. The students must be motivated and encouraged to discover best practice for themselves and this can be encouraged through the use of translation diaries for evaluation.

For some regions, there are periods when language graduates are likely to encounter translation during their careers. It is therefore necessary to have some form of translation training within language degrees. It has to be recognised that this will not produce professional translators, but can produce competent translators who will be able to play an active role in the wider market until the market no longer requires the services of less-qualified ones.

## Notes

1. An increasing number of Slovak companies are now in foreign ownership and have non-Slovak higher management.

2. This was a particularly difficult term for our students since few had any experience of air travel and Slovakia has no hub airport of its own for comparison.

## References

BBC (2001). *BBC Education – Languages – Languages of Europe*. London: BBC. Available online at http://www.bbc.co.uk/education/languages/european_languages/languages/index.shtml Cited at 9:40 GMT, 5th June 2001.

Gile, D. (1995). *Basic Concepts and Models for Interpreter and Translator Training*. Amsterdam and Philadelphia: John Benjamins.

Gromová, E. & Müglová, D. (2001). "New Trends in Translator Training in Slovakia". In *Proceedings from III Conference on Training and Career Development in Translating and Interpreting*. Madrid: Universidad Europea de Madrid.

Kiraly, D. (2000a). *A Social Constructivist Approach to Translator Education: Empowerment From Theory to Practice*. Manchester: St. Jerome.

Kiraly, D. (2000b). "Summary of Discussion on Collaboration, Teamwork and Group Work". In *Innovation in Translator and Interpretor Training (ITIT). An on-line symposium 17–25 January 2000*. Taragona. Available online at http://www.www.fut.es/~apym/symp/s-team.html. Cited at 11:20 GMT, 18th May 2001.

Mackenzie, R. (1998). "The Place of Language Teaching in a Quality Oriented Translators' Training Programme". In K. Malmkjær (Ed.), *Translation and Language Teaching: Language Teaching and Translation*. Manchester: St. Jerome.

Nord, C. (1998). "Textanalyse: pragmatisch/funktional". In M. Snell-Hornby (Ed.), *Handbuch Translation* (p. 350). Tübingen: Stauffenburg-Verlag Brigitte Narr GmbH.

Pym, A. (1992). "Translation Error Analysis and the Interface with Language Teaching". In C. Dollerup & A. Loddegaard (Eds.), *Teaching Translation and Interpreting: Training Talent and Experience*. Amsterdam and Philadelphia: John Benjamins.

SME (2004). "EÚ chýbajú z nových krajín audítori, právnici i sekretárky" ("EU Lacks Audtiors, Laywers and Secretaries from Accession Countries"). In *SME Online: Európska Únia*. Bratislava. Available online at http://eu.sme.sk/clanok.asp?cl=1250688. Cited at 6:20 GMT, 23rd March 2004.

Weatherby, J. (1998). "Teaching Translation into L2". In K. Malmkjær (Ed.), *Translation and Language Teaching: Language Teaching and Translation*. Manchester: St. Jerome.

# Corpus-aided language pedagogy
# for translator education

Silvia Bernardini

## 1.   Introduction

The pedagogic uses of language corpora have become a major research area in recent years, following faster and faster technological progress and an ever increasing belief in the role of lexicalisation and memorisation in language performance. For similar reasons, corpora are nowadays also enjoying increasing popularity in translation theory and practice, filling a notorious lack of tools and methods in these areas. At the cross-roads between language pedagogy and translation studies, translator education would seem to be potentially one of the areas to gain most profoundly from corpus use, and indeed a number of researchers so far have testified to the important role of corpora as aids in translation teaching (Bowker 2000; Gavioli 2001; Varantola 2003; Zanettin 1998).

In this paper I would like to take a different though closely related perspective, and look at the role of corpora in *language pedagogy for translator education*, rather than *translation teaching*. My conclusion will be that corpora have an important role to play in the education of translators, first as translating aids, as testified in the literature, secondly as sources of learning activities and of knowledge about the language, and thirdly and more importantly perhaps, as instruments through which approaches to language teaching and to translation teaching can be integrated into a coherent whole, with common aims and methods specific to this pedagogic setting.

Before moving on to discussing the pedagogic and translational issues that are closest to these concerns, I would like to briefly introduce the notion of *corpus* and the linguistic approach which provides a theoretical motivation for its analysis.

## 2. Why *corpus* linguistics?

Corpus linguistics is, in very general terms, an approach to language description and theorisation based on the computerised analysis of large samples of language use. The theoretical premise underlying it is a belief in the primacy of communicative competence and performance over linguistic competence as the objects of study of linguistics. In order to explain how this view differs from other, equally well argued views of the object of study and priorities of linguistics, we should probably embark on a history of linguistic thought ranging, at least, from de Saussure to the present day, an endeavour clearly well beyond the scope of this paper. Suffice to say that corpus linguistics follows from the work of ethnographically- and socioculturally-oriented linguists like J.R.R. Firth and Dell Hymes, who rejected the idea that "language equals grammar", or that "linguistic theory is concerned with an ideal native speaker-listener, in a completely homogeneous speech community, who knows his language perfectly..." (Chomsky 1965:3). The above scholars claimed that the notion of "ideal native speaker", secluded from the influence of culture and society, is a less than ideal generalisation if linguistics is to play a role in the real world. This is because

> for each social role we routinely play, we do not make up our lines as we go along, rather, to a large extent, they are already there for us, stereotyped and narrowly conditioned by our particular type of culture.      (Firth 1935:69)

If language is patterned, and its use more a matter of remembering than one of putting together from scratch, as claimed by a number of other linguists (e.g. Bolinger 1976; Pawley & Syder 1983), it follows that linguistics should be concerned more with studying large repositories of written or spoken texts than with questioning native speakers about the grammaticality of a decontextualised sentence. Hence the emphasis on corpus analysis.

Theoretical arguments apart, the success of corpus linguistics depends considerably on the exponential growth in computer technology we are currently witnessing. In particular, inexpensive storage space, fast processing, and availability of texts in electronic form, standardised for ease of interchange, have all contributed to making the construction and/or analysis of corpora possible not only to large companies and research laboratories, as was generally the case in the past but also to single individuals. Furthermore, this wider number of users can take advantage of a wider range of tools, as the horizons of computer-aided linguistic research are being stretched to include access to textual and contextual features like sound and (moving) images (McEnery & Wilson 1997; Hofland 2003).

The variety of available tools and the increasing ease of construction have resulted in a wealth of original approaches to corpus use, some more theoretical, some more pragmatic in nature. Corpus-derived insights and analytical methods have proved to be promising for, among many other areas lexicography (most recent dictionaries of English claim to be corpus-based, following the pioneering *Collins Cobuild* series), register analysis (Stubbs 1996), forensic linguistics (Coulthard and French, eds.), and more cogently for our concerns, translation studies and language pedagogy.

## 3. Corpus-based translation studies

Corpus-based translation studies have nowadays become a well-established and promising approach to the study of translation, with descriptive, theoretical and applied branches. Laviosa (1998), for instance, analyses a monolingual, multi-source comparable corpus (the English Comparable Corpus, or ECC) and identifies the following patterns as typical of translated narrative and newspaper texts in English and, potentially, of translated English in general, as opposed to non-translated comparable texts:

1. Lower lexical density
2. Higher percentage of high frequency words
3. Higher levels of repetition of frequent words
4. Fewer lemmas

Kenny (2000) reaches conclusions regarding lexical normalisation in translated texts that are in accord with Laviosa's: employing a different methodology, involving this time a bilingual parallel corpus of English and German and two reference corpora for the source and target languages, she finds a tendency for translated texts in her corpus to be "sanitised" through a process of neutralisation of negative semantic prosodies present in the source texts.

Descriptive studies of translation such as the ones just mentioned feed into the more theoretical branch of corpus-based translation studies, contributing empirical data to a number of research issues such as the ongoing search for translation norms (Toury 1995). According to Baker (1999) corpora are an especially powerful research tool in theoretical translation studies insofar as they can provide a way of relating the expectations of the receivers of a translation with the statements of translation researchers and the practices of professional translators, these being interrelated aspects of translation research that an integrated and fully-fledged approach cannot ignore.

Lastly, corpora, both parallel (Source texts in Language 1 – Target texts in Language 2) and bilingual comparable (Source texts in Language 1 – Source texts in Language 2), have been used in the translation classroom. Provided that they are large and varied enough, the former can provide students with examples of translation practices (i.e. how certain problems have been solved by others in the past) and consequently favour the observation and evaluation of translation strategies (Pearson 2003). The latter, on the other hand, can "help learners investigate the respective expectations, experience and knowledge of the linguistic communities involved" (Zanettin 1998:618), without the potential bias due to the specific constraints of the translation activity. Also, they provide background information about a certain topic area, which may help learners understand the text to be translated better. The value of this type of corpus work in the classroom becomes even more obvious when one considers the difficulties involved in settings such as teaching/learning technical translation or translation into the L2, in which intuitions about stylistic/discourse acceptability and/or area knowledge are often lacking.

## 4.   Corpus-based language pedagogy

The considerations just made about the role of language patterning, expectations, and acceptability in translation pedagogy apply even more cogently to language pedagogy (see Wray 2000 for a theoretical overview and Partington 1998 for examples of classroom practice). Participation in discourse involves an awareness of the "rules of use" regulating a given community (Hymes 1972). These are more appropriately definable in terms of tendencies than categorical rules such as those of grammar. Being more difficult to identify and describe, they are seldom and unsystematically included in foreign language textbooks and materials (Römer 2004). Yet they appear to orient the behaviour of the speakers and influence their acceptability judgements substantially. We shall see some examples below of such tendencies. Since corpora can provide access to the spontaneous behaviour of native speakers of a foreign language, and consequently a vantage viewpoint to observe appropriate use of such a language in context, they can make a valuable pedagogic aid. Furthermore, they can provide a valid support in curriculum design. In the words of Kennedy (1992:335):

> Corpus linguistics can tell us not just what is systemically possible, but what is actually likely to occur [...] potential usefulness and likelihood of occurrence have been seen as relevant for deciding what to teach or learn.

We should be careful, however, not to conclude that corpora and corpus linguistics insights should alone shape language pedagogy, or, in other words, that descriptive adequacy should be equated with pedagogic relevance. This view, held, among others, by supporters of the *lexical syllabus* (Willis 1990), has been criticised by Widdowson (e.g. 1984:240) on the grounds that:

> authenticity is not achieved by simply working from genuine texts. It has to be a function of an engagement with discourse whereby students exercise their capacity for making indexical meaning out of signs in utterances. [...] Authenticity is not a matter of selection but of methodology.

Widdowson's objections do not apply to the use of corpora in language pedagogy as such, but, as he has himself repeatedly pointed out, to the view that the new, compelling insights gained thanks to the use of corpora should alone inform language courses or, in other words, that theoretical and descriptive linguistics observations should override applied linguistics considerations.

A different approach from the lexical syllabus, which is more in line with Widdowson's position and more relevant to the views expressed here, is Johns's *data-driven learning*, in which corpora and corpus tools are treated as pedagogic instruments in their own right, not just as repositories of descriptive facts about the language. In this approach (described, for instance, in Johns 1991), there is a direct (albeit teacher-mediated) involvement of learners with corpora. They access authentic corpus data (selected and simplified by the teacher) in order to interpret them and arrive inductively and through discussion at the solution to a linguistic problem which makes the subject of the lesson.

One can easily see how this approach differs from more traditional, teacher-centred formats in which corpora operate as sources of information about the language. Here the correctness of the solution arrived at is not meant to be absolute but relative: the results of corpus work of this kind are partial, qualified generalisations, which may not be entirely correct descriptively/theoretically, but are pedagogically and contextually adequate for each learner at each stage of her learning process. More importantly, learners construe their own interpretations of the data instead of passively memorising a rule explained by the teacher, and in the process are forced to focus jointly on meaning and form, thus reconciling these aspects of language use that have sometimes been treated as separate variables.

## 5.   Corpus-aided discovery learning and the education of translators

Following Johns, I would argue that the most authentically pedagogic value of corpora lies in the chances of inductive learning they can offer, rather than in the descriptively sound insights they can provide. My work, like his, has therefore focused more on the interaction between learners and corpora than on the insertion of corpus-derived descriptive insights into language teaching/learning.

In what I would call "corpus-aided discovery learning", learners are given or asked to come up with a relatively unstructured task involving corpus analysis. This can be quite straightforward, like investigating the meaning and use(s) of a word or phrase in the foreign language, or more complex, like analysing the use of, say, animal-related fixed expressions in economics texts. There are endless possibilities, depending on the size and type of corpora available, and on the imagination of learners and teachers. The crucial point is that the task should provide a stimulus rather than a goal, and on completion should be evaluated in terms of what chances of learning one has been able to recognise and take advantage of, rather than on the basis of a more or less correct answer to the initial problem/stimulus. In operational terms, the only instructions learners are given deal with (a) the stimulus; (b) the minimum amount of time they should spend browsing the corpus; (c) the requirement to report on the learning experience and describe their findings and consequently (d) the advice to make notes of the steps taken as well as of any observations that could be useful in view of a presentation/discussion.

This procedure may seem rather unorthodox since it encourages learners to stray from their intended path and indulge in whatever may strike their attention, hardly a standard pedagogical practice in many settings. Yet corpus-aided discovery learning has a number of interesting pedagogical implications:

1. It is authentic, because tasks are selected by the learners according to their current concerns (they may choose the stimulus, the research procedure, the format of the report);
2. It is "authenticating", in the sense that it provides opportunities for discourse production as well as discourse observation;
3. Putting the learner in charge, it may lead to increasing autonomy and motivation (Crabbe 1992);
4. It is based on inductive "reasoning-gap" activities, which have been suggested to have a high communicative potential whilst being less face-threatening than other types of activities (Prabhu 1987);

5.  It has an important consciousness-raising function, as learners are sensi-
    tised to the existence of such phenomena as collocational restrictions and
    semantic prosodies (see below) and become increasingly skilled at "seeing
    through language" (Carter 1993), at recognising the intentions and strate-
    gies behind a text by setting it against the backdrop of the culture of which
    it is a product;
6.  It provides a perfect setting for learning how to learn; through practice,
    learners become more experienced corpus users, develop confidence in the
    potential of this resource and get more out of it, initiating a bootstrapping
    process that leads them to being able to analyse larger amounts of data
    faster and more efficiently as they accumulate experience and develop
    procedures for querying the corpus and analysing the results obtained.
    In my experience, corpus use then becomes an everyday activity for most
    learners, to check on a doubt or hunch much as they would consult a native
    speaker or a dictionary;
7.  It helps learners focus jointly on lexical and discoursal perspectives, and
    see the interrelations between the two.

Although discussion of the technicalities of this approach would exceed the
scope of this paper, I have spent some time listing its advantages because I
believe it to be particularly suitable for the education of language mediators in
general, and of translators in particular.

This is because, I would suggest, language teaching for translators can be
considered as a non-standard variety of LSP. As I understand it, the main aim
of a standard LSP course is that of teaching specific linguistic competencies,
relative to a given subject domain. The education of translators, on the
other hand, involves first and foremost the development of specific capacities
required by the translating process in its widest sense (including, for instance,
documentation, proof-reading, project-management and so on). Far from
being the exclusive province of translation classes, the development of these
capacities is also, I believe, a major priority of foreign language courses geared
at future translators.

Thanks to its focus on capacity as well as competence, its orientation towards the learning process rather than the learning product, its
autonomy-fostering and consciousness-raising preoccupations, discovery (language) learning with the aid of one or more corpora can offer a valid comple-
ment to translation pedagogy, whose aims it largely shares. I shall illustrate this
with reference to a few areas where corpus-aided discovery learning appears to
be particularly well tuned to translator education.

Example 1: Raising the learners' awareness

The development of linguistic, socio-cultural and discoursal awareness is probably the most obviously relevant among these areas. It is not possible here to consider the many ways in which corpora can be used to elicit this type of knowledge. I shall only mention four theoretical constructs which have been described by linguists and investigated mainly through corpus analysis, namely *collocation, colligation, semantic preference,* and *semantic prosody* (Hoey 1997; Louw 1993; Sinclair 1991). I shall concentrate on the phrasal level for ease of discussion, although discoursal perspectives are also relevant (Bernardini 2000; Hoey 1991; Stubbs 1996).

In the course of a discovery learning seminar offered to fourth year students of translation and interpreting at the School for Translators and Interpreters of the University of Bologna, a small group of participants decided to look at the nouns *cause* and *reason* in the British National Corpus (BNC), in order to check whether the negative semantic prosody of the verb *to cause* discussed in the literature (e.g. by Bublitz 1995) also applies to the noun, and whether this trait can be used to distinguish between the (near-)synonyms under examination. They ended up concentrating especially on instances in which the nouns were followed by the preposition *for,* and reported, among a number of other interesting observations, that:

1. *cause for* would indeed seem to show a tendency to "collocate" with negatively connotated nouns; however, a few positively connotated nouns (*hope, celebration*) also appear quite frequently in the concordance, hinting, maybe, at the existence of lexicalised units that run counter to the negative "semantic prosody" of the expression;
2. *reason for* would seem to show a tendency to "colligate" with "*ing*-form" verbs, which *cause for* does not share;
3. *cause for* would seem to show a "semantic preference" for abstract nouns referring to mental/psychological states which *reason for* does not share.

A few concordance lines should clarify the points just made (Concordance 1).

The learners' observations, as can be seen, have nothing of the clarity and economy of the theoretician. Rather, they look like partial, rule-of-thumb generalisations, to be checked, revised and enriched as further evidence is encountered. What matters in a learning-how-to-learn, awareness-raising perspective is that learners become sensitised to such phenomena as collocations, colligations, semantic preferences and prosodies, and to their role in the production and understanding of an idiomatic text.

lambs she fed with youthful pride. Her family saw no cause for alarm — — how could it do her any harm w
classical recourse of the bourgeois in trouble or with cause for complaint was to exercise or ask for perso
ofessional tournament tennis), Tretorn has justifiable cause for concern. It has it in writing from the LTA tha
an and Diana Travers. On the face of it there was no cause for concern. Theresa Nolan, after having a me
n set, but even now she managed to retain sufficient cause for indignation, and the quality of her feeling fc
ss, and also children. Children were recognized as a cause for long-lasting happiness, so they are include
ı bacterial decomposition, is very seldom indeed the cause for worry. Nitrogen shortage normally shows o
ˈestriction. I can't agree with any of those things. The reason for bringing forward this policy was because i
ᵢrything quicker and saves money so there is a good reason for businesses to switch to EDC,' says Micha
didn't care a fig what she looked like, but that was no reason for him to tighten the purse-strings. ' Don't be
within a social context of some kind. The immediate reason for not using Labov's concept is that the verni
at lack of scientific certainty should not be used as a reason for postponing cost-effective measures to ha
ıuth of the Tropic of Cancer was not to be taken as a reason for resuming hostilities in Europe. This clausε
these pieces often speaks for itself, and is the main reason for them being collectable. Unfortunately, the
nce, loving Brief Encounter is one such marker. One reason for this, I would suggest, is that Brief Encounl
t rear cross member instead of the angled type. The reason for this is the provision of lifting eyes on the e

Concordance 1. Some examples of occurrences of "cause for" and "reason for" in the
BNC

To take another example, awareness of formal and distributional variation
at the phraseological level can also develop as a result of corpus work. One
of the most obvious advantages is that users learn to rely on contextual and
co-textual signals to predict the meaning and function of a lexical item. One
participant in the seminar talked to the class about her analysis of the pattern
*the x behind the y*, which she had found to have an interesting discoursal
function. She reported on the kinds of nouns that normally appear in the *x*
and in the *y* position, and on the types of texts in which it would seem to
be more widely used. Looking at the data together with the rest of the class,
we reached the conclusion that there seem to exist two main overlapping but
distinct uses of this pattern. The first one is often signalled by three features:
(1) thematic position/focusing function; (2) text type = academic prose; (3) an
abstract noun occupies the *x* position. Examples:

1.  The intention behind the book is furthering...
2.  The rationale behind the changes was to reduce...
3.  The theory behind the methods utilising these bases is described...

Alternatively, this expression can be used to refer to an individual or institution
(in the *x* position) responsible for the entity denoted by the noun in the *y*
position. This second figurative use does not seem to be associated specifically
with any position or function, even though stylistically it may seem to be
somewhat typical of journalistic prose (see Concordance 2).

   Again, it can be seen that the perspective here is not that of the descriptivist,
whose objective is total accountability, but that of the learner, who works
with useful generalisations and prototypical cases. Corpora hardly ever give

'ee persons of the Christian Trinity. It is this being, the power behind the throne who acts as the unifying force
· the Elephant & Castle, waiting for Guy Chadwick, the mastermind behind The House Of Love, purveyors of :
. Lachman president Ron Lachman was of course the force behind the creation of WABI, Sun Microsystems
·m those at the centre who seek control. However, the thinking behind the FMI was that if the budgetary proce
·loper and investor Ewart. Burton Property Trust is the developer behind the Cornmill shopping centre in Darli
·els has been expressed in many quarters. This is the reason behind the launch of Amity News Service, publi
for prestige commercial and architectural lighting. The aim behind the range is to incorporate well-proven, st:
·w have to be fulfilled by a team from Manchester. The theory behind the cuts was that there was no point in h
·eem blindingly obvious, one non-NHS member of the team behind the strategy points out: 'Irrespective of th·
·orturer. The word is bald, impersonal. But what of the person behind the label? How did Andres Valenzuela ·
·, semiconductors, and aqueous solutions of salts. The chemistry behind the formation of zeolites is still not c
·inded something historic in Yorkshire. Barnes was the brain behind the South West's first Divisional 29-9 triur
·ndidate for Parliament in the Maryhill Division, was the eminence grise behind the 'Hall of Laughing Mirrors' ar

Concordance 2.  Some examples of occurrences of "the _ behind the" in the BNC

access to the complete picture, but rather present glimpses of it. I would suggest this to be an advantage rather than a limit, for two reasons: first, because learning proceeds through successive approximations consistent with the learners' own developmental states, as recommended by a number of scholars in the Vigotskian tradition (see for instance Krashen 1979) and, second, because learners may gain a better understanding of the probabilistic nature of language organisation (as discussed in Section 2), often hidden by the artificial dichotomies of pedagogy.

## Example 2: Developing communication skills

Besides its wide-ranging awareness-raising function, corpus-aided discovery learning has another important role in the education of translators, namely that of providing a perfect setting for the development of communication- and learning-oriented skills.

As a communicative event, albeit a very special one, translation is bound to rely substantially, though not exclusively, on the same skills required by successful communication in general. Discovery learning creates the conditions for learners to practice intensively these same skills. Let us consider, for instance, the list of communication capacities provided by Beaugrande and Dressler (1981:210):

1. Problem-solving
2. Planning
3. Generating, testing and revising hypotheses
4. Pattern-matching
5. Processing-ease for expected or probable occurrences
6. Processing depth for non-expected or improbable occurrences

7. Reducing complexity to meet processing limitations
8. Selective focus of attention
9. Maintaining continuity of experience
10. Projecting or inferring these various dispositions and activities among other participants in interaction

Discovery learning activities overtly require the engagement of all these capacities for completion. Planning the queries to interrogate the corpus, managing the data (selecting relevant lines, ordering them, expanding contexts), formulating and testing hypotheses when interpreting them, and so on are cognitively demanding activities that systematically exercise, and consequently stretch, all the capacities listed above. Furthermore, by providing stimuli for authentic, motivated interaction with other learners (reporting on the activity, discussing results, raising objections, motivating decisions etc.), discovery learning activities also covertly favour the engagement of these capacities in actual discourse.

## Example 3: Developing learning skills

One last point worth making with regard to the role of discovery learning in translator education relates to the issue of learning itself. Learning capacities should score high in the priority list of any course for translators, given the constant necessity to acquire new knowledge and develop technical (if not cognitive) skills in the course of professional life (see Bernardini this volume). As claimed by Kiraly (2000: 182):

> [O]ur primary goal is to help [translation students] become competent, self-confident, autonomous professionals for today and life-long learners for tomorrow.

Skehan's work (1996, 1998), for instance, suggests that language learning proceeds through a constant cycle of analysis and synthesis, and a balanced focus on form, meaning, and on the interrelations between the two. Whilst *accuracy* develops mainly through analysis and focus on form, and *fluency* mainly through synthesis and focus on meaning, *restructuring* or "willingness and capacity [...] to reorganize [one's] underlying and developing language system" (Skehan 1996: 22) requires analysis and synthesis operating together, and a joint focus on meaning and form. Activities such as those described here can favour the development of:

> *accuracy*, providing stimuli and opportunities for the analysis of formal features of the language;

*fluency*, through report and discussion activities;

*restructuring* skills, since they provide an opportunity for relating formal and functional/semantic observations through data analysis and synthesis of results.

Among the many learning skills that future translators may require, it is also worth mentioning, as a way of concluding this section, "noticing skills". A number of scholars have worked on the hypothesis that language learning cannot be subliminal, but depends on focal awareness, or noticing of formal features of the input (Schmidt 1990; Robinson 1995; Fotos 1993; Leow 2000). These features should carry information crucial to the task in order to be noticed, and should ideally be already present in the learners' consciousness. Under such conditions, learners are more likely to pick up target language forms and encode them in short-term memory. For learning to take place, these must subsequently be moved on to long-term memory. According to Robinson (1995:298)

> More permanent encoding in long-term memory is a consequence of the level of activation of information in short-term memory, itself the result of rehearsal and elaboration.

Corpus-aided discovery learning tasks can favour *noticing* thanks to their focus on formal features which are relevant for task completion (because the task itself is centred around linguistic analysis) and present in the learner's consciousness (because they are encountered over and over again in the concordance outputs). Also, they can favour subsequent remembering, or encoding in long-term memory, because of the cognitive effort required for their completion, which are likely to result in high levels of activation of the information in short-term memory.

It is not possible here to mention all the advantages of discovery learning activities in the education of translators. I hope that the few examples provided can give an idea of the wealth of possibilities available.

## 6.   Conclusion

Summing up the present discussion, corpora would seem to have a lot to offer future translators, not only as translating aids, but also as sources of discovery learning activities. As I hope to have shown, they can offer opportunities for students (a) to increase their linguistic, socio-cultural and discoursal awareness, (b) to develop a number of skills required to communicate (and consequently also to translate) successfully, and (c) to learn how to learn more effectively and autonomously, thus becoming successful language users and language learners today, and laying the bases for becoming successful language professionals tomorrow.

Translation pedagogy and language pedagogy have traditionally been considered as separate disciplines. This is not surprising if one looks at translation as a transcoding process, and at translation pedagogy as a training process. However, if we agree that translation is an act of mediation and that future translators should be educated, not trained, then language teaching should become an integral part of this educational process and, together with translation teaching, should form a coherent whole, with common aims and methods specific to this pedagogic setting.

The educational bet in translation pedagogy would now seem to be that of determining the specificities of this pedagogic setting, identifying the requirements of translation students (professional and educational) in terms of skills and competencies (socio-linguistic and cognitive), and subsequently developing an integrated and theoretically thought-out approach in which translation classes, language classes and any other class in the course of studies tend towards these goals. By offering foreign language learning tasks geared specifically at students of translation, the aim of which is increasing language competence alongside communication, learning and translation capacity, corpus-aided discovery learning would seem to make a valid first step in this direction.

## References

Baker, M. (1999). "The role of corpora in investigating the linguistic behaviour of professional translators". *International Journal of Corpus Linguistics, 4* (2), 281–298.

Bernardini, S. (2000). *Competence, Capacity, Corpora. A Study in Corpus-aided Language Learning*. Bologna: CLUEB.

Bolinger, D. (1976). "Meaning and memory". *Forum Linguisticum, 1* (1), 1–10.

Bowker, L. (2000). "Towards a methodology for exploiting specialized target language corpora as translation resources". *International Journal of Corpus Linguistics, 5* (1), 17–52.

*British National Corpus Version 1.0*. Oxford: Oxford University Computing Services.

Bublitz, W. (1995). "Semantic prosody and cohesive company: Somewhat predictable". *Universität Duisburg Gesamthochschule, L.A.U.D.*, 1–23.

Carter, R. (1993). "Language awareness and language learning". In M. Hoey (Ed.), *Data, Description, Discourse* (pp. 139–149). London: Harper Collins.

Chomsky, N. (1965). *Aspects of the Theory of Syntax*. Cambridge, MA: MIT Press.

Coulthard, M. & French, P. (Eds.). *Forensic Linguistics. The International Journal of Speech, Language and the Law*. Birmingham: Birmingham University Press.

Crabbe, D. (1993). "Fostering autonomy from within the classroom: The teacher's responsibility". *System, 21* (4), 443–452.

Firth, J. R. (1935). "On sociological linguistics". Extracted from Firth, J. R. *The Technique of Semantics – Transactions of the Royal Society*. Reprinted in Hymes, D. (Ed.). (1964), *Language in Culture and Society* (pp. 66–70). New York: Harper International.

Fotos, S. (1993). "Consciousness-raising and noticing through focus on form: Grammar task performance versus formal instruction". *Applied Linguistics, 14* (4), 385–403.

Gavioli, L. (2001). "The learner as researcher. Introducing corpus concordancing in the classroom". In G. Aston (Ed.), *Learning with Corpora* (pp. 108–137). Houston, TX: Athelstan.

Hoey, M. (1991). *Patterns of Lexis in Text*. Oxford: Oxford University Press.

Hoey, M. (1997). "From concordance to text structure: New uses for computer corpora". In B. B. Lewandowska-Tomaszczyk & P. J. Melia (Eds.), *Practical Applications in Language Corpora – Proceedings* (pp. 2–23). Lodz: Lodz University Press.

Hymes, D. (1972). "On communicative competence". In J. B. Pride & J. Holmes (Eds.), *Sociolinguistics* (pp. 269–293). London: Penguin.

Johns, T. (1991). "Should you be persuaded – Two samples of data-driven learning materials". In T. Johns & P. King (Eds.), *Classroom Concordancing. ELR Journal, 4* (pp. 1–16). Birmingham: University of Birmingham.

Kennedy, G. (1992). "Preferred ways of putting things with implications for language teaching". In J. Svartvik (Ed.), *Directions in Corpus Linguistics* (pp. 335–373). Berlin: Mouton de Gruyter.

Kenny, D. (2001). *Lexis and Creativity in Translation*. Manchester: St. Jerome.

Kiraly, D. (2000). *A Social Constructivist Approach to Translator Education*. Manchester: St. Jerome.

Laviosa, S. (1998). "Core patterns of lexical use in a comparable corpus of English narrative prose". *Meta, 43* (4), 557–570.

Leow, R. P. (2000). "A study of the role of awareness in foreign language behavior: Aware versus unaware learners". *Studies in Second Language Acquisition, 22* (4), 557–584.

Louw, B. (1993). "The diagnostic potential of semantic prosodies". In M. Baker, G. Francis, & E. Tognini Bonelli (Eds.), *Text and technology* (pp. 157–176). Amsterdam and Philadelphia: John Benjamins.

McEnery, T. & Wilson, A. (1997). "Multimedia corpora". In B. Lewandowska-Tomaszczyk & P. J. Melia (Eds.), *Practical Applications in Language Corpora – Proceedings* (pp. 24–33). Łódź: Łódź University Press.

Partington, A. (1998). *Patterns and Meanings*. Amsterdam and Philadelphia: John Benjamins.

Pawley, A. & Syder, F. H. (1983). "Two puzzles for linguistic theory: Native-like selection and native-like fluency". In J. C. Richards & R. W. Schmidt (Eds.), *Language and Communication* (pp. 191–227). London: Longman.

Pearson, J. (2003). "Using parallel texts in the translator training environment". In F. Zanettin, S. Bernardini, & D. Stewart (Eds.), *Corpora in Translator Education* (pp. 15–24). Manchester: St. Jerome.

Prabhu, N. S. (1987). *Second Language Pedagogy*. Oxford: Oxford University Press

Robinson, P. (1995). "Attention, memory, and the 'noticing hypothesis'". *Language Learning*, *45* (2), 283–331.

Römer, U. (2004). "Comparing real and ideal language learner input: The use of an EFL textbook corpus in corpus linguistics and language teaching". In G. Aston, S. Bernardini, & D. Stewart (Eds.), *Corpora and Language Learners* (pp. 153–170). Amsterdam and Philadelphia: John Benjamins.

Schmidt, R. W. (1990). "The role of consciousness in second language learning". *Applied Linguistics, 11* (2), 129–155.

Sinclair, J. (1991). *Corpus, Concordance, Collocation*. Oxford: Oxford University Press.

Skehan, P. (1996). "Second language acquisition and task-based instruction". In J. Willis & D. Willis (Eds.), *Challenge and Change in Language Teaching* (pp. 17–30). Oxford: Heinemann.

Skehan, P. (1998). *A Cognitive Approach to Language Learning*. Oxford: Oxford University Press.

Stubbs, M. (1996). *Text and Corpus Analysis*. Oxford: Blackwell.

Toury, G. (1995). *Descriptive Translation Studies and Beyond*. Amsterdam and Philadelphia: John Benjamins.

Varantola, K. (2003). "Translators and disposable corpora". In F. Zanettin, S. Bernardini, & D. Stewart (Eds.), *Corpora Translator Education* (pp. 55–70). Manchester: St. Jerome.

Widdowson, H. G. (1984). *Explorations in Applied Linguistics 2*. Oxford: Oxford University Press.

Willis, J. D. (1990). *The Lexical Syllabus*. London: Collins.

Wray, A. (2000). "Formulaic sequences in second language teaching: Principle and practice". *Applied Linguistics, 21* (4), 463–489.

Zanettin, F. (1998). "Bilingual comparable corpora and the training of translators". *Meta, 43* (4), 616–630.

# Developing professional translation competence without a notion of translation

Christina Schäffner

## Introduction: Translation as an object of research and as practice

A central issue for any discipline is to define its object of research. As the object of research of translation studies, translation has been defined in various ways (for detailed discussions see *e.g.* Stolze 1994; Munday 2001; Schäffner in press), which have subsequently influenced research methodologies and data selection. For example, Koller (1979, 1993) differentiates between translation proper and adaptation, arguing that translation needs to be defined with reference to equivalence relations between source text (ST) and target text (TT). In his view, translation scholars need to determine objective criteria for such equivalence relations. Only then can translations (i.e. translations proper) be set clearly apart from other cases of derived text production. Toury, on the other hand, argues against setting criteria as a first step of any research. For him, a translation is "that which is regarded as a translation by a certain cultural community at a certain time" (Toury 1995: 32). In a similar way, Hermans (1985: 13) argues that a translation researcher should "work without preconceived notions of what actually constitutes 'translation' or where exactly the dividing line between translation and non-translation is to be drawn". In his opinion, "such notions would inevitably reveal themselves to be normative and restrictive" (*ibid.*).[1]

For research purposes, defining translation in a specific way may indeed be restrictive since certain texts will be excluded from the beginning and insights into the phenomenon of translation as a social and cognitive activity may thereby be limited. But translation is not only an object of research, it is also a practice and a profession which many now join after they have followed a course of education and training, and courses in translation tend to be predicated on a fairly well defined notion of translation. Neubert (1997:85) argues that the "traditional wisdom that one only learns to translate by translating [...] is in need of a significant correction or rather reassessment", and I have argued repeatedly that if translation competence is developed within a theoretical framework, students will be better able to make informed decisions in their future, professional translation practice (cf. Schäffner 2000; Schäffner with Wiesemann 2001). Students who practice translation need to know something about the processes of translating, and about what is expected of the products of the processes, i.e. translations as target texts. This does not mean, however, that in the training process a definition of translation (ideally, in my view, an understanding of translation as a purposeful activity, cf. Nord 1997) needs to be provided from the beginning of a course. On the contrary, in this chapter I would like to argue for two methodological approaches which defer definition until much later.

## Developing translation competence in the academic environment: Two scenarios

Students who choose to study translation at university usually do so because they have enjoyed translating in the past. They arrive with a notion of translation mainly acquired at school and possibly reaffirmed or modified at university, where translation is practised as a pedagogical exercise as part of language learning modules. They are normally not at all familiar with the requirements of the contemporary translation profession, which relies heavily on technology, strives to comply with quality assurance standards recognised and used by the rest of industry and working to extremely tight deadlines. Students as trainee translators need to be prepared for these real-world conditions. This can be done in one of (at least) two ways, depending on the type of translation programme the students are following.

### Scenario 1: Teaching translation as part of a language programme

At the University of Aston, final year students on undergraduate language programmes are able to follow modules on Advanced Translation. They have typically spent a year abroad, so their knowledge of the second language (I use German for illustration here) and their cultural competence are generally very good. They can be expected to have practised translation as part of written language modules in previous years and also to be required to translate in their written language classes in their final year, although in those modules, translation is mainly intended to:

–   show whether students have understood the content and the linguistic structure of an L2 source text which is translated into L1
–   show whether students can produce well-structured L2 texts when translating from their L1, conforming to linguistic rules and conventions of the L2
–   show whether students have fully understood the message of a text in L2 and whether they can reproduce this message in a well-structured text in L1, conforming to the rules and conventions of the L1.

In contrast, the aim of the Advanced Translation module is to introduce students to aspects and requirements of professional translation, i.e. to develop translation competence. Since there is not likely to be much time available (around two hours per week for 12 weeks), an efficient way has to be found to achieve this aim. In my experience, the following model proves effective:

In the first week, students are asked to consider a list of statements like the following, most of them slight modifications of statements that occur in Hönig and Kussmaul (1991: 15–16), and to rate them as: "true", "not true", or "don't know":

(1)   If we do not know the readership for a text, we can not translate it.

(2)   If it is obvious that a text is a translation, then it is a bad translation.

(3)   Translating a scientific or technical text is more difficult than translating general or everyday texts, because scientific or technical texts contain many more unfamiliar words.

(4)   It is always riskier to do a free than a literal translation because translating freely can easily lead you away from the proper meaning of a word.

(5)   Translators need a bilingual dictionary because it tells them which word to use in the text and where to use it.

(6)   It cannot be the task of the translator to make a translated text easier to understand for the readers than the original text is for its readers.

(7)   Ideally, a back translation will reproduce the original text.

(8)   In every language there are some words which are untranslatable.

(9)   Even if two experienced translators translate one and the same text, their translations will be different. This shows that subjectivity and individual taste play such an important role in translating that it is probably not possible to explain the phenomenon on the basis of an objective model.

(10)   The source text is the yardstick by which the quality of a translation is measured.

When the students have ticked their choices, they compare answers and listen to the arguments with which those answers are backed up. This results in interesting and very lively debates, the aim of which is to establish what the students' preconceived notions of translation are. There is normally a tendency to disagree with statement (1) and agree with statements (2), (3), and (9), while the remaining statements are greeted variously, including with uncertainty ("don't know"). The debates reveal that the students normally see translation as a close reproduction of the source text, both in content and in form. This is not the notion of translation I would like them to leave the module with, but what is important in this first session is not to provide an answer to the statements but to use the ensuing discussions to raise students' awareness of a number of issues and to encourage them to continue to reflect on the statements.[2]

In later sessions, translations are produced of several texts, representing genres such as tourist information, film reviews, instructions for use, political speeches, popular science, legal texts, literary texts, and advertising. For each, a specific translation assignment is given. On the basis of research (*i.e.* researching translation studies literature), for each genre students give short presentations about recurring translation problems posed by the genre in question and the strategies to consider in producing the target text. In commenting on the target texts, *i.e.* discussing their appropriateness, we refer back – explicitly or implicitly – to the statements discussed above. For example, in discussing instructions for use for a hairdryer, we reflect on genre conventions (*e.g.* use of infinitives in German but imperatives in English for giving instructions, or conventional phrases such as *Für Kinder unzugänglich aufbewahren!* – 'Keep out of the reach of children'). We also reflect on voltage and wiring instructions and after-sales service in the source and target cultures. For tourist information, we discuss strategies for dealing with proper names and culture-specific terms (*e.g.* keeping the names of places of interest in German to ensure that tourists will find their way; how much information to give for culture-specific concepts). For legal texts, we discuss how to deal with cross-references to legal documents, reflecting on the addressees of the text (*i.e.* the relevance of a reference to German Civil Code differs depending on whether a company operates in the UK or in Germany). For political speeches, *e.g.* a televised New Year address by the German Chancellor, we reflect on the changing purpose of the text (persuasive text for the German public versus informative text for British politicians) and consequences for translation. For literary texts, we reflect on considerations of style, rhythm, rhyme (for example, the students translated a song from Brecht's *Dreigroschenoper* into English, where the fact that the text will have to be sung posed a major problem). For an advertising text we discuss advertising strategies (selling a product – selling an image) and the relationship between verbal and non-verbal information. In these discussions about (degrees of) appropriateness of the TTs produced by the students, we thus take the following into consideration:

– the purpose of the target text
– its addressees
– their culture-specific background knowledge
– their expectations about genre conventions
– aspects of time and place of text reception, *etc.*

We also comment on the most effective use of reference tools, such as various types of dictionaries, parallel texts, encyclopedias, specialist literature, human resources, the Internet *etc.* For example, parallel texts, *i.e.* "L$_2$ and L$_1$ texts of equal informativity which have been produced in more or less identical communicative situations" (Neubert 1985:75), have proved useful for practically all genres, but especially for instructions for use and tourist information. For tourist information, maps of the respective towns are helpful in getting a sense of direction (*e.g.* to follow visually the path from the east bank of the Rhine across the Hohenzollern bridge into the famous shopping area in Cologne). The Internet has proved a highly effective tool for searches of all kinds. For example in the case of film reviews, the Internet can be used to search for reviews of the same film in both German and English.

We also have one session devoted to translation quality assessment and translation criticism, where we look at authentic translations and discuss their quality. In this session, we refer to quality standards such as DIN 2345, the result of an agreement between translator training institutions, professional translator organisations and clients, and introduced in Germany, Austria and Switzerland in 1996 as a guideline to customers and translators for organising translation projects (*cf.* Schmitt 1998). In the final session, we return to the ten statements, and try to provide answers. It becomes clear in these concluding discussions that the students have changed their view of translation. They demonstrate their newly acquired competence in the examination, which for this specific module consists of a take-away paper requiring them to translate two texts of about 400 words each within 48 hours, from German into English. A translation brief is provided, and students are expected to use all tools available to them, but they must work individually. The results are usually reasonably good and show that the students have indeed acquired an acceptable degree of professional competence, though some worry that such a relatively free approach – as they see it – to the text might impact negatively on the mark they get for their translations. Introducing annotations as a compulsory element of the exam may go some way to alleviating this sense of insecurity since it allows students to comment on their solutions. Another possibility is to let students evaluate and mark previous exam papers.

As mentioned above, students only begin to view translation as purposeful activity in the course of the module. However, internalising the steps and procedures and actually applying them to the task are developmental processes which cannot be completed within the available time. Moreover, the placement of the module alongside language skills modules where translation exercises are practised for language learning purposes, contributes to the limited success in achieving the aims. Since the students are following language programmes, it is likely that only some of them may want to embark on careers as professional translators, but in any case, it is not until the final year that students are actively made to realise that translation is more than the simple replacement of source language words and syntactic structures by target language words and syntactic structures.

In view of the increasing demands of the translation industry, this process of developing translation competence needs to be speeded up, as is reflected in the introduction of translation programmes at undergraduate level in UK universities from the final decade of the 20th century. In the following section I present a model of such a programme.

## Scenario 2: Teaching translation in a translation programme

At Aston, it is also possible to study Modern Languages with translation at undergraduate level. This programme offers a translation specific core of modules accounting for around one third of the programme, and students are introduced to professional aspects of translation from the beginning of the course of study.

These students, too, have a preconceived notion of translation, stemming from their experience of translation exercises at school. In addition, they follow the language skills modules together with other students on language programmes, and translation exercises as part of language learning are used in the written language classes. The aim of the translation programme, in contrast, is to introduce them as quickly as possible to a more functionalist approach to translation.

In year one, students are introduced to basic concepts of translation studies and approaches to translation in order to develop an understanding of theoretical concepts which underpin systematic analysis and decision-making in the translation process. That is, the course is intended to develop some initial competence which will be enhanced over the following years. In the first seminar, students discuss the need for translation and translators and their own experience of translations and translating: whether they have read anything in translation, how they knew it was a translation, what they would expect of a translation. The discussions usually reveal that students in their first year believe that source text and target text should be identical in content, that the TT should be a reproduction of the ST in another language, and that the TT should read well and be understandable.

Next, the students are asked to translate a text in their L2 into English as homework, using whatever dictionaries and other resources they desire. The specific text used in this exercise is taken from a small card which guests receive in a hotel. In class, students compare and discuss their translations before comparing the latter with the German source text and the English and French translations that were actually printed on the card:

> *Für Telefongespräche ausserhalb des Hauses drücken Sie bitte die Taste "Amt/Self Dial" und die Taste "Rezeption" verbindet Sie mit dem Empfang.*
>
> *Die Haftung für im Zimmer belassene Wertsachen und Geld ist nach BGB Bestimmungen beschränkt. Ein Safe steht Ihnen unentgeltlich zur Verfügung.*
>
> *Am Tage Ihrer Abreise ersuchen wir Sie, das Zimmer bis 11.45 Uhr zu räumen.*
>
> For outgoing calls please press the button "Amt/Self Dial", if you have any questions touch the key "Rezeption".
>
> You are requested not to leave money or valuables in your room, since our liability is limited by law. They may be kept in our safe, free of charge.
>
> The day of your departure kindly vacate the room by 11.45.
>
> *Pour téléphoner vous pressez le buton "Amt/Self Dial" pour une ligne ex-térieure et la touche "Rezeption" si vous avez des questions.*
>
> *L'hotel n'est pas responsable d'argent et des objects de valeur dans la chambre. A la disposition de nos clients se trouve un coffre-fort.*
>
> *Le jour de votre depart nous vous prions de libérer la chambre avant 11.45.*

The students notice differences both between their own versions and the authentic English TT, and between the three versions of the text on the card. In the ensuing, interesting debates, questions like the following typically arise:

Why does the German text have only *Taste* whereas the English text has two words ('button' and 'key')? Why do we find '*Amt*/Self Dial' and '*Rezeption*' in both texts? Why have these terms not been translated? Why has the reference to *BGB* (*Bürgerliches Gesetzbuch*, 'German Civil Code') in the German text not been represented in the French text, and why does the English text mention only an unspecified, general 'law'? After some prompting, the students also notice differences in the degree of formality and politeness (the English text is more personal, as reflected in the use of personal pronouns; the German text is more formal and authoritative), and differences in the syntactic structures.

The discussion sooner or later culminates in the questions: is this a good translation? And: is this a translation at all? Or would we need another name, e.g. adaptation, re-writing? The answers are mostly that it is not a proper translation because there are too many differences in the surface structures of the texts, but that the English text does make sense and the readers get the most important information they need. We introduce some key concepts into the debate, such as addressees, function, situation, culture, conventions, readers' knowledge and expectations, and I encourage the students to continue to bear these concepts in mind.

During the remaining weeks (twelve weeks in all), we discuss the following topics, constantly coming back to the hotel key text and bringing in additional texts:

- A short overview of the history of translation and of the contributions made by translators to home languages and cultures (based on Delisle & Woodsworth 1995).
- Linguistic concepts, translation as interlingual transfer; translation and equivalence (with references to Vinay & Darbelnet 1958; Newmark 1981; Kade 1968).
- Textlinguistics and translation, text typology, genre conventions and translation (with references to Reiss's 1971 translation-oriented text typology and to Neubert's 1985 concept of parallel texts).
- Functionalist approaches to translation: translation as intercultural communication, translation as purposeful activity (with reference to Vermeer's 1996 notion of *skopos*, to Nord's 1991, 1997 four types of translation problem, to Chesterman's 1997 translation strategies, to Hönig & Kussmaul's 1991 notions of *Funktionskonstanz* and *Funktionsveränderung* ('same function', 'different function') and to Holz-Mänttäri's 1984 notion of translatorial action).

The students are also introduced to tools for translators (including various types of dictionaries, but above all the possibilities offered by the Internet). Since in this module the focus is on actually producing translations, the important contributions of Descriptive Translation Studies and Cultural Studies (e.g. notions such a norms, foreignisation and domestication) are only briefly introduced.

Most of the time is devoted to translation-oriented text analysis, *i.e.* identification and discussion of text-external and text-internal features and their relevance for translation; identifying translation problems according to the types they belong to (pragmatic, intercultural, interlingual, text-specific, cf. Nord 1991) and discussing potential translation solutions; identifying genre specific conventions in a text and translating extracts by making use of parallel texts. For all the exercises we always use authentic texts and make sure that a translation assignment is provided. Since the students are at the same time improving their language skills, we often use source texts and authentic translations on the basis of which we comment on the translation strategies applied and their effectiveness in view of the (assumed) purpose. Multilingual texts are especially useful in this respect. We practise the use of labels for translation strategies, initially Vinay/Darbelnet's (1958) terms, and subsequently the labels Chesterman (1997: 92–116) employs. For example:

(i) 'by scientifically capturing' – *en capturant de façon scientifique – es ist uns gelungen . . . mit wissenschaftlichen Methoden einzufangen*

Example (i) above illustrates modulation (specification/explicitation) for both French and German (i.e. the notion of *method* has been added: *façon*, *Methoden*) in addition to transposition for German (where the English and French texts have gerunds, the German text has an indicative verb form; the agent has been added, which results in personification)

(ii) 'cools and uplifts tired eyes' – *apaise et tonifie les yeux fatiqués – kühlt die Augenpartie und macht müde Augen wieder munter*

Example (ii) illustrates modulations in the German text, *e.g.*, specification ('*die Augenpartie*), antonymic translation ('tired', *fatiqués* as opposed to *munter*) and alliteration and allusion (*macht müde Augen wieder munter* is an allusion to a well-known slogan *Milch macht müde Männer munter*, 'milk makes tired men awake').

(iii) 'please note' – *veuillez noter – zur Beachtung*

Example (iii) illustrates the varied forms which are required by genre conventions in different languages.

(iv)   'Slip thumbs inside a leg and gather to the stitching at the toes' – *Rollen Sie nun ein Strumpfbein bis zur Spitze zusammen - Glissez vos pouces à l'intérieur d'une des jambes de votre collant. Retroussez cette jambe jusqu'à son extrémité*

Example (iv) illustrates a distribution change (implicitation) in the German text as compared to the English and the French texts, the French text being even more specific than the English ST.

By working with translations in this way, students discover for themselves that translation is a decision-making process, and that the decisions need to be made on the basis of reflection about addressees, the purpose of the TT, situational and contextual aspects and genre conventions. Students come to appreciate, at the same time, that what they do in their written language classes is a specific kind of translation (philological translation) which serves a specific purpose (language learning). They do not experience translation in translation modules and translation in language modules as conflicting and contradictory, but as activities fulfilling different purposes.

For the examination, the students translate a text of 250 words into their mother tongue. They choose the text and the source language themselves and they have several weeks in which to produce the target text, which must be submitted towards the end of the teaching period. In the last week, there is an oral exam lasting between fifteen and twenty minutes during which students 'defend' their translation. They are asked to comment on three or four translation problems in the text and give reasons for the translation strategies they employed, to be backed up by evidence where appropriate (e.g. illustrating on the basis of parallel texts that they were dealing with a feature which is genre specific, or how they accounted for different background knowledge on the part of the addressees, or what kind of research they carried out, or what types of dictionaries they used). The translation accounts for 60% of the mark and the oral exam for 40%. At this early stage of their studies, the students do not produce flawless target texts; however, they demonstrate emerging translation competence (see also Schäffner 2000).

In the subsequent years, specific modules build on the knowledge gained and the skills acquired in the first year. In the second year, textual competence, i.e. knowledge of regularities and conventions of texts, genres and text types is further developed in the module 'Translation-oriented intercultural text comparison' (cf. Schäffner 2002); and the relevance of domain specific competence, i.e. knowledge of an area of expertise, is illustrated in the module

Terminology for translators. The third year is an obligatory year abroad, and students follow translation classes at exchange universities and/or do an annotated translation into their L1 as year abroad project. In the final year, modules in Advanced Translation, LSP-Translation, Interpreting, and Contemporary Translation Theories are designed to consolidate translation competence.

## Evaluation of the two scenarios

What both scenarios described above have in common is that at the beginning of the course the students have a notion of translation which sees translation pretty much as reproduction of the source text as closely as possible. In the course of time, i.e. during the module, they begin to change their perception, gradually developing a notion of translation which sees translation as text production for specified purposes, taking account of situational and cultural aspects, addressees' knowledge and expectations, and genre conventions, in addition to reflecting on the linguistic means available. They also gradually change their research strategies, adding different types of tools (e.g. parallel texts, Internet, reference books) to the bilingual dictionary they usually start out with. At the end of the modules, therefore, the result is the same, i.e. students (are beginning to) realise that translation competence is a complex notion which involves an awareness of and conscious reflection on all the relevant factors for the production of a target text that appropriately fulfills its specified function for its target addressees. The difference between the two scenarios, however, is one of time: in scenario one, students have twelve weeks available to adopt a new notion of translation before they embark on a professional career (though few will take up jobs as translators immediately after graduation); whereas in scenario two, an initial twelve weeks are followed by a further three years during which this newly acquired notion can be consolidated. Although final year students have a better developed linguistic and cultural competence, which is helpful in understanding the source text, they have to 'unlearn' their translation procedures and change their approach to translating. First year students, although not yet competent in language and cultural aspects, are introduced to the complexity of the notion of translation competence and are encouraged to apply the required research skills right from the beginning, thus developing linguistic, cultural, textual, research and translation competence in parallel.

In the case of both scenarios, it proves useful, methodologically, to present definitions of translation towards the end of the course instead of at the beginning, the advantage being that in the course of our discussions, the students become aware of the importance of genre conventions, addressees' knowledge, text functions, etc., and it is much easier for them to accept definitions such as the following:

> To translate means to produce a text in a target setting for a target purpose and target addressees in target circumstances.   (Vermeer 1987:29)

> Translation is the production of a functional target text maintaining a relationship with a given source text that is specified according to the intended or demanded function of the target text (translation skopos).   (Nord 1991:28)

Such a discovery procedure allows for the conscious acquisition of knowledge (reflective learning) as opposed to an imposition of knowledge. As such, it helps us achieve the aims and objectives of undergraduate translation programmes such as those described here: The development of translation competence through reflective practice within the theoretical framework provided by functionalist approaches to translation.

The title of this paper could therefore be rephrased in a more programmatic way as: Developing translation competence by developing a notion of translation in a process of critical reflection about the activity of translation.

## Notes

1. I tend to agree with Vuorinen (1996:21) who argues that "it may be questioned whether research 'without preconceived notions' is at all possible. In fact, such a research attempt would seem to represent naive empiricism."

2. Answers, with extensive comments, can be found in Hönig and Kussmaul (1991:147–153). Their preferred answers, based on a functionalist approach to translation, are "true" for the first statement and "not true" for all the rest except 9, in the case of which "not quite true as it stands" would be more appropriate.

## References

Chesterman, A. (1997). *Memes of Translation*. Amsterdam and Philadelphia: John Benjamins.

Delisle, J. & Woodsworth, J. (Eds.). (1995). *Translators through History*. Amsterdam and Philadelphia: John Benjamins, UNESCO Publishing.

Hermans, T. (Ed.). (1985). *The Manipulation of Literature: Studies in Literary Translation*. London: Croom Helm.

Holz-Mänttäri, J. (1984). *Translatorisches Handeln. Theorie und Methode*. Helsinki: Suomalainen Tiedeakatemia.

Hönig, H. & Kussmaul, P. (1991). *Strategie der Übersetzung. Ein Lehr- und Arbeitsbuch.* Tübingen: Narr.

Kade, O. (1968). *Zufall und Gesetzmäßigkeit in der Übersetzung* (Beiheft I zur Zeitschrift *Fremdsprachen*). Leipzig: Enzyklopädie.

Koller, W. (1979). *Einführung in die Übersetzungswissenschaft.* Heidelberg: Quelle & Meyer.

Koller, W. (1993). "Zum Begriff der 'eigentlichen' Übersetzung". In J. Holz-Mänttäri & C. Nord (Eds.), *Traducere Navem. Festschrift für Katharina Reiss zum 70. Geburtstag.* Tampere: Tampereen Yliopisto (studia translatologica A 3).

Munday, J. (2001). *Introducing Translation Studies. Theories and Applications.* London and New York: Routledge.

Neubert, A. (1985). *Text and Translation* (Übersetzungswissenschaftliche Beiträge 8). Leipzig: Enzyklopädie.

Neubert, A. (1997). "Teaching Translation as text". In H. Drescher (Ed.), *Transfer. Übersetzen – Dolmetschen – Interkulturalität.* Frankfurt/Main: Peter Lang.

Newmark, P. (1981). *Approaches to Translation.* Oxford: Pergamon

Nord, C. (1991). *Text Analysis in Translation.* Amsterdam: Rodopi.

Nord, C. (1997). *Translating as a Purposeful Activity. Functionalist Approaches Explained.* Manchester: St. Jerome.

Reiss, K. (1971). *Möglichkeiten und Grenzen der Übersetzungskritik.* München: Hueber.

Schäffner, C. (2000). "Running before Walking? Designing a Translation Programme at Undergraduate Level". In C. Schäffner & B. Adab (Eds.), *Developing Translation Competence.* Amsterdam and Philadelphia: John Benjamins.

Schäffner, C. with Wiesemann, U. (2001). *Annotated texts for translation: English-German. Functionalist Approaches Illustrated.* Clevedon: Multilingual Matters.

Schäffner, C. (2002). "Entwicklung von Übersetzungsorientierter Textkompetenz". In C. Feyrer & P. Holzer (Eds.), *Translation: Didaktik im Kontext.* Frankfurt Main: Peter Lang.

Schäffner, C. (in press). "Systematische Übersetzungsdefinitionen". In A. P. Frank, N. Greiner, T. Hermans, H. Kittel, W. Koller, J. Lambert, & F. Paul (Eds.), *Übersetzung – Translation – Traduction. An International Handbook of Translation Studies.* Berlin: de Gruyter.

Schmitt, P. A. (1998). "Qualitätsmanagement". In M. Snell-Hornby, H. G. Hönig, P. Kussmaul, & P. A. Schmitt (Eds.), *Handbuch Translation.* Tübingen: Stauffenburg.

Stolze, R. (1994). *Übersetzungstheorien. Eine Einführung.* Tübingen: Narr.

Toury, G. (1995). *Descriptive Translation Studies and Beyond.* Amsterdam and Philadelphia: John Benjamins.

Vermeer, H. J. (1987). "What does it mean to translate?" *Indian Journal of Applied Linguistics, 13*, 25–33.

Vermeer, H. J. (1996). *A Skopos Theory of Translation (Some Arguments For and Against).* Heidelberg: TEXTconTEXT.

Vinay, J.-P. & Darbelnet, J. (1958). *Stylistique comparée du français et de l'anglais. Méthode de traduction.* Paris: Didier.

Vourinen, E. (1996). *Crossing Cultural Boundaries in Internaitonal News Transmission – a Translational Approach.* University of Tampere, unpublished Licentiate thesis.

# Are L2 learners more prone to err when they translate?*

Anne Schjoldager

## Introduction

In Denmark, as in many other countries, it has long been a tradition to include translation as a compulsory component in the teaching and testing of foreign languages, both at university and lower levels. Interestingly, though recent years have seen at least some reappraisal of the role of translation in the language classroom, this practice is not in accordance with current thinking within the field of language teaching. Thus, most scholars who write on language teaching still seem to regard translation as an inadequate, even harmful, teaching and testing tool. This view is usually mirrored by translation scholars, who simply take for granted that language learning, on the one hand, and learning about professional translation, on the other, are two rather different activities: linguistic knowledge is a means, not an end, if one wishes to translate, just as knowledge of cultures and subject area is.

Is translation then a valuable component of the foreign-language (L2) curriculum? Practice seems to indicate that it might be, theory that it is not. Unfortunately, the issue is still largely unexplored empirically and we still lack necessary evidence to decide which position is more correct. Though I do not pretend to contribute any definitive answers, I hope that this paper will add some useful fuel to the ongoing debate about the possible merits and dangers of translation as an activity for L2 learners.

I shall start by looking more closely at the role of translation in language teaching, giving a brief overview of past and current thinking, citing arguments for and against it and discussing a few empirical studies on the issue. Then I shall describe the aims, rationale, procedure, and some preliminary results of my own investigation. In this study, I compare translations from Danish into

English (the subjects' L2) with comparable picture verbalizations in English, in order to carry out product-oriented error analyses. The subjects are university students and secondary-school students (*gymnasieelever*). Preliminary results indicate that, in absolute numbers, those who translated were more prone to err than those who did picture verbalizations. For the secondary-level students there was an overrepresentation of so-called interference errors in the translations, whereas the university students showed some tendency to err more in the picture verbalizations.

## The role of translation in language teaching

In this section, I shall look briefly at past and current thinking on language teaching in general before providing an overview of current practice in Denmark.

### Past and current theory

Though it cannot properly be termed a theory (Richards & Rodgers 1986:5), the grammar-translation method seems to have dominated pre-20th-century thinking on language teaching. According to this method, modern languages should be taught using the same procedures as those used in the teaching of Latin, namely through rote learning of abstract grammar rules and lists of vocabulary and the translation of isolated sentences constructed to illustrate grammatical points (Richards & Rodgers 1986:2). There was little interest in teaching the students any oral skills in L2, and as a matter of course the language of instruction was the students' native language (L1).

The grammar-translation method no longer dominates language-teaching theory. It was first attacked theoretically in the mid- and late 19th century, when members of the Reform Movement began to argue that the focus of language teaching should be changed: languages should no longer be taught by means of abstract grammar rules and lists of vocabulary. Instead, grammar should be taught inductively, and new vocabulary should be acquired through establishing associations within L2, rather than by establishing associations with L1; whole texts, not isolated sentences, should be studied; the skills of speaking and listening should be emphasized; and the language of instruction should now basically be L2. As a logical consequence of these views, translation was to be avoided (Richards & Rodgers 1986:8).

According to Richards and Rodgers (1986:4), the ideas of the Reform Movement meant that the grammar-translation method ceased to dominate the practice of language teaching around the 1940s, but this does not mean that it no longer exists. As already mentioned, the grammar-translation method continues to be practised, in a more or less modified form, especially in secondary schools, in many parts of the world (see e.g. Richards & Rodgers 1986:4–5; Cook 1998:118).

The ideas of the Reform Movement led to the formation of the direct method, the most widely known of the so-called natural methods (Richards & Rodgers 1986:9–13). As its name suggests, the direct method is the teaching of an L2 without reference to L1. The underlying idea is that L2 learning is – and should be – similar to natural L1 learning, which means of course that the use of translation as a tool is impossible.

As almost all current theories tend to be related to the direct method (Cook 1998:118), many influential scholars still condemn the use of translation as a teaching tool. However, there are signs that the area is warming up to a reappraisal of the merits of translation (Cook 1998:119). As the direct method has been criticized for overemphasizing and distorting similarities between natural L1 learning and classroom L2 learning, it is now widely acknowledged that an exclusive use of L2 in the classroom is neither practical nor recommendable. And if L1 should play a role after all – why not in the form of translation between L1 and L2?

## Current practice

In a discussion of the role of translation in language teaching, it is important to remember that the grammar-translation method is just one way of using translation as a pedagogical tool – a fact that many who condemn the use of translation in the L2 classroom tend to overlook (Cook 1998:119). For the purposes of this paper, I shall therefore distinguish between three kinds of teaching activities which all involve translation, but which – at least in theory – use translation in different ways: Language teaching, translation teaching and translator training. In each case, I shall cite examples from the teaching of English in Denmark.

### Language teaching
Using a more or less modified version of the grammar-translation method, teachers may view translation mainly as a means of teaching and testing L2 proficiency. Translations from L1 into L2 are supposed to test L2 production

skills, whereas translations the other way, i.e. L1 translations, are supposed to test comprehension skills.

It is my impression that translation plays hardly any role at the primary (*folkeskole*) level of language teaching in Denmark, whereas its role is still rather significant at the secondary (*gymnasie-*) level at least as far as English is concerned. In accordance with ministerial rules and regulations (*Bekendtgørelse om gymnasiet, studenterkursus og enkeltfagseksamen* 1999, Bilag 9, ENGELSK), most exams still contain a compulsory element of translation, which is supposed to function as a supplementary test of the student's L2 proficiency. Thus, all oral exams contain an element of L1 (sight) translation, and most written exams contain an element of L2 translation.

*Translation teaching*
Translation may also be taught as a separate component in a language programme. Translation may still be used as a means of teaching and testing L2 proficiency, but since the activity is given a more independent status, there is more room for teaching translation as an end in itself.

In Denmark, such translation classes are quite common at the tertiary level, for instance in most language departments of the University of Aarhus. In the department of English, translation (both ways) is a one-semester course in the third year and is the only compulsory upper-level (MA) course.[1] Though we may try to focus on translation as a skill in its own right in this course, we cannot escape the fact that the overall aim of the final exams is (probably) still to test L2 proficiency. At least, the exam regulations make no mention of testing translational competence, but merely stipulate that students must be proficient in the written translation (between Danish and English) of non-specialized texts which are particularly difficult with regard to syntax, style, lexicon and idiomatic expressions (*Studieordning Engelsk Kandidatuddannelse* Jan. 1999, §52).

*Translator training*
Finally, translation can be taught for professional purposes. Though such courses may also involve some degree of language teaching, language is no longer – supposed to be – the main concern (see e.g. Schäffner 1998:131–132). Typically, institutions which offer such vocational training for would-be translators are members of CIUTI (Conférence International d'instituts Universitaires de Traducteurs et Interprètes), and their MA graduates within translation are entitled to become authorized translators and interpreters.

Whereas this kind of translation is often taught at universities in other countries, Danish universities usually confine themselves to using translation as a pedagogical device in their language programmes, though often in separate classes (see above).[2] In Denmark, vocational studies for translators at the MA level are found at other university-level institutions, namely the business schools of Aarhus and Copenhagen, the only CIUTI members in Denmark. In the rest of this article, I shall not deal with translator training as, by definition, linguistic knowledge is a means, not an end in such classes.

## Arguments for and against translation

Before we look at some specific arguments for and against the use of translation in language teaching, I would like to mention some rather practical reasons both for the perseverance with this use of translation and for it being so severely criticized.

Why is translation so widely used? First of all, the influence of tradition is still immensely strong (Pedersen 1974: 21): in Denmark, for instance, translation has been used as a teaching and testing tool in the L2 classroom for so long that many teachers and decision makers tend to take it for granted that this is how it should be. Another factor may be that some people actually like the grammar-translation approach. No doubt, in its purer forms, this method makes few demands on teachers, who can use the same material year after year, making the same corrections again and again because students tend to make exactly the same mistakes as their predecessors did (see Richards & Rodgers 1986: 4; Coleman 1986: 102). Furthermore, with its emphasis on grammatical analysis and learning rules by heart, the grammar-translation method may be rather appealing to teachers and students who enjoy this approach to language.

Why is translation so widely criticized? An important reason seems to be the way the grammar-translation method was – and perhaps is - implemented. No doubt, when practised rigorously, teaching based on this method may seem rather boring, irrelevant, and even disturbing to the average student. Thus, for instance, giving a comprehensive overview of the history of language teaching, Richards and Rodgers (1986: 4) write this about the grammar-translation method:

> Its worst excesses were introduced by those who wanted to demonstrate that the study of French or German was no less rigorous than the study of classical languages. This resulted in the type of Grammar-Translation courses

**Table 1.** Arguments for and against the use of translation in language teaching

| AGAINST | FOR |
| --- | --- |
| Translation is useless | Translation is useful |
| Translation strengthens L1 interference | Translation counteracts L1 interference |
| L2 translation is unethical | L2 translation is not unethical |

remembered with distaste by thousands of school learners, for whom foreign language learning meant a tedious experience of memorizing endless lists of unusable grammar rules and vocabulary and attempting to produce perfect translations of stilted and literary prose.

However, though the grammar-translation approach still seems to dominate the way most people think about translation in the L2 classroom, we need more substantial arguments if we wish to either defend or reject any pedagogical use of translation. I shall now mention some of the more common arguments put forward. For the sake of convenience, they will be presented as three sets of contradicting arguments, as shown in Table 1.

## Arguments against translation

As already mentioned, an important reason for the general dislike of translation is probably rooted in the way the grammar-translation approach was – and is – carried out. We shall now look at some arguments that go beyond this.

### Translation is useless

A prevailing argument is that translation as a pedagogical tool is inefficient, even useless. On a general level, Gatenby (1948/1967:70) asserts that the use of translation is a waste of time and asks: 'Why use two languages when the time allowed for learning one is so short?' Lado (1964:53) emphatically asserts that translation is different from language practice, the real aim of language teaching. Similarly, after a brief analysis of the grammar-translation method, Krashen (1987:129) simply concludes that it 'should result in very low amounts of acquired competence'.

Translation classes into L2 are particularly criticized in this respect. Generally, such classes are supposed to promote L2 proficiency, but, the argument goes, by using translation in this way they fail to achieve the objective. Thus, according to Marsh (1987:24–25), in using L2 translation almost exclusively as a teaching tool we run the risk of believing that we are teaching students how to communicate in L2, but what we really teach is merely knowledge of the language system. Coleman (1986: 101) puts it even more strongly when he characterizes the resulting exam as 'a kind of stationary driving-test, consisting of questions on the Highway Code'.

## Translation strengthens L1 interference

It is of course a serious enough accusation that translation classes are useless. But even more serious is the claim that the use of translation as a pedagogical tool is actually counterproductive. First of all, it is said to hinder the learning process by allowing students to rely on processing via L1, which strengthens L1 interference (negative transfer). For example, Gatenby (1950/1967: 2) describes the use of translation in this way as 'bad pedagogy', because it forces students to think in L1 when they should really be brought to a stage where they can use L2 'without having to think'. Similarly, Lado (1964: 54) explains that translation is unnatural because it is contrary to what natural bilinguals do: translation creates 'a subordinate, overly complex functional organization of the second language'; instead, two coordinate systems should be created.

Secondly, an exclusive use of translation assignments is claimed to be counterproductive because it has a negative effect on the way students think about language. According to Lado (1964: 53–54), for instance, translating misleads students into thinking that two expressions in two languages correspond completely (see also Malmkjær 1998: 6). Lado (1964: 54) also argues that if students are allowed to produce word-for-word translations (which he obviously thinks they are), this leads to the production of incorrect language. Irons (1998: 28) mirrors this view when lamenting that translation assignments seem to instill a belief in his students (training to become English teachers in Danish primary schools) that the only correct translation is a direct one, which to Irons is a contradiction in terms. In line with this, Coleman (1986: 102) argues that L2 translation 'may encourage the acquisition of habits and the development of strategies that are actually harmful to overall linguistic competence': translation leads to an obsession with the individual word.

## L2 translation is unethical

The practice of L2 translation is particularly vilified by the critics. Apart from the above-mentioned arguments, a weighty argument is that L2 translation is contrary to a professional norm of only translating into one's L1 (e.g. Marsh 1987: 24; Irons 1998: 29). The basis of this norm is obviously the widely held belief that only L1 translators reach professional standards. In other words, it is not only considered useless or even counterproductive to employ L2 translation in the L2 classroom, it is also thought to be unethical because it may lead students to think they are qualified to do such translations professionally.

## Arguments in favour of translation

As already mentioned, there are signs that the field is warming up to a reappraisal of the role of translation in language teaching (Cook 1998:119). Indeed, a considerable number of scholars have actually begun to defend the use of translation. We shall now consider some of their arguments.

### Translation is useful

It is important to note that many who speak in favour of translation are not referring to the grammar-translation method. Thus, for instance, whereas translation was a dominant tool in the grammar-translation method, the scholars mentioned in this section take for granted that translation is just one of several tools in the L2 classroom (e.g. Malmkjær 1998:9). Furthermore, whereas translation was formerly thought to be relevant for all levels of language teaching, many now accept that it may be advisable only to use it at the advanced level (e.g. Snell-Hornby 1985:21), though this view is not shared by all (e.g. Stibbard 1994:13). Also, it is worth pointing out that most authors who find translation useful do not see translation as an exercise in grammar. In fact, many stress that translation should, of course, be viewed as text production, ie a special kind of communication.

Fraser (1996) sees no conflict between contemporary views on L2 teaching and the use of translation as a teaching tool. To her, L1 translation (which is the sole concern of her paper) is an opportunity for students not only to add to their passive knowledge of L2, which is the traditional role of L1 translation, but also to reflect on 'the different ways in which L1 and L2 achieve the same communicative end' (Fraser 1996:122). As a consequence of this, Fraser (1996:127) strongly recommends that students are not asked to translate in a vacuum, as it were, but are given a brief, that is that they are given specific information about the situation and aims of their translation assignment. In continuance of this, Klein-Braley and Franklin (1998:59) emphasize that only those texts that may realistically be translated in real life should be chosen as material for the translation class. This recommendation is very much in line with modern translation studies, especially the *skopos* theory (e.g. Vermeer 1989; Nord 1997).

This view of translation is quite compatible with communicative language teaching, which appears to have 'assumed the status of orthodoxy in British language teaching' (Richards & Rodgers 1986: 83). Thus, for instance, in a book entitled Teaching Language as Communication, Widdowson (1978/1983) first asserts that grammar-translation types of assignments, with their emphasis on literal translation, merely operate at the level of the language system, which he refers to as 'usage'. Practised in this way, translation is useless, even harmful: 'A methodology which concentrates too exclusively on usage may well be creating the very problems which it is designed to solve' (Widdowson 1978/1983: 18). However, if the learner recognizes translation as an act of communication, translation can play a valuable role in language teaching, for instance by making students translate knowledge which they have acquired in other subjects in the school curriculum (Widdowson 1978/1983: 158).

To sum up, the basic argument is that translating increases one's linguistic knowledge (Sewell 1996: 142), linguistic accuracy (Duff 1989/1992: 7) and verbal agility (Sewell 1996: 142) and that it promotes thoughtful, critical reading (Stibbard 1994: 15). Specifically, L1 translation is a time-saving way of checking comprehension (Stibbard 1994: 15) and helping students add to their passive knowledge of L2 (Fraser 1996: 112); L2 translation perfects 'knowledge about and active mastery of' L2 (Snell-Hornby 1985: 21). The reason why translation is such an asset for the L2 classroom is that it involves a beneficial constraint on the writing process: the learner is not free to choose the meanings that s/he must express and therefore may be forced to venture into unknown areas of the L2 system (e.g. Duff 1989/1992: 7; Cook 1998: 119; see also Campbell 1998: 58).

*Translation counteracts L1 interference*
It is beyond dispute that L1 is bound to influence the learning of L2 and that some degree of L1 interference (negative transfer) is inevitable (Færch & Kasper 1989; Campbell 1998: 12). Similarly, nobody would disagree that the objective of any language class is to enable students to perform in that language with as little L1 interference as possible. What is disputed, however, is how best to achieve this aim and, specifically, what role translation should play in the L2 classroom. I have already mentioned that many scholars argue that translation should be banned from the L2 classroom because it encourages L1 interference. I shall now cite some scholars who think that translating is actually necessary to counteract L1 interference – at least at the advanced level. Though they do emphasize the importance of working with whole texts rather than isolated sentences, these scholars are probably less interested in teaching language as communication (at least at the point in time when I quote them below) than they are in achieving linguistic correctness.

Subscribing to a contrastive approach, Knud Sørensen is a great advocate of translation as a means of counteracting the influence of L1 on L2. For instance, in a paper entitled 'Translation as a Unifying Discipline', on the teaching of English to Danish university students, Sørensen (1990:57) writes: 'It is [...] extremely valuable for the student to contrast the two languages he is concerned with, by developing skills in translating from his native language and vice versa'. This activity makes advanced students aware of 'tricky dissimilarities and incongruities' between languages (Sørensen 1988:202; see also Sørensen 1991).

Snell-Hornby (1985) advocates a similar approach to language teaching. In a paper entitled 'Translation as a means of integrating language teaching and linguistics', she mentions several examples, based on her own teaching experience, of the usefulness of translation in highlighting contrastive aspects for German university students of English. Much in line with Sørensen's recommendations, Snell-Hornby (1985:24–25) makes it clear that such classes must be conducted in a systematic and rational way. This is undoubtedly important: if carried out intuitively, translation classes may be more likely to lead students to the naive view that every expression in one language has an exact equivalent in another, but if approached systematically and rationally they may actually discourage such naiveté (see also Cook 1998:119).

Similarly, Titford (1985:82) argues that L2 translation not only allows (university) teachers to correct L1-induced errors, but also 'gives us a context within which to explain them with a minimum of metalinguistic apparatus', and Harvey (1996:56) points to the usefulness of translation as a way of making (advanced) learners 'aware of how errors in L2 can result from the unconscious superimposing of L1 structures'.

*L2 translation is not unethical*
I have already mentioned that L2 translation is particularly vilified by the critics because it is contrary to a professional norm. However, though some authors, who are generally in favour of translation as a pedagogical tool, take for granted that only L1 translation is professionally relevant (e.g. Duff 1989/1992; Fraser 1996), others argue that L2 translation should not be ignored in university departments, because it is a skill that students will be called upon to perform in real life (e.g. Larsen 1990:95; Klein-Braley & Franklin 1998:54–55). Particularly, translations into English undoubtedly outnumber those from English, and given the relative lack of interest in foreign language learning in Britain and the United States (see Barbour, this volume) it is unlikely that a sufficient number of L1 translators of English will be available for a

considerable time to come. McAlester (1992) for instance suggests that this is the case with translations from Finnish into English – and I would suggest the same in connection with Danish-English translations.[3]

## Empirical studies

Let us now revert to the question with which we started: Is translation a valuable component of the L2 curriculum, or is it not? As will be apparent, opinions differ greatly. Unfortunately, there is little empirical evidence to support either position. We may think that translation is either good or bad for our students' acquisition of L2 proficiency, but we cannot know for certain because we still lack sufficient evidence.

However, the field is not completely unexplored, and I discuss a few of the empirical studies that exist below. Although it is mostly taken for granted that their findings will have a bearing on the teaching situation as a whole, most scholars tend to focus on translation as a testing tool and there are very few empirical studies which focus specifically on translation as a teaching tool (notable exceptions are Berggren 1972; Uzawa 1996; and, especially, Källkvist this volume). This may not be surprising as the testing feature is probably more readily isolated than other features of translation in the L2 classroom. Also, I have seen very little evidence to either support or reject the relevance of L2 translation for vocational reasons. Finally, in the few empirical studies on translation as a component of the L2 curriculum, there is a marked tendency towards ignoring L1 translation. This may be because L1 translation tends to be practised orally (i.e. as sight translation), at least at lower levels, which is probably regarded as less interesting – and less controversial – because of its transient nature. Thus, in the context of language teaching, L2 translation appears to be central and is therefore often the only object of investigation.[4]

I shall discuss three empirical studies whose aims are rather similar to that of my own investigation (see below), in so far as they all deal with L2 translation as a testing tool, comparing it with other L2 writing tasks. However, whereas my own data derive from an experimental setting, the investigations mentioned below all base their findings on exam papers; and whereas I shall attempt a comparison between the tertiary and secondary levels, the scholars mentioned below focus on the tertiary level.

Klein-Braley (1987) investigates the objectivity, reliability and validity of L2 translation as a testing tool of L2 proficiency. Her data derive from tests written by German students of English at the University of Duisburg, where students were tested partly by means of L2 translation and partly by some other tests. According to Klein-Braley (1987:118), 'it is no great technical problem to ensure the objective scoring of translation tests', but a lot of work is required. Even when such objectivity was achieved, only moderate reliability scores emerged; and, as far as validity was concerned, the translation tests always scored lowest. Klein-Braley's (1987:128–129) general conclusion is therefore that though L2 translation does seem to test general L2 proficiency, it appears to be the least satisfactory and the least economical of the tests examined. Specifically, Klein-Braley (1987:129) suggests that translation tests are 'two-dimensional' in that they measure other features as well, including capacity to translate, which may be unrelated to L2 proficiency. This leads her to conclude that translation should not be used as the only test of language proficiency. (See also Klein-Braley & Smith 1985; Klein-Braley 1996; Klein-Braley & Franklin 1998.)

Larsen (1990) is similarly interested in exploring the possible discrepancy between students' performances in L2 translation and other tasks. The starting point for her investigation was her impression that students often perform less well when translating than when writing a free essay. Her investigation is based on exam papers written by Danish university students of English. The exam (which existed until 1986) consisted of three parts – a summary, a translation and an essay – and its aim was to test the candidate's 'ability to write fluent, correct and idiomatic English' (Larsen 1990:97). Larsen's findings more or less confirm her initial feeling that translation is no reliable test of L2 proficiency. As one possible explanation for this, Larsen suggests that 'in some instances the source language, which confronts the student in black and white, intervenes to such an extent that [the student] translates directly without having recourse to the whole of his knowledge of the target language' (Larsen 1990:107). This argument is implicit in much criticism of translation as a testing tool, but it is rarely made explicit in the way Larsen does.[5]

In her PhD dissertation on lexical form-class effects in L2 learning, Källkvist (1997) compares free compositions, written retellings and translations, most of which are exam papers written at the English department of Lund University. Regarding the translations (from Swedish into English), she sets out to examine Weller's (1989:45) claim that 'the same kinds of errors attributed to translation also occur when learners produce target language utterances without setting out from the native language' (see Källkvist 1997:143). Of particular interest is her finding that the same lexical errors are found in the three tasks, but the distribution is different in compositions and retellings, on the one hand, and translation, on the other. Thus, for instance, those who translated wrote more non-existent words and, generally, made more meaning errors, the reason for this probably being that the translation task made them unable to avoid difficult L2 items. This leads Källkvist (1997:218) to conclude that Weller's above-mentioned claim is only partly true, and her general conclusion supports Klein-Braley's view that translation cannot stand alone as a test of general L2 proficiency, which also concurs with Larsen's (1990) findings. (For a summary of her results regarding translation, see Källkvist 1998:84–85; her 1997 PhD dissertation was published in a revised and condensed version as Källkvist 1999, which has less emphasis on the translation data).

## The experiment

In this section, I shall briefly discuss the aims, rationale, procedure, and some preliminary results of a small-scale experiment.

## Aims

My starting point is that L2 translation is generally assumed to invite errors that other L2 writing tasks do not. There are at least three related reasons for this, which have all been mentioned above:

- L1 interference is enhanced, because the student may be led to think in L1.
- The 'hypnotic' pressure from the L1 ST prevents the student from making full use of his/her linguistic capacity in L2.
- Because of the constraints of translating, the student may be forced to venture into unknown areas of the L2 system.

On this basis, I shall attempt to clarify the relationship between L2 translation competence and L2 proficiency in general. In the form of a product-oriented error analysis, I shall compare L2 translations (Danish into English) with L2 picture verbalizations with a view to answering these specific questions: Are there more errors in the translations? Are some errors more prevalent? Are there different kinds of errors? May these be the result of L1 interference? Of 'hypnotic' pressure from the ST? May the picture verbalizations generally be described as more successful?

In addition, I wish to consider whether the learner's general level of L2 competence as well as the nature of the language course may play a role. I shall therefore compare two kinds of data: at university level, which I define as translation teaching, and the secondary level, which I define as language teaching (see above). Specifically, I shall try to answer the question: Are university students less susceptible to the 'dangers' of translation? And, if so, is this simply because they are more advanced than the secondary-level students or is it because their approach to translation is different?

## Rationale

In this investigation, translation and picture verbalization are regarded as different, yet comparable writing tasks. Borrowing Jakobson's (1959/1989:55) much-quoted definitions, the former may be described as "interlingual translation or *translation proper*" and constitutes "an interpretation of verbal signs by means of some other language". The latter may be defined as "intersemiotic translation or *transmutation*" and constitutes an interpretation of non-verbal signs by means of verbal signs (though Jakobson mentions the reverse process).

In other words, the two tasks may both be regarded as a kind of translation, that is a controlled writing task in which the subject is asked to interpret and express somebody else's ideas. However, they differ crucially in at least two ways. Firstly, translation is based on a verbal, language-specific ST whereas picture verbalization is not. This means that L1 interference might play a stronger role in translation than in picture verbalization and that the ST asserts verbal pressure in translation, whereas there is no such pressure in picture verbalization. Secondly, in picture verbalization it may be easier than in translation to get around problems by choosing a different wording or giving up on a concept altogether, that is to make use of so-called 'avoidance' or other 'compensatory' strategies (though this should be more difficult in picture verbalization than in, for instance, free composition). In addition, the two tasks may also differ cognitively: the mental processing involved in translation may be rather different from that in picture verbalization. However, though such differences may have a bearing on the comparability of my data, I have no means of defining them at present and shall not discuss this further.

Finally, I should mention that, in my investigation, the use of dictionaries and other reference tools is not considered a necessary component of translation. Though I agree that it is a natural strategy for any translator to seek such help, I made my subjects work without access to reference tools in order to rule out as many external factors as possible. Admittedly, my subjects were not used to this, and many, especially the secondary-level students, seemed rather frightened by the prospect of having to work without reference tools.

## Procedure

The experiment was carried out in seven stages.

1.  Spring 2000. A picture story was selected, Pia Thavlov's (1996) *Familien Bartoldy. Frokost i det grønne*, a children's book, published for Libero by Gyldendal. This book tells a charming story about a family picnic exclusively by the means of well-made, very detailed colour pictures. Pages 1–6, three double-page pictures, were selected for the elicitation of data.
2.  Spring 2000. Four native speakers of Danish wrote a text to be read aloud on the radio as a story for children (approximately 8 years old) on the basis of the three pictures. For their information, they were also given copies of the remaining four double-page pictures. These texts were synthesized into one text of 426 words, which was used as a ST for the translation task.[6]
3.  Spring 2000. Eight third-year students of English in my own translation class did the translation, instructed (in Danish, in writing) to pretend that they were translating a text to be read aloud on the radio as a story for children, not to use any reference tools, and not to discuss the task with anybody.
4.  Spring 2000. Eight MA students of English in my Translation Studies class did the picture verbalization, with the same instructions (but in English) as the native speakers of Danish, but were also told, like those who translated, that they must not use any aids, etc.
5.  Spring and summer 2000. Four native speakers of English did the picture verbalization, with the same instructions (but in English) as the native speakers of Danish. These texts function as so-called 'parallel texts', ie texts used 'for assessing how the same kind of factual material is verbalized in different languages' (Snell-Hornby 1988:86), in order for me to use them as a source of reference in the ensuing error analysis.
6.  Summer 2000. The above-mentioned data were used in a pilot study in order to prepare for the collection of the main data. The result was that the two tasks seem sufficiently comparable.
7.  Autumn 2000. The main data for the investigation were collected. Subjects were final-year secondary-level students specializing in languages (*Sproglig linje*) at Risskov Amtsgymnasium (RA); and third-year students of English taking the compulsory translation course at the University of Aarhus (AU). Nine subjects were my own students, but the others were unknown to me. The subjects were not allowed to work in their own time, but worked under exam-like conditions (still without reference tools), and they were given a maximum time-limit, 75 minutes for RA students and 65 minutes for

AU students, which was determined by their respective timetables. Table 2 shows the distribution.

All subjects had Danish L1 and English L2, were brought up in Danish families in Denmark and had learned English as a foreign language.[7]

In both groups, there was an overrepresentation of female students: 14 females out of 21 in the RA group; and 27 out of 32 in the AU group, but this is representative of the situation in general among students who specialize in languages.

There was a marked age difference between the two groups. The RA students were all between 17 and 19 years old. The age span of the AU group ranged between 25 and 46, with the majority in their twenties. Again, this is representative of the two types of group.

I did not carry out any pretests of general level of L2 proficiency (*cf.* Källkvist this volume) and it was quite accidental who happened to do the translation and who did the picture verbalization. Therefore, though I am trying to remedy this partly by looking at the subjects' general marks,[8] I cannot know for certain how comparable the various groups are in terms of level of L2 proficiency, but shall simply assume that my data are sufficiently representative in this respect too.

## Preliminary results

The results presented below are based on my own marking and a preliminary error analysis of the subjects' scripts. Later I intend to ask a panel of colleagues to assess the texts, using a method similar to that of Källkvist (1997).

For the preliminary analyses, errors were divided into the following categories: Formal errors, incl. spelling and typing errors; grammatical errors including word order and concord errors; lexical errors, including Danish words, non-English words, wrong words and missing words; illegible or otherwise uncategorizable words. It is important to note that these are considered errors of language, as opposed to translational errors, which would be based on a comparison with the sources (pictures and ST).

Table 2.

| Subjects | Translation | Picture verbalisation | Total |
|---|---|---|---|
| RA | 10 | 11 | 21 |
| AU | 16 | 16 | 32 |
| Total | 26 | 27 | 53 |

Table 3.

| No. errors | Translation | Picture verbalisation | All |
|---|---|---|---|
| RA | 418 | 241 | 659 |
| AU | 291 | 184 | 475 |
| Total | **709** | 425 | 1134 |

Table 4.

| % Errors | Translation | Picture verbalisations | All |
|---|---|---|---|
| RA | 63% | 37% | 100% |
| AU | 61% | 39% | 100% |
| Total | 62% | 38% | 100% |

Table 5.

| Errors: Danish | Translation | Picture verbalisation | Total |
|---|---|---|---|
| RA | 19 | 2 | 21 |
| AU | 6 | 16 | 22 |

Table 6.

| Errors: non-English | Translation | Picture verbalisation | Total |
|---|---|---|---|
| RA | 23 | 12 | 35 |
| AU | 2 | 4 | 6 |

As mentioned above, I set out to answer a number of research questions. In the initial stage of the analyses, I have concentrated on the first two questions: Are there more errors in the translations? Are some errors more prevalent?

There were clearly more errors in the translations. Of a total of 1134 errors, 709 were committed by those who translated, as opposed to only 425 errors in the picture verbalizations, as shown in Table 3.

Dividing the total numbers of errors by the total numbers of subjects (709 and 425 by 26 and 27) gives an average number of errors per student in the translations of 27.3. In the picture verbalisations, the average number is only 15.7.

This overall tendency was not stronger in the RA group than in the AU group: In the RA group, 63% of all errors were committed by those who translated; in the AU group, the figure was 61%, as shown in Table 4.

When looking at individual errors, one would expect there to be an overrepresentation of so-called interference errors, namely instances of Danish ('non-translation') and non-English words, *etc.*, in the translations. But this assumption is only supported by the RA group, as the AU group actually shows some tendency in the opposite direction. Thus, in the RA group, out of a total of 21 instances of Danish words, *etc.*, 19 occurred in the translations; in the AU group the corresponding figures were only 6 out of 22, as shown in Table 5. Similarly, in the RA group, out of a total of 35 instances of non-English words, *etc.*, 23 occurred in the translations; in the AU group, the corresponding figures were, perhaps, rather insignificant: only 2 out of 6, as shown in Table 6. Since these are rather small figures, I have chosen not to indicate mean values or percentages.

## Discussion

There are at least three caveats which need to be considered in connection with the above-mentioned results.

Firstly, individual differences in all groups (RA vs. AU; translation vs. picture verbalization) are considerable and relative differences are therefore not sufficiently significant for me to generalize at this point.

Secondly, the analysis is based on instances of 'non-textual' errors. If textual features, such as coherence and well-formedness, were taken into account, the results might change slightly: because less 'textual responsibility' rests with the translator than with the writer in picture verbalization, one might expect there to be relatively more errors of this kind in the picture verbalizations. Interestingly, however, many picture verbalizations produced by the RA group are actually quite good in textual terms, and this seems to be relatively less so in the AU group. Thus, though one might expect the AU group to be better in all respects, there is some evidence that the picture verbalizations produced by the AU group are, relatively speaking, less superior than their translations are.

Thirdly, and this is linked with the previous caveat, the RA and the AU students may have approached the tasks in rather different ways. Judging from what they told me afterwards (in the weeks following the data collection, when I gave them feedback in the form of a class), I would say that most AU students seemed to enjoy translation and preferred this to picture verbalization, whereas most RA students did not. In line with this, some RA students complained that they felt frustrated and lacked self-confidence in connection with the translation (and perhaps with translation in general) because it was more difficult and too restrictive; some AU students said that they felt confident doing the translation because it was a controlled, textual task and some said that they did not like the picture verbalization because they 'lacked the imaginative powers' to do it properly. This difference may not be surprising since the AU students had been attending a *translation* class, whereas the RA students knew translation mainly as a teaching and testing tool. Also, perhaps the younger students (the RA group) generally liked picture verbalization more because they were more in touch with their 'inner child', finding it easier to use their imagination; and perhaps the older students (the AU group) had focussed so much on academic topics, learning verbal, textual skills, that they were now less interested in doing a narrative based on pictures, which they may have perceived as rather unacademic.

## Concluding remarks

Are learners who translate more prone to err? In terms of 'non-textual' errors, my subjects certainly seem to be, regardless of general level of L2 proficiency. If textual features, such as coherence and well-formedness, were taken into consideration, the result might change, though. Is there an overrepresentation of errors caused by L1 interference in translation? There is some support for this in the group of secondary-level students, but the evidence is somewhat inconclusive for the university students and actually points in the opposite direction. This could mean that the university students are less susceptible to the 'dangers' of translation, in the sense that they tend to commit fewer 'translation-induced' errors, but it is far from certain. The study provides no definitive evidence as to the usefulness of translation in the L2 classroom, but I would like to think that this paper provides information that may be useful in the ongoing debate.

There are weighty arguments both for and against the use of translation in the L2 classroom, but it is time that the issue received more scholarly attention and that it was investigated more thoroughly. Such empirical evidence would be specifically relevant to those who (have to) use translation as a teaching tool and those who teach translation as an end in itself. And it would be generally relevant for those who need to decide whether to discourage, condone or recommend translation in the L2 classroom.

## Notes

* I should like to thank Inge P. Windeballe, who was brave and open-minded enough to give me access to her English classes and to let me use her secondary-level students (*gymnasieelever*) as subjects in my investigation. I would also like to thank Poul Tornøe, Shirley Larsen, Tim Caudery, and Marie Källkvist for their helpful and kind criticism of the contents and language of various versions of this paper. Needless to say, all remaining defects are my own responsibility.

1. Other departments have several compulsory translation classes, at both lower and upper levels. Interestingly, however, in the department of German, translation is not mentioned explicitly in the curriculum (*læseplan*) but is an integral part of the teaching and testing of written language proficiency at all levels.

2. I should mention that the Centre for Translation Studies and Lexicography at the English Department of the University of Copenhagen offers an academic course for would-be TV subtitlers (e.g. Gottlieb 1992, 1996).

3. Within translation studies, this issue is often discussed under the heading of directionality. For an overview, see Lonsdale (1998). For an assessment of the state of the art in translation studies regarding L2 translation, see Stewart (1999).

4. For one of very few investigations into the qualities of L1 translation as a testing procedure of comprehension, see Buck (1992), who – to his own surprise and regret – finds that it works fairly well.

5. Wilss' (1982:207) claim that the ST asserts 'hypnotic pressure' is rather similar, but his context is somewhat different: firstly, he is dealing with L1 translation, and, secondly, he is mainly concerned with discussing the relative instability of native tongue competence in translation.

6. This ST is somewhat longer than the texts that the subjects usually translate in their regular classes – especially the secondary-level students, who were used to STs of approximately 150 words. However, though it is a point worth noting, I do not regard it as an invalidating factor.

7. All subjects filled in a questionnaire with questions about their (linguistic) background. On the basis of their answers, several subjects had to be excluded from the corpus. Thus, for instance, one student was excluded because of an American parent, and several were excluded because Danish was not their L1.

8. If one is to believe their general marks in English proficiency in the autumn, it seems that the RA students who did the translation were mainly average-achievers, whereas the group who did the picture verbalization may have had a slight overweight of high-achievers. I am currently trying to monitor my AU subjects in a similar way.

# References

*Bekendtgørelse om gymnasiet, studenterkursus og enkeltfagsstudentereksamen (Gymnasiebekendtgørelse)* (1999). Undervisningsministeriet. htttp://www.uvm.dk/lov/bek/1999/0000411.htm – available on 26/5/00

Berggren, I. (1972). *Does the use of translation exercises have negative effects on the learning of a second language? A pilot study based on an experiment with two methods of teaching carried out on the beginners in the autumn term 1971. Rapport 14.* University of Gothenburg: Department of English.

Buck, G. (1992). "Translation as a language testing procedure: Does it work?" *Language Testing, 9* (2), 123–148.

Campbell, S. (1998). *Translation into the Second Language.* London and New York: Longman.

Coleman, J. A. (1986). "Requiem for the Prose?" *Modern Languages in Scotland, 29,* 98–105.

Cook, G. (1998). "Use of translation in language teaching", In M. Baker (Ed.), *Routledge Encyclopedia of Translation Studies* (pp. 117–120). New York and London: Routledge.

Dollerup, C. & Loddegaard, A. (Eds.). (1992). *Teaching Translation and Interpreting: Training, Talent and Experience.* Amsterdam and Philadelphia: John Benjamins.

Duff, A. (1989/1992). *Translation.* Oxford: Oxford University Press.

Fraser, J. (1996). "'I Understand the French, But I Don't Know How to Put It Into English': Developing Undergraduates' Awareness of and Confidence in the Translation Process". In P. Sewell & I. Higgins (Eds.), *Teaching Translation in Universities: Present and Future Perspectives* (pp. 121–134). London: CILT.

Færch, C. & Kasper, G. (1989). "Transfer in Production: Some implications for the interlanguage hypothesis". In H. W. Dechert & M. Raupauch (Eds.), *Transfer in Language Production* (pp. 173–193). Norwood: Ablex.

Gatenby, E. V. (1948/1967). "Translation in the Classroom". In W. R. Lee (Ed.), *E.L.T. Selections 2. Articles from the journal English Language Teaching* (pp. 65–70). London: Oxford University Press.

Gatenby, E. V. (1950/1967). "Popular Fallacies in the Teaching of Foreign Languages". In W. R. Lee (Ed.), *E.L.T. Selections 2. Articles from the journal English Language Teaching* (pp. 1–8). London: Oxford University Press.

Gottlieb, H. (1992). "Subtitling: A new university discipline". In C. Dollerup & A. Loddegaard (Eds.), *Teaching Translation and Interpreting: Training, Talent and Experience* (pp. 161–170). Amsterdam and Philadelphia: John Benjamins.

Gottlieb, H. (1996). "Billedmedieoversættelse på Engelsk Institut". In *Årsberetning 1996 Engelsk Institut Københavns Universitet* (pp. 41–51). Københavns Universitet.

Harvey, M. (1996). "A Translation Course for French-speaking Students". In P. Sewell & I. Higgins (Eds.), *Teaching Translation in Universities: Present and Future Perspectives* (pp. 45–65). London: CILT.

Irons, J. (1998). "Der var saa deiligt ude paa Landet...". *Sprogforum, 4* (11), 26–32.

Jakobson, R. (1959/1989). "On Linguistic Aspects of Translation". In A. Chesterman (Ed.), *Readings in Translation* (pp. 53–60). Helsinki: Finn Lectura.

Klein-Braley, C. (1987). "Fossil at Large: Translation as a Language Testing Procedure". In R. Grotjahn, C. Klein-Braley, & D. K. Stevenson (Eds.), *Taking Their Measure: The Validity and Validation of Language Test* (pp. 111–132). Bochum: Studienverlag Dr. N. Brockmeyer.

Klein-Braley, C. (1996). "Teaching Translation, a Brief for the Future". In P. Sewell & I. Higgins (Eds.), *Teaching Translation in Universities: Present and Future Perspectives* (pp. 15–30). London: CILT.

Klein-Braley, C. & Franklin, P. (1998). "'The Foreigner in the Refrigerator'. Remarks about Teaching Translation to University Students of Foreign Languages". In K. Malmkjær (Ed.), *Translation and Language Teaching: Language Teaching and Translation* (pp. 53–61). Manchester: St. Jerome.

Klein-Braley, C. & Smith, V. (1985). "Incalculable and full of risks? Translation L1 to L2 as a testing procedure". In C. Titford & A. E. Hieke (Eds.), *Translation in Foreign Language Teaching and Testing* (pp. 155–168). Tübingen: Narr.

Krashen, S. D. (1987). *Principles and Practice in Second Language Acquisition*. New York: Prentice-Hall International.

Källkvist, M. (1997). Lexical Form-Class Effects in Foreign Language Learning: A Study of the English Produced by Advanced Swedish Learners. Unpublished PhD Dissertation, University of Cambridge.

Källkvist, M. (1998). "How Different are the Results of Translation Tasks? A Study of Lexical Errors". In K. Malmkjær (Ed.), *Translation and Language Teaching: Language Teaching and Translation* (pp. 77–87). Manchester: St. Jerome.

Källkvist, M. (1999). *Form-Class and Task-Type Effects in Learner English. A Study of Advanced Swedish Learners*. Lund: Lund University Press.

Lado, R. (1964). *Language Teaching. A Scientific Approach*. New York, San Francisco, Toronto and London: McGraw-Hill Inc.

Larsen, S. (1990). "Testing the Test: a preliminary investigation of translation as a test of writing skills". In S. Larsen (Ed.), *Translation. A Means To An End* (pp. 95–108). Aarhus: Aarhus University Press.

Lonsdale, A. B. (1998). "Direction of translation (directionality)". In M. Baker (Ed.), *Routledge Encyclopedia of Translation Studies* (pp. 63–76). New York and London: Routledge.

McAlester, G. (1992). "Teaching translation into a foreign language – status, scope and aims". In C. Dollerup & A. Loddegaard (Eds.), *Teaching Translation and Interpreting: Training, Talent and Experience*. Amsterdam and Philadelphia: John Benjamins.

Malmkjær, K. (1998). "Introduction: Translation and Language Teaching". In K. Malmkjær (Ed.), *Translation and Language Teaching: Language Teaching and Translation* (pp. 1–11). Manchester: St. Jerome.

Marsh, M. (1987). "The value of L1 > L2 translation on undergraduate courses in modern languages". In H. Keith & I. Mason (Eds.), *Translation in the Modern Languages Degree: Proceedings of a conference held at Heriot-Watt University, Edinburgh, 5–7 Jan. 1986* (pp. 22–30). Edinburgh: CILT.

Nord, C. (1997). *Translating as a Purposeful Activity: Functionalist Approaches Explained*. Manchester: St. Jerome.

Pedersen, V. H. (1974). "Oversættelse og sprogundervisning". *Meddelelser fra Gymnasieskolernes Engelsklærerforening, 70*, 21–36.

Richards, J. C. & Rodgers, T. S. (1986). *Approaches and Methods in Language Teaching.* Cambridge: Cambridge University Press.

Schäffner, C. (1998). "Qualifications for Professional Translators: Translation in Language Teaching Versus Teaching Translation". In K. Malmkjær (Ed.), *Translation and Language Teaching: Language Teaching and Translation* (pp. 117–133). Manchester: St. Jerome.

Sewell, P. (1996). "Translation in the Curriculum". In P. Sewell & I. Higgins (Eds.), *Teaching Translation in Universities: Present and Future Perspectives* (pp. 135–159). London: CILT.

Snell-Hornby, M. (1985). "Translation as a means of integrating language teaching and Linguistics". In C. Titford & A. E. Hieke (Eds.), *Translation in Foreign Language Teaching and Testing* (pp. 21–28). Tübingen: Narr.

Snell-Hornby, M. (1988). *Translation Studies: An Integrated Approach.* Amsterdam and Philadelphia: John Benjamins.

Stewart, D. (1999). "Translators into the Foreign Language: Charlatans or Professionals?". *Rivista Internazionale di Tecnica della Traduzione, 4*, 41–67.

Stibbard, R. (1994). "The use of translation in foreign language teaching". *Perspectives: Studies in Translatology, 2* (1), 9–18.

*Studieordning Engelsk Kandidatuddannelse Januar 1999* (1999). Aarhus: Det Humanistiske Fakultet. Aarhus Universitet.

Sørensen, K. (1988). "Cognate, but *sui generis*: Difficulties confronting advanced Danish Students of English". In M. Powell & B. Preisler (Eds.), *English Past and Present. A Selection Of Essays By Knud Sørensen Presented To Him On His Sixtieth Birthday* (pp. 201–230). Aarhus: Aarhus University Press.

Sørensen, K. (1990). "Translation as a Unifying Discipline". In S. Larsen (Ed.), *Translation. A Means to an End* (pp. 57–68). Aarhus: Aarhus University Press.

Sørensen, K. (1991). *English and Danish Contrasted. A Guide for Translators.* Copenhagen: Munskgaard.

Titford, C. (1985). "Translation – a postcommunicative activity for advanced learners". In C. Titford & A. E. Hieke (Eds.), *Translation In Foreign Language Teaching And Testing* (pp. 73–86). Tübingen: Narr.

Uzawa, K. (1996). "Second language learners' processes of L1 writing, L2 writing, and translation from L1 into L2". *Journal of Second Language Writing, 5* (3), 271–294.

Vermeer, H. J. (1989). "Skopos and Commision in Translational Action". In A. Chesterman (Ed.), *Readings in Translation* (pp. 173–187). Helsinki: Finn Lectura Ab.

Weller, G. (1989). "Some Polemic Aspects of Translation in Foreign Language Pedagogy Revisited". In P. W. Krawutschke (Ed.), *Translator and Interpreter Training and Foreign Language Pedagogy* (pp. 39–50). State University of New York at Binghamton.

Widdowson, H. G. (1978/1983). *Teaching Language as Communication.* Oxford: Oxford University Press.

Wilss, W. (1982). *The Science of Translation: Problems and methods.* Tübingen: Narr. Translation of Wilss, W. (1977), *Übersetzungswissenschaft. Probleme und Methoden.* Tübingen: Narr.

# Students buzz round the translation class like bees round the honey pot – why?

Penelope Sewell

This paper is meant to be polemical: it explores the apparent lure of the translation class by setting it against the apparent turn-offs of the communicative language class. To do this effectively, it deliberately caricatures both types of class. The reader is of course invited to take the caricatures with a pinch of salt, especially as they are based on intuitive observation rather than research findings. It is hoped, nonetheless, that by polemicizing, the paper will throw some light on the intriguing phenomenon of the unfailing popularity of the optional translation course, at least as it has been observed in my institution (Birkbeck, University of London).

The communicative approach grew out of the most solid of theories and observations. It was a child both of Chomskyan notions of competence and performance, and of structuralism. The latter theory told us how language hung together as a system, each word dependent for its meaning on a whole host of others. According to this view, language did not need to refer to anything outside itself (such as etymology or Latin and Greek, or even "objective" reality), it was seen as autonomous and self-sufficient. In his *Cours de linguistique générale*, published posthumously in 1916, De Saussure focused on languages as internally coherent systems of signs. There follow two consequences to this principle. Firstly, a concept takes its meaning from other related concepts as they are expressed in a given language. For instance, the word *arbre* in French draws its meaning from the fact that it is different from *arbuste, arbrisseau* and *buisson* (all small versions of trees). Secondly, concepts have culturally defined referents. The image that the word *arbre* conjures up in a French person's mind is of a tree as a projection of French imagination, carrying with it the connotations attributed to it in French culture. An English tree has a different representation and different connotations. It follows that signs in different languages cannot be seen as exact equivalents of one another since they are dependent for their meaning on their place in a given culture. (De Saussure gave the example of the French word *mouton* covering the referents of the English words "sheep" and "mutton", De Saussure 1979: 160.) From this one must surely deduce that to learn a language well it is better to enter its system and culture, and not try to access it via one's own.

Up to that point, language teaching had been based on the premise that access to the target language in a formal learning situation was via the first language of the learner. Structuralism brought in its wake the revolutionary idea that access should be direct, with little or no reference to the first language. The idea of "communicative competence", first discussed in depth by Dell Hymes (1971), was the goal learners were asked to aim for, and there were many proponents of this approach. Leon Jakobovitz, J. B. Carroll, Paul Pimsleur, Joshua Fishman, Bernard Spolsky, Robert Lado, H. G. Widdowson, all, to a greater or lesser degree, emphasise the need for students to acquire an awareness of the pragmatics of the foreign language, and thus become autonomous in the language. To that end, methods used (audio-lingual, audio-visual, direct...) played down, or even eliminated, all reference to the students' first language (L1); students were not overtly taught grammar rules, rather they were left to deduce them from the living language they were manipulating. Oral work came into its own. Language laboratories were new, and we teachers devised endless structure drills for our students to intone into the microphones, in the firm belief that we had at last cracked it: this method would certainly produce the brilliant linguist we knew lurked under every school child's grin.

Central to the communicative method was the idea of role-play and simulation. Students were trained to act out little scenes of the sort they might encounter in the foreign country. They had to pretend, for instance, that they had tooth-ache, that they wanted to book a hotel room, that they had lost their way, or that they were ordering a meal. In spite of all the other attributes of the communicative method, it seems that it is this, the need for simulation, the need for the individual to act a part, which lies at its heart. Even if such specific role-play situations are not a major feature of language-learning in higher education, the communicative method involves students engaging in discussions, debates, summary-writing and other such activities, as if they were fluent in the target language. The role-play is thus more of a generalized principle. The learner's role is to pretend to be a native of the language being learnt.

It is fair to say today, forty years after the heady pioneering days, that the hoped-for miracle has not happened: the lurking linguists have not manifested themselves, and we have not found the panacea in terms of language teaching. It is true that language learning is now far less exclusive than it was fifty years ago, and we have opened up languages to a far greater number of people, especially of school age. Almost every school child in the UK can utter a few words of a foreign language – now increasingly Spanish as opposed to French. But, in our excitement, we swung from one extreme to the other – we threw out the old "excluding" grammar translation method and assumed that the new "including" communicative method was the best for everyone. We assumed that everyone learned in the same way, instead of realising that individuals differ in the way they learn. We produced some excellent linguists, but we also produced some semi-literate parrots who perhaps communicated adequately, but often in a series of approximations and with little understanding of how the foreign language worked as a system. The tendency of British learners to reduce all definite articles in French to [lœ] (*le maire, le mer* – what's the diff?) is a case in point.

So much for the background to this paper. The communicative method, which is epitomised in the need for role-play, is the foil against which I wish to set the activity called translation. At this College of the University of London, in the Department of French, students continually ask to do translation, even when they have very well-taught communicative classes available to them. (These classes are open-ended, entirely conducted in French and involve role-play in the sense described above.) Why is it that students clamour for translation? What does translation offer that the communicative class does not? Do the students think they can make real progress in their language learning, and are they justified in thinking so? I propose to approach these questions from five different, but complementary, angles, showing why I believe translation is perceived as the answer to some very deep-seated impulses felt by many language-learners. The five angles are:

a.   the need for confidence and self-esteem
b.   the need not to lose face
c.   the need to be rewarded
d.   the need for certainty, for closure, for autonomy
e.   the needs arising from any introversion in our personalities.

## The need for confidence and self-esteem

Communicative methods require students to assume roles, put themselves into make-believe situations. But role-play can infantilise us, it can take us back to the time when we used to play mummies and daddies, or doctors and nurses. Aren't we, as teenagers and adults, a little ashamed of all that? Yet that is what we are expected to do: book rooms in virtual hotels, write letters to non-existent people, make pretend telephone calls, conduct artificial conversations and debates... Many of us cannot cope with that, and even if we can, we prefer not to have to because role-play can do serious damage to our self-image and our confidence.

If you think about the procedure in written translation, however, you will agree there is always a source text (ST), there is a translator, and there is a target text (TT). The translator stands between and outside both the ST and the TT: not being the source of the original message, he/she has no stake in the direct, immediate act of communication, and his/her self-image is therefore not challenged. The common perception is that the translator is in *control*, he/she takes the ST and fashions it with skill into the TT. There is no immediate oral feedback, and because of that, no social pain or embarrassment. The activity is extremely *satisfying*, since the translator has the luxury of taking the time to improve the TT at will. At least in the short term, his/her self-esteem is secure, even bolstered.

What do the specialists have to say about the need for confidence and self-esteem? The satisfaction derived from translating would be music to the ears of psychologists Bednar and Peterson (1995) who focus on clinical theory and practice, and bring out the centrality of the notion of self-esteem. This, of course, is not new. An early example is Diderot (1762:46), who makes Rameau's nephew say, "Et puis le mépris de soi; il est insupportable" ("Disgust with oneself is unbearable."). In Bednar and Peterson's words (1995:1), "The absence of a healthy sense of self-appreciation seems to be one of the basic warning signs of a dysfunctional personality."

It is therefore with surprise that I note that the word "confidence" is not in the subject index of Ellis (1994); even "self-esteem" gets only scant reference. Ellis mentions that Gardner and Lambert (1972) failed to find a significant relationship between self-esteem and language learning, but that Heyde (1979) found that self-esteem correlated positively with oral production. However, Ellis does devote several pages to *anxiety* and the way it can affect second language (L2) acquisition or performance. Anxiety also concerns Spolsky (1989), who says that anxiety can facilitate second language acquisition (SLA), but that it can also inhibit it. According to Spolsky, anxiety is most often focused on listening and speaking, and is largely influenced by the threat to a person's self-concept (1989: 113–114). Discussing reading tasks, MacIntyre, Kimberley and Clément (1997) seem to confirm Spolsky's intuitions, since they conclude that reading tasks are not so clearly linked with anxiety because when one reads, one's "face" is not threatened. They also point to a more far-reaching theory, which is that individuals who can avoid ruminating over affective reactions can concentrate better on task demands. They are under no illusion as to the important role that self-perceptions play in anxiety and achievement (1997: 280).

These are mere snippets from the literature on Second Language Acquisition, but most do support my thesis that an activity such as written translation – at least as it is perceived by the non-specialist translator – offers greater opportunity for the student to enjoy enhanced self-esteem than the communicative class which is constantly challenging his/her self-image.

### The need not to lose face

Imagine you are playing a role in which you have to ask the way and respond to what you are told. You do not know what your partner is going to answer. In that sense, the role-play situation is *open-ended* and therefore *unpredictable*. You, the student, are therefore in a *vulnerable* position, as, if you respond inappropriately, you stand to *lose face* not only in your partner's eyes (or the teacher's), but more importantly, in your own eyes. Your mistakes are plain for all to see.

Translation, on the other hand, gives the impression that students are *in control*. Students can see the whole task from start to finish. They know they are required to transform the ST into the TT, observing criteria of accuracy and appropriacy. Students work at home, far from the vagaries of social intercourse. If they are worried about losing face, they will work harder, to ensure that they will not be caught out in public.

If the literature on SLA does not yield very much on the importance of being in control, or at least believing you are in control, it does flag up the names of Brown and Levinson (1978). Brown and Levinson are interested in politeness and how it affects human interaction. They start from the premise that politeness phenomena are universal principles, and are reflected in language. Their critics take them to task on the notion of universality, which may be legitimate, but I remain convinced that the notions of politeness and "face" are fundamental to much of human interaction. Brown and Levinson posit the idea of a "Model Person" (MP). All MPs have *positive face*, and all MPs have *negative face*, and all MPs are *rational agents*, that is, they choose means that will satisfy their ends (1978:59). Positive face is the want of every MP that his/her wants be desirable to at least some others, and negative face is the want of every MP that his/her actions be unimpeded by others (1978:62). Brown and Levinson seem to be saying that every interaction can be categorized in terms of the effect it has on the positive and negative face of both MPs involved. Events are usually supportive of face, or threatening to face. The values put on these events vary from culture to culture.

My contention is that communicative methods have not taken into account the need for us not to lose face. The methods ask students to suspend normal psychology and lay themselves open to face-threatening acts (FTAs). Not many students feel comfortable doing that, which is hardly surprising, given that in all learning situations there is a threat to face and self-esteem. When one translates, however, the threat is deferred, and may even be transacted in written form, which is far less traumatic. Once again, translation, as a satisfying and reassuring activity, wins hands down.


## The need to be rewarded

Not only do we need to have our self-image bolstered, but we also need rewarding frequently! At least, this is the thesis I would like to explore in this section. Role-play and other interactive situations are, by their nature, totally dependent on another person. Whatever is achieved is the result of at least two people's contribution. The process is hazardous because dependent on the unpredictable, and the result has to be shared. These are not, *a priori,* the characteristics of a very satisfying or rewarding experience. Translation, on the other hand, is immensely satisfying. It is analogous to cooking – you end up with a product you can call your own, the fruit of your individual, sustained labour. Your ST is the basket of ingredients which you "treat" in various ways in order to produce your delicious dish. The production of the dish constitutes the "reward" or satisfaction you get out of the process.

Another analogy is with little computer toys given to children to help them learn spelling and mental arithmetic. When the child gets the answer right, the machine emits a delightful pinging sound, but when it gets it wrong the machine makes a rude noise of disapproval. The child is likely to go on playing in a way that will gain him/her the maximum number of "pings", since the pings are the mark of approval, the reward.

I. P. Pavlov worked in Russia in the late nineteenth century, establishing scientifically the phenomenon of the conditioned reflex, using reward as the way of conditioning the reflex. The work, which was pioneered on animals (mainly dogs), was seen to be applicable to humans and introduced the idea that the physiological and the psychological were closely linked. This school of psychology, known as behaviourism, was also developed in the United States by J. B. Watson, (early twentieth century) and led to theories of education such as those proposed by J. Dewey. A fellow American, B. F. Skinner published *Verbal Behaviour* in 1957, the product of work carried out in the 1930s. He is known for his experiments using pigeons, and developed the idea of instrumental conditioning (or selection by consequences) – which was not dependent on unconditional or inborn reflexes – and then applied his findings to verbal behaviour. Skinner's ideas paved the way for the structure drills developed for students to work through in the language laboratory, used because it was thought reflexes could be conditioned that way. What interests me about these scientists is less their denial of human volition and their finding that behaviour can be modified, than their discovery of the power of reward. Now, contrary to the hazards of unpredictable role-play situations, the activity of translation holds within it considerable opportunity for reward. It may be illusory, but it is certainly perceived to be there. Have we not all been triumphant when we have solved a problem posed by the ST, or when we have found the target language word or phrase we think best renders the meaning of a word or phrase in the ST? Not only can we be proud of our final product, but also we have had the opportunity of many delightful "pings" along the way!

## The need for certainty, for closure, for autonomy

I shall start this section by discussing some perceived characteristics of the role-play situation, and go on to link these with the need for certainty, which I believe to be a facet of the need for autonomy.

Communicative methods require the student to complete a variety of tasks, entirely in the target language and heavily dependent on learned appropriate responses. If you are required to play a role, say going to a chemist's shop with a minor medical complaint, who is to say whether you have played the role satisfactorily? There is nothing concrete to measure your performance against, since you are not actually in a chemist's shop. The role was invented, it is artificial, serving only to make you operate in the target language. You cannot use it to evaluate your own performance. You are entirely reliant on the teacher who is the sole arbiter of whether your language skills were adequate or not. The role is pure ephemera: it came out of thin air, and it returns to thin air. You have no handle on it; on the contrary, you have to dance to its tune and risk losing face when your teacher tells you what went wrong. Role-plays are by definition open-ended and unpredictable.

Now think of translation: it is, of course, usually written, but above and beyond that, it has a *product*, which can be *measured* against a visible yard-stick, the ST. It is thus rock-solid as an activity, reassuring in that the student holds a far greater number of keys for success than with role-play. Translation is seen as a closed-ended activity, texts for translation have clear beginnings and clear endings, and the student is in charge.

Does not this state of affairs correspond to every student's need for autonomy? There is a growing literature on student autonomy, the notion that students should take charge of their own learning. Key to the notion is that students can pace themselves, predict what is required, make decisions about how best to learn. I believe that translation taps into these requirements. The activity is, to the relatively unsophisticated at least, entirely transparent, no "content" or "ideas" have to be supplied or evaluated, and the learner can presume him/herself to be in possession of all the attributes needed to be autonomous.

Educational psychologists have developed the notion of closed and open skills, and these seem to be applicable here. Positing that foreign language skill is an open skill, Segalowitz (1997: 100–101) defines both closed and open skills as follows:

> Closed skills are those that take place in a relatively stable environment and primarily involve accurate repetition of particular physical or cognitive acts (e.g. weight lifting; mental calculation). Open skills, on the other hand, are those that take place in a relatively unpredictable environment and involve bringing about certain effects on that environment. [...] The performer of a closed skill does not need to be continuously alert for unexpected changes in the environment; the performer of an open skill, on the other hand, must always be prepared for surprises that might interfere with his or her performance intentions.

Such statements correspond to my own understanding of the situation, and support the notion that students might express preferences about the way they learn. This thesis does, admittedly, beg the question of the perceived goals of the language-learner (e.g. good oral ability? Good written ability? Just passing examinations?), but, not concerned at present with goals, I am merely pointing out the advantages that the "closed-ended" activity of translation has over the open-ended activities promoted by the communicative method of language teaching.

## The needs arising from any introversion in our personalities

Within the context of considering communicative methods and translation, I wish here to focus on, firstly, learning styles, and secondly, introversion and extraversion. Taken in their purest form, the two language-learning "methods" each assume an *undifferentiated learning style*, with all students responding positively regardless of their individual psychological make-up. On reflection, however, communicative methods would seem to favour *risk-taking, extraverted personalities* and high levels of *interaction*, whereas, translation seems to favour *reflection, introverted personality traits* and low levels of interaction. Rixon (1984:28) writes:

> Typically, communicative methodology revolves around activities which encourage students to take risks, in order to help them develop strategies for making the most of their small stock of language.

The writer goes on to point out the deficiencies of students taught by the grammar translation method, but that is not what is at issue here, since I am only seeking to isolate those characteristics of the activity of translation which seem to make translation more attractive to students than communicative activities.

There clearly are many different learning styles, just as there are many different personality traits. Busato et al. (1999) study the relation between learning styles, personality traits and achievement motivation in higher education. Their subjects were psychology students. Busato et al. sought to match "the Big Five" personality traits:

extraversion
conscientiousness
openness to experience
neuroticism
agreeableness

with four different learning styles as defined by Vermunt (1994), namely: meaning-directed; reproduction-directed; application-directed; and undirected. It is the concepts of the personality traits and the learning styles which are of interest here, but for the record (1994:137),

> The highest, as well as unpredicted, correlation was between *the meaning-directed learning style* [students wish to find out what is meant exactly in their study material, interrelate what they have learned and try in a critical sense to develop their own view (1994:130)] and *openness to experience* [openness involves motivation and the need for variety, cognition, sentience and understanding]. (my emphasis)

How these concepts might apply to language learning is as yet undetermined, but intuitively, they do seem plausible, even illuminating.

In contrast, some work on personality and speech production has focused on L2 acquisition and performance. Drawing on a number of different sources, Dewaele and Furnham (2000:356) have this to say about people exhibiting extraverted personality traits:

> Studies by personality psychologists [...] show that extraverts have a better short-term memory; are more stress-resistant and are less anxious in second language production.

They go on,

> Introverts tend to be more socially anxious, and a high anxiety leads to increased attentional selectivity and reduced attentional capacity. M.W. Eysenck also argues that the higher anxiety of the introverts could further reduce the available processing capacity of working memory. "This would explain why introverts take longer to access information from long-term memory or permanent storage". (Eysenck 1982)

Dewaele and Furnham refer to Matthews and Dorn (1995) who suggest that the extraverts' better resistance to stress may result from their "low autonomic arousability [...] and the insensitivity to punishment signals [...]" These "processing characteristics of extraverts may assist them in dealing with high information flows (particularly of verbal stimuli) and time pressure". Dewaele and Furnham (2000:362–363) conclude:

> Our findings suggest that the formality of the situation, or rather the interpersonal stress that it provokes, has the strongest effect on the speech production process of the introverts. [...] The stress of the formal situation could cause an excessive degree of arousal in the brain of the introverts, which would overload

their short-term memory and affect efficient incremental processing, hence a breakdown of fluency.

However, the authors also hypothesize that foreign language anxiety is not a stable personality trait, that it is a complex phenomenon linked also to societal factors such as the relative prestige of the language being learned. Nonetheless, the evidence seems very strong indeed that people with predominantly introverted personalities are at a disadvantage both when it comes to speech production, and, by extension, when they are obliged to learn by communicative methods. It could be that there is a link between introversion, and all four of the preceding points on my list (need for confidence and positive self-image, need not to lose face, need for reward, need for autonomy), and that it is perhaps those sorts of people (i.e. with predominantly introverted personalities) who are most likely to be in higher education studying for a languages and culture degree. That would explain why translation is so popular, because it appears to fulfill all those needs.

I say "appears" because I am well aware that most people have a distorted view of what translation involves, and, with Déjean le Féal (1994, 1996), I can see many inescapable disadvantages of using translation as a language-learning method, not least that it tends to focus on the *product* and the notion of surface equivalences between languages, brushing aside the all-important cognitive dimension of the activity of translation. I am not evaluating the methods, merely pointing out student preferences.

In conclusion, starting from an observation, I have suggested five possible explanations for that observation, and tried to support my suggestions by referring to the literature on second-language acquisition. I have been discussing higher education, and would not wish to extend these ideas to the secondary sector, where other factors are paramount. I hope I have gone some way in exploring what makes translation such a pleasurable activity for a large number of students (and colleagues). However, the predominant teaching method remains communicative. Maybe we should try to adapt the tasks we set to cater for more of the needs of the introvert.

## References

Bednar, R. L. & Peterson, S. R. (1995). *Self-esteem. Paradoxes and Innovations in Clinical Theory and Practice.* American Psychological Association.
Brown, P. & Levinson, S. (1978). *Politeness: Some Universals in Language Use.* Cambridge: Cambridge University Press.

Busato, V., Prins, F., Elshout, J., & Hamaker, C. (1999). "The Relation between Learning Styles, the Big Five Personality Traits and Achievement Motivation in Higher Education". *Personality and Individual Differences, 26*, 129–1401.

De Saussure, F. (1979). *Cours de linguistique générale*. Paris: Payot (first published 1916).

Déjean Le Féal, K. (1994) "Pédagogie raisonnnée de la traduction". *Terminologie et Traducation, 3*, 7–66. Luxembourg: Office des publications officielles des communautés européennes.

Déjean Le Féal, K. (1996). "La Formation de traducteurs professionnels". In P. Sewell & I. Higgins (Eds.), *Teaching Translation in Universities* (pp. 31–44). London: AFLS/CILT.

Dewaele, J.-M. & Furnham, A. (2000). "Personality and Speech Production: a Pilot Study of Second Language Learners". *Personality and Individual Differences, 28*, 355–365.

Diderot, D. (1762). *Le Neveu de Rameau*, Nouveaux Classiques. Paris: Larousse 1972.

Ellis, R. (1994). *The Study of Second Language Acquisition*. Oxford: Oxford University Press.

Eysenck, M. W. (1982). *Attention and Arousal, Cognition and Performance*. Berlin: Springer-Verlag.

Hymes, D. H. (1971). *On Communicative Competence*. Philadelphia: University of Pennsylvania Press. Preprinted in J. Pride & J. B. Holmes (Eds.), *Sociolinguistics* (1972). London: Penguin.

MacIntyre, P., Kimberley, N., & Clément, R. (1997). "Biases in Self-Ratings of Second Language Proficiency – the Role of Language Anxiety". *Language Learning, 47* (2).

Matthews, G. & Dorn, L. (1995). "Cognitive and Attentional Processes in Personality and Intelligence". In D. H. Saklofske & M. Zeidner (Eds.), *International Handbook of Personality and Intelligence* (pp. 367–396). New York: Plenum Press.

Pavlov, I. P. (1926). *Lectures on Conditioned Reflexes*.

Rixon, S. (1984). "Language Learning Theories and their Implications for the Classroom". In D. Sidwell (Ed), *Teaching Languages to Adults*. London: CILT.

Segalowitz, N. (1997). "Individual Differences in Second Language Acquisition". In A. de Groot & J. Kroll (Eds.), *Tutorials in Bilingualism*. New Jersey: Lawrence Erlbaum Associates.

Skinner, B. F. (1957). *Verbal Behaviour*. New York: Appleton-Century-Crofts, Inc.

Spolsky, B. (1989). *Conditions for Second Language Learning*. Oxford: Oxford University Press.

Vermunt, J. (1994). *Inventory of Learning Styles in Higher Education; Scoring Key for the Inventory of Learning Styles in Higher Education*. Tilburg: Tilburg University.

# The effect of translation exercises versus gap-exercises on the learning of difficult L2 structures

## Preliminary results of an empirical study

Marie Källkvist

## Introduction

Translation has been used for centuries in language learning settings, and, as Malmkjær (1994: 123) says, arguments for and against the use of translation are "well rehearsed". In stark contrast, the issue of using translation for enhancing L2 proficiency is rarely addressed empirically. At a time when universities all over the world seem to be faced with financial cut-backs resulting in a reduced number of teaching hours, it seems more important than ever that we evaluate our teaching and learning materials.

The present study was launched in the light of the absence of empirical work on the effect of translation on L2 proficiency. It examines the effect of L1-to-L2 translation exercises versus exercises directly in L2 on the morphosyntactic accuracy of advanced, adult Swedish (L1) learners of English (L2). There is reason to believe that exercises involving the comparison of the L1 and L2 (i.e. translation) lead to deeper and more elaborate cognitive processing and thus enhanced memory retention compared to exercises which involve no such comparison (see discussion in Hummel 1995). The aim of this study is to find out whether such enhanced memory retention can be traced in tests of the morphosyntactic accuracy of students who have been exposed to translation exercises. The purpose is not to advocate using the so-called Grammar Translation method, but rather to establish whether translation has a place at all in the L2 classroom, and if it does, what its proper place may be.

I will in the following bypass the arguments often expressed for and against the use of translation in linguistically homogenous groups of foreign language learners as they are clearly outlined in Malmkjær (1998) and in Schjoldager (this volume). Instead I will move straight into previous attempts at shedding empirical light on this issue before presenting preliminary results of my own study.

## Existing empirical work

When it comes to L2 learners and translation, research has been carried out with the aim of uncovering the processes and strategies employed by L2 learners and professional translators when translating (e.g. Barbosa & Neiva 2003; Fraser 1995, 1996; Enkvist 1994; Krings 1987; Lörscher 1993; Omura 1996; Uzawa 1994, 1996). The *effect* of translation on L2 learners' accuracy has been given less attention, however. Extensive literature searches yielded only two previous studies (Berggren 1972; Slavikova 1990).[1] Both were carried out on learners receiving classroom instruction in a foreign language.

Slavikova (1990) studied the effect of L2 (Italian) > L1 (English) translation exercises on the proficiency of beginner adult English-speaking learners of Italian. Slavikova addressed the following question: is there a correlation between the use of translation and learners' progress in L2? Her subjects were divided into two groups, one of which was exposed to translation for three months whereas the other group was not. At the end of three months' instruction Slavikova tested both groups on what she calls "three aspects of proficiency" (1990:101), by which she means "morphosyntactical abilities" and "semantic and sociolinguistic abilities" (1990:102). Her translation group scored higher on the latter two (semantic and sociolinguistic abilities) whereas the group who did no translation performed somewhat better on morphosyntactic ability. None of these differences identified in her test results was statistically significant, however, so the instruction given to her subjects had no differential effect on the aspects of proficiency she tested in her test instruments.

The second study, Berggren (1972), focused on lexical matters. She investigated the use of "eight words and expressions" (1972:12) in L2 (English) before and after a 45-minute lesson by 120 Swedish undergraduate students of English (advanced learners: approximately eight years of classroom instruction in English prior to data collection).

Berggren's 120 subjects were divided into 16 groups which received two different types of instruction based on a short text: 57 students (eight groups) were asked to translate a text in Swedish into English, whereas 63 students (the remaining eight groups) carried out close reading of the same text in English. The text was based on a picture series, and was originally written in English by two native speakers. The total instruction time was 45 minutes. Several different teachers were involved but all of them had been given detailed instructions regarding what words, phrases, and structures to bring up for discussion with the students. Thus, both 'translation' and 'close reading' students were exposed to the same phrases and words, but only students in the translation groups compared these with their Swedish translation equivalents. Prior to the 45-minute lesson, all 120 students had written a description of a picture series. A week later, all students wrote a description of the same picture series again; it was thus possible to measure progress (or lack of progress) between their first and second attempts at the same description task.

Berggren concludes that the use of translation "did not have a negative effect" (1972:19) in that the number of interference errors was lower in the translation groups than in the close reading groups. Further she states that "[a] comparison of the number of expressions used correctly before the teaching but incorrectly afterwards indicates that the translation exercise has been more effective than the intensive reading exercise" (1972:19). Unfortunately, Berggren does not evaluate the differences in her post-test statistically.

It is not surprising that students exposed to translation committed fewer interference errors since their attention was specifically and explicitly drawn to the words and phrases which, according to Berggren (1972:9), have "different usage in Swedish and English". Students in the close reading groups were taught the same words and phrases, but there was no explicit comparison with Swedish.

One can conclude that Slavikova's and Berggren's studies leave the issue of the effect and value of translation for the enhancement of L2 proficiency very much unresolved.


## Introducing a new project: Focus and research questions

This study, which is still in progress, focuses solely on L2 morphosyntax (leaving lexis aside). The reason for concentrating on morphosyntax is that the aim of using translation exercises for enhancing L2 learning in my case was to make learners apply their explicit knowledge of a grammatical rule repeatedly in exercises so that they develop an ability to generalise from the rule and use the target structure correctly and with increasing automaticity. Vocabulary (for example culture-specific items) can indeed be dealt with using translation exercises, but teaching/learning vocabulary is quite a different matter. It would involve raising learners' awareness of certain words, rather than aiming at restructuring part of their L2 grammatical system (by learning, for example, "in English, use the zero article with uncountable nouns whose reference is generic rather than specific").

The primary research question addressed is the following:

1.  Do students who have been exposed to translation exercises perform equally well on morphosyntactic accuracy in English as students who have done exercises in the L2 only (but targeting the same structures) in writing (a) when *translating* from Swedish into English, and (b) when *operating directly* in English?

On the basis of previous research and on logic, my hypothesis was that two groups of subjects exposed to the same explicit grammar instruction, and where only the ensuing exercises differed, would perform similarly in tests on morphosyntactic accuracy. In an attempt to test whether this was true, it was decided to expand the study by including a third group of learners of the same proficiency level who were studying English but *without* a grammar component. This group will be referred to as the 'NoG' (for 'No Grammar') group. Their English course consisted in reading fiction in English and writing papers based on their reading. At no point was their attention drawn to grammar.

The second research question addressed reads:

2.  Do students who have had input through extensive reading and writing in English as L2, but no explicit instruction in the use of morphosyntactic structures, perform equally well as students who have had 'translation exercises' or 'target-language-only exercises' on morphosyntactic accuracy in writing (a) when *translating* from Swedish to English and (b) when *operating directly* in English?

## Methodology

Experimental methodology was adhered to as far as possible for research question 1, and data were collected in an authentic educational environment at a Swedish university. All students (approximately 55) admitted to studying English (first-term level) were randomly assigned to two groups for the purposes of this research. The instructional treatment was given to them in their subcourse in English grammar. One group was consistently given translation exercises targeting structures presented in their grammar book; this group will be referred to as the 'T' group (for 'Translation group'). The second group was given exercises in L2 targeting the same structures the same number of times, and will be referred to as the 'NoT' group (for 'No Translation') group.

The grammar course constitutes one of several courses they took during their first term of English; it accounted for 15% of their credits gained at the completion of this, their first term. The course content of other sub-courses they took during this term was identical for both groups (phonetics and English phonology, British and American culture and society, history of English literature and literary analysis, spoken proficiency, and essay writing).

Including the NoG group meant departing from the experimental design, however; several variables apart from translation differ between this group and the T and NoT groups: the NoG students were in their final year of upper-secondary school, and were taught by a different teacher. Moreover, they were an intact group (no random assignment), and were taking other subjects apart from their English classes. For these reasons, any differences in results between the NoG and the two experimental groups are hypothesis-generating rather than conclusive.


## Subjects

All subjects were native speakers of Swedish. Those in the experimental groups (T and NoT) ranged in age from 19–37 (although few were older than 25).

**Subjects in the experimental groups:**

30 Swedish-speaking advanced learners of English → 'Translation group' (T): 15 students

→ 'No Translation group' (NoT): 15 students

**Subjects in the NoG group:**

14 advanced-level Swedish learners of English

**Figure 1.** Distribution of subjects across the three groups

Students in the NoG were 18–19 years of age. All subjects were at the advanced stage since they had had 8–9 years of classroom instruction in English prior to data collection. The distribution of subjects was as shown in Figure 1.

Only students who had 100% attendance over all thirteen weeks were included as subjects of this study. The fact that both T and NoT comprise 15 students is coincidental.

## Instructional treatment

The instruction and exercise material that students in the T group and NoT group were exposed to in the grammar course can be described as follows: the aim was to introduce students to the grammatical analysis of the English language, and to improve their proficiency in English through explicitly teaching them certain structures and then having them do production exercises.[2] The course progressed along traditional lines (being based on a presentation of word classes covering the main contrastive differences between Swedish and English). Following a short presentation of the target structures, students were asked to complete a number of exercises. The instructional treatment covered 13 weeks and included fifteen 90-minute lessons.

Students in the T group were consistently provided with exercises involving translation of a full (but short) text, of full sentences, or in some cases, part of a sentence. All exercises were done in class with students working in pairs or small groups before the teacher conducted a full class discussion.

Students in the NoT group were provided with exercises targeting exactly the same structures the same number of times, but these exercises never involved translation; rather, students were required to fill in a missing word or manipulating the word order of English sentences. When target structures were presented and discussed in class with the NoT group, no mention was made of differences between English and Swedish.

The NoG group read fiction in English, discussed works read in class and wrote essays which were handed in for marking.

## Testing procedure

In the first lesson in week one, all students completed a pre-test battery consisting of three tasks: (a) a multiple-choice test, (b) a translation test, and (c) a written retelling. When treatment ended in week 13, students completed

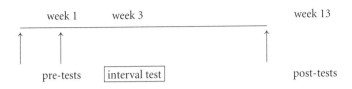

**Figure 2.** Research schedule

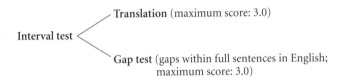

**Figure 3.** The two parts of the interval test

the same tasks again (i.e. the pre-test battery was identical to the post-test battery). In addition to the pre-tests and post-tests, students were asked to complete two considerably shorter tests in week 3. These tests will be referred to as the 'interval tests'. The purpose of the interval tests was to measure learning over one week and covering one grammatical structure (as opposed to the pre-tests and post-tests which covered several grammatical structures over 13 weeks). This chapter will report the results of the *interval test* since analysis of the pre-test and post-test data is still ongoing. The research schedule is illustrated in Figure 2.

The interval test was administered on one occasion only (i.e. not as pre-test and post-test) in the third week of instruction. The purpose of this test was to measure the learning of one structure only (the use of the zero versus the definite article in English noun phrases) over the course of one week. As the target structure of the interval test was included in the pre-test (translation part) as well, pre-test scores for each student and each group for this particular structure were calculated and compared to their interval test scores.

The interval test consisted of two parts: a translation test (included in Appendix 1), and a gap test in English (in Appendix 2).[3]

Exactly the same structures were tested in both tests. The gap test in English was actually a translation (made by a native speaker of English) of the translation task. Students were first asked to do the translation task, which was then collected by the teacher. Following this, students were given the gap task, which was a translated version of the Swedish text they had just translated, and were asked to fill in the definite article when necessary.

The NoG group completed the same pre-tests, post-tests, and interval tests under identical circumstances (i.e. with 13 weeks intervening between the pre-tests and post-tests, and with the interval test in the third week).

## The target structures and the teaching material

The following structures were targeted and tested using the interval tests:

- the use of the zero versus the definite article in English in conjunction with non-count nouns with generic reference (e.g. *British industry*), and with countable nouns in the plural with generic reference (e.g. *food prices*)[4]

The following treatment was given to the two experimental groups: the T group was asked to translate 19 sentences as production practice, whereas the NoT group was given 19 sentences containing gaps where they had to decide whether to add the definite article or not. This is illustrated by the following examples (example (2) is a translation of example (1)):

(1)   Föroreningarna utgör ett hot mot miljön.

(2)   _____ pollution is a threat to _____ environment.

As stated above, the NoG group had no explicit grammar instruction.

Before considering the results, it is necessary to discuss some problematic aspects inherent in this kind of research.

## Challenges and persistent problems

The results to be presented below for the T and NoT groups are based on a study examining the effect of two different treatments on two different groups of subjects. This is a methodology frequently used in the natural sciences and in medicine, where controlling variables other than the one under investigation can be relatively straightforward. When conducting a longitudinal study of human learning, however, exerting control over unwanted variables that may affect the results is more challenging. Such unwanted variables affecting the results of this study may be the following: firstly, learners may have individual characteristics that affect learning, such as aptitude and motivation, and secondly, they can engage in activities outside class time that affect learning.

These factors can never be fully controlled for and their effect can never be ruled out. In an attempt to partly control for them, information on motivation, work effort, prior exposure to English and study habits was elicited from students using questionnaires. For example, it was of course important to ensure that students in the NoT group were not doing extra exercises using translation in their spare time at home. This turned out not to be the case at all since students found the work load of the entire course in English extremely heavy.

In the questionnaire, students were asked to indicate their levels of motivation and work effort on a scale ranging from 1 to 5, to describe the nature and frequency of their exposure to English in their free time, and to indicate length of time spent in English-speaking countries and their activities there. They were aware that their responses (and their results on the pre- and post-tests) would be used for a research project, and it was explained that it was vital for the validity of the research that they be honest when giving this information. When checking their responses for motivation and work effort, I found that their information was in accordance with my own impression built up over the fifteen 90-minute lessons. Even so, there is still room for a certain amount of subjectivity in students' self-reported estimates.

There are persistent problems, however, in that certain factors cannot be controlled for in a study like this. For example, it is not possible to gain complete control over students' different attention span patterns in lessons, or whether the attention level of a particular student was low for an entire lesson due to fatigue or stress, for example. In addition, the students' individual levels of language aptitude were not controlled for as this would have involved a time-consuming testing procedure.

The following factors were controlled for, however: students' prior command of the target structures, the teacher factor (for the two experimental groups), and attendance (through attendance lists).

## Results 1: The translation and gap interval tests

The interval tests were administered to the two experimental groups (T and NoT) disguised as an exercise, which I marked and returned in the next lesson. Students in the NoG group were simply asked to complete the two tasks. Both the interval translation test and the interval gap test contained 3 test items, and the maximum score was therefore 3.0 on both. The results of the test (and

**Table 1.** Group mean pre-test scores for the target structure, mean scores for motivation and work effort, and mean scores on the interval translation test and interval gap test

|  | T group (N = 15) | NoT group (N = 15) | NoG group (N = 14) |
|---|---|---|---|
| Pre-test score (max. 4.0) | 0.27 | 0.33 | 0.67 |
| Motivation (max. 5.0) | 4.20 | 3.80 | 3.40 |
| Work effort (max. 5.0) | 3.80 | 3.30 | 3.20 |
| Translation test (max. 3.0) | 1.53 | 1.53 | 0.73 |
| Gap test (max. 3.0) | 2.00 | 2.40 | 1.00 |

students' pre-test scores for this target structure, motivation and work effort) are illustrated in Table 1.

The table shows, first of all, that all three groups had similar *pre-test mean scores* for the target structure: out of a maximum 4.0, the T group had a mean of 0.27. The mean for the NoT group was 0.33, and for the NoG group it was 0.67. These figures are based on four test items in the translation part of the pre-test, and, evidently, learners in all three groups showed poor command of this structure prior to treatment.

As for motivation, the T group had the highest mean (4.2 out of a maximum 5.0),[5] compared to 3.8 and 3.4 for the NoT and NoG groups respectively. Also for work effort, the T group had the highest average (3.8 out of a maximum possible of 5.0),[6] compared to 3.3 for the NoT group, and 3.2 for the NoG group. Thus, students in the T group were, on average, more motivated and reported the highest mean score for work effort. Learners in the NoG group were, in comparison, the least motivated and reported the lowest level of work effort.

We are now ready to consider the results in the two tasks that make up the interval test, presented in the bottom two rows in Table 1. In the interval *translation* test, students in the two experimental groups (T and NoT) have identical mean accuracy scores, 1.53 out of the maximum 3.0. The NoG group, on the other hand, performed worse, achieving a mean of 0.73 out of the maximum 3.0. They show virtually no improvement compared to the pre-test translation test (0.67 out of a maximum 4.0).

On the interval *gap* test, all groups achieved better results. The NoG group, again, performed more poorly however (a mean of 1.0 out of 3.0) than the experimental groups (T: 2.0, and NoT: 2.4).

The most important results revealed in Table 1 are the following: (1) the NoT group performed as well as the T group in the interval *translation* test,

(2) the NoT group did better than the T group in the interval *gap* test, and (3) all groups performed better on the interval gap test than on the interval translation test. These must, however, be considered tentative findings as the number of test items is extremely low (only 3). Since the number of subjects is also limited, inferential statistical analysis was not carried out, and the differences in results between the three groups may thus be due to chance. Two of the findings make sense on logical grounds, however: the NoG group showed poorer performance as they had no explicit grammar teaching and no practice using the target structure, and the NoT group had a better result on the gap test (which has the same format as their exercises).

Since the data include values for learners' level of motivation and work effort, it is possible to partly control for motivation and work effort, i.e. calculate results separately for students who reported the same level of motivation and work effort. Mean scores were therefore computed for students who had indicated that their level of motivation was 5 on the five-point scale. This leaves us with very small samples of subjects: five students in the T group, five in the NoT group, and three in the NoG group.

Table 2 reveals that these reduced T and NoT groups share highly similar characteristics: they have an identical pre-test mean score (0.4 out of 4.0). Their mean level of motivation is identical, and their mean level of work effort is similar (4.2 for T, and 4.0 for NoT).

The most interesting result is that the T group had a *lower* mean accuracy score for the interval *translation* test (1.6) than the NoT group (2.6). Thus, the NoT students who indicated the highest possible level of motivation were capable of performing very well in the interval translation test despite not having been prompted to use the target structure in translation exercises at all. This is a surprising finding that merits closer attention. Did this result arise due to one or a few students performing particularly poorly or particularly well?

Table 2. Mean scores for students reporting 5 for motivation

|  | T group (N = 5) mean | NoT group (N = 5) mean | NoG group (N = 3) mean |
|---|---|---|---|
| Pre-test score (max. 4.0) | 0.4 | 0.4 | 0.7 |
| Motivation (max. 5.0) | 5.0 | 5.0 | 5.0 |
| Work effort (max. 5.0) | 4.2 | 4.0 | 4.0 |
| Translation (max. 3.0) | 1.6 | 2.6 | 0.7 |
| Gap test (max. 3.0) | 2.2 | 2.6 | 1.0 |

## Results 2: The interval *translation* test in more detail

Table 3 provides descriptive statistics for the interval *translation* test for all five highly motivated students (motivation = 5) in the T group.

The most important results in Table 3 are in the forth column (in bold). This column gives the 'learning' score for each student, arrived at in the following manner: the student's *pre-test score* (which was rarely more than 0 out of 4.0: only subject T6 achieved more than 0) was subtracted from the student's *interval translation test score* (max. 3.0). This gives us the learning score for each highly motivated T student and a mean learning score for the highly motivated T group: 1.2. It is then possible to calculate how much this group of students improved ('learned') from the pre-test to the interval translation test by dividing their total learning score, which is 6,[7] by the total number of *possible* learning scores, which is 13.[8] This gives us a total learning score for this group of 6/13 = 46%. This means that they improved (from the pre-test score to the interval translation test score) by 46% of the maximum improvement possible.

Table 4 presents the equivalent results for the five highly motivated NoT students (who, as a group, outperformed the five T students).

These students' mean learning score is 2.2 (bottom row in the fourth column) compared to 1.2 for the five T students). The same calculations carried out for the highly motivated T students were then made, which revealed the following: the highly motivated NoT group improved from the *pre-test score* to *the interval translation test score* by 85% of the maximum improvement possible (compared to 46% for the five T students).

**Table 3.** Results for each highly motivated T group student

| Student (N = 5) | Pre-test score (max. 4.0) | Interval translation test score (max. 3.0) | 'Learning' (difference between pre-test score and interval translation test score) | Motivation (ranging from 1 to 5) | Work effort (ranging from 1 to 5) |
|---|---|---|---|---|---|
| T2 | 0 | 3 | 3 | 5 | 4 |
| T4 | 0 | 2 | 2 | 5 | 4 |
| T6 | 2 | 2 | 0 | 5 | 5 |
| T10 | 0 | 0 | 0 | 5 | 4 |
| T12 | 0 | 1 | 1 | 5 | 4 |
| Mean | 0.4 | 1.6 | 1.2 | 5.0 | 4.2 |

**Table 4.** Restults for each highly motivated NoT group student

| Student (N = 5) | Pre-test score (max. 4.0) | Interval translation test score (max. 3.0) | 'Learning' (difference between pre-test score and interval translation test score) | Motivation (ranging from 1 to 5) | Work effort (ranging from 1 to 5) |
|---|---|---|---|---|---|
| NoT 3 | 2 | 2 | 0 | 5 | 5 |
| NoT 4 | 0 | 3 | 3 | 5 | 4 |
| NoT 12 | 0 | 2 | 2 | 5 | 5 |
| NoT 13 | 0 | 3 | 3 | 5 | 3 |
| NoT 15 | 0 | 3 | 3 | 5 | 3 |
| Mean | 0.4 | 2.6 | 2.2 | 5.0 | 4.0 |

**Table 5.** Restults for the less motivated T student (N = 10)

| Student (N = 10) | Pre-test score (max. 4.0) | Interval translation test score (max. 3.0) | 'Learning' (difference between pre-test score and interval translation test score) | Motivation (ranging from 1 to 5) | Work effort (ranging from 1 to 5) |
|---|---|---|---|---|---|
| T1 | 0 | 1 | 1 | 4 | 4 |
| T3 | 0 | 2 | 2 | 4 | 3 |
| T5 | 0 | 2 | 2 | 4 | 4 |
| T7 | 0 | 0 | 0 | 4 | 4 |
| T8 | 0 | 1 | 1 | 4 | 4 |
| T9 | 0 | 2 | 2 | 3 | 2 |
| T11 | 0 | 1 | 1 | 3 | 3 |
| T13 | 0 | 2 | 2 | 4 | 4 |
| T14 | 2 | 2 | 0 | 4 | 4 |
| T15 | 0 | 2 | 2 | 4 | 4 |
| Mean | 0.2 | 1.5 | 1.4 | 3.8 | 3.6 |

These results invite the question of whether a similar difference, 85% versus 46%, holds also for the rest of the T and NoT groups, i.e. for students who reported a level of motivation that was lower than 5. In order to find this out, we need to consider each individual student's learning score. Table 5 gives these scores for the ten T students.

These less motivated T students actually had a higher mean learning score (1.4) compared to the highly motivated T students (1.2). Their improvement

**Table 6.** Restults for the less motivated NoT students (N = 10)

| Student (N = 10) | Pre-test score (max. 4.0) | Interval translation test score (max. 3.0) | 'Learning' (difference between pre-test score and interval translation test score) | Motivation (ranging from 1 to 5) | Work effort (ranging from 1 to 5) |
|---|---|---|---|---|---|
| NoT 1 | 0 | 0 | 0 | 3 | 3 |
| NoT 2 | 0 | 1 | 1 | 4 | 3 |
| NoT 5 | 1 | 1 | 0 | 2 | 2 |
| NoT 6 | 0 | 1 | 1 | 4 | 4 |
| NoT 7 | 2 | 2 | 0 | 3 | 3 |
| NoT 8 | 0 | 1 | 1 | 3 | 3 |
| NoT 9 | 0 | 3 | 3 | 4 | 3 |
| NoT 10 | 0 | 1 | 1 | 2 | 1 |
| NoT 11 | 0 | 0 | 0 | 3 | 3 |
| NoT 14 | 0 | 0 | 0 | 4 | 4 |
| Mean | 0.3 | 1.0 | 0.9 | 3.2 | 2.9 |

from the *pre-test score* to the *interval translation test score* was 46% of the maximum improvement possible, which is identical to the corresponding figure for the highly motivated T students.

Table 6 gives us the results for the less motivated NoT students.

The results for these less motivated NoT students point in the direction one would expect: their mean learning score is considerably lower (0.9) than that of the highly motivated NoT students (2.2), and lower than that of the less motivated T students (whose learning score was 1.4).

The other important result, i.e. the improvement out of possible improvement was 26% for the less motivated NoT students, compared to 46% for the less motivated T students, which, again, would be expected. For ease of reference, Table 7 provides the results in per cent for *improvement out of possible improvement* for the four groups of students (1. highly motivated T students, 2. highly motivated NoT students, 3. less motivated T students, and 4. less motivated NoT students).

These results show that there is something remarkable about the highly motivated NoT students as they so clearly outperform the highly motivated T students. This impressive performance by the highly motivated NoT students is not at all matched by the *less* motivated NoT students, who were outperformed by the less motivated T students (26% compared to 46%).

Table 7. Relative improvement of the four groups

| Group | Improvement in per cent (out of possible improvement) max. 100% |
|---|---|
| T highly motivated (N = 5) | 46% |
| NoT highly motivated (N = 5) | 85% |
| T less motivated (N = 10) | 46% |
| NoT less motivated (N = 10) | 26% |

## Discussion

This study shows that, with regard to the use of the zero versus the definite article in English noun phrases with generic versus specific reference, highly motivated learners exposed to L2 exercises can perform as well as, or even better, on a translation task than a group of similarly highly motivated learners who have done translation exercises. The results also show that the learners in the experimental groups perform rather similarly in the tests, whereas students in the NoG group perform considerably worse. The latter results support the hypothesis that the T and NoT groups would perform similarly. It was, in all likelihood, the absence of explicit grammar instruction with ensuing production practice that made the results of the NoG stand out as being worse.

These findings could lead one to assume that grammar exercises involving translation may be inferior to non-contrastive exercises. It seems that the T group had a great deal going for it: higher mean scores for both motivation and work effort, yet they do not perform better than the NoT group, not even in the interval translation test. However, caution is necessary when interpreting these results. Both the number of subjects and the number of test items are restricted, and inferential statistical analysis was not carried out. This study needs to be replicated and expanded, in terms of test items and number of subjects, to permit conclusions to be drawn.

What this study has shown, however, is that four highly motivated adult L2 learners *can* use newly learned and difficult L2 structures correctly in a translation task despite not having been exposed to translation exercises. These four students make up 27% (4/15) of the entire NoT group.

One may wonder whether properties of the exercise material other than that of 'translation' or 'no translation' could lead to enhanced learning. Consider the following four Swedish sentences used with the T group and compare with the gap exercises done with the NoT group:

1. Matpriserna har gått upp med 10 procent på tio år.
   *Gloss*: [Food prices have gone up by 10 per cent over the last ten years.]
2. Den brittiska industrin håller på att ändras; stålindustrin får en allt mindre betydelse.
   *Gloss*: [British industry is changing; the steel industry is no longer as important.]
3. Den svenska ekonomin är i gott skick och arbetslösheten minskar.
   *Gloss*: [The Swedish economy is in good shape and unemployment is dropping.]
4. Föroreningarna utgör ett hot för miljön.
   *Gloss*: [Pollution is a threat to the environment.]

---

1. This year, _____ food prices have gone up by 2 per cent.
2. _____ British industry is changing; _____ steel industry is no longer very important.
3. _____ Swedish economy is doing well and _____ unemployment is dropping.
4. _____ pollution is a threat to _____ environment.

It seems reasonable to assume that students working with full sentences to be translated are faced with a greater cognitive load in that they need to deal with more potential difficulties simultaneously than do students who are asked to consider gaps within sentences in L2. In addition to being in the L2, the gap exercises are more focused on the target structure. The focus inherent in the gap exercises may be one factor contributing to enhanced learning. In order to properly address the issue of the effect of translation versus no translation, exercises would have to be designed in such a way that there is an identical or at least similar degree of focus.

Another reason for the superiority of the gap exercises may be the fact that the target structure is of a binary kind, i.e. either you use the definite article or you do not. Gap exercises may work particularly well for this kind of target structure.

What is remarkable about the four NoT top achievers is probably the following: they are very motivated and they were given highly focused practice at using the target structure. It is, after all, not surprising that a high level of motivation coupled with sharply focused production exercises produce outstanding results. In addition, the highly successful NoT learners may have high levels of aptitude; we do not know: aptitude was not controlled for by this study (and controlling this would indeed have been very difficult).

Motivation may be a particularly potent factor for success in the kind of focused test of explicit knowledge of a grammatical structure of which the interval test is an example. One would assume that highly motivated students pay more attention in class and are more likely to ask questions about their erroneous attempts at solving a particular exercise. In addition to this, highly motivated learners may be more careful when completing tests. Perhaps motivation is a particularly potent factor leading to success in classroom settings which require concentrated and focused learning efforts on specific L2 structures.

## Conclusion

This study has shown that four of the highly motivated learners in this study performed very well on a translation task targeting a binary grammatical structure despite not having been exposed to translation exercises.

Weaknesses of this study include the fact that the data are limited in size, that differences between groups were not analysed statistically, and that only the learners' explicit knowledge was tapped in that tests and exercises focused exclusively on form. We do not know how well the top achievers of this study would have performed if using the target structures in a task where they would need to generate the propositional content as well as encode the language.

The results imply that if translation is used in the L2 classroom, it should be used only in conjunction with exercises in the target language[9] which allow for a sharp focus on difficult L2 structures. As this study was designed, it was of course the researcher in me (rather than the teacher in me) that forced two extremes on the two experimental groups (one group – only translation exercises, the other group – exercises in the target language only). If we expect our students to do well both when translating and when operating directly in L2, we need to stimulate their minds using a range of exercises. Some of these may require translation, whereas some should make learners operate directly in the L2. Exercises to be used initially should be designed in such a way that there is a sharp focus on the target structure.

However, as this study is conducted in an area which is very much unexplored empirically and therefore not highly developed with regard to research methodology, a great deal still remains to be done. For example, we need to find out whether a particular type of exercise is suitable to a certain kind of structure. Further, through focusing translation exercises more clearly on the target structure, we can develop a more precise way of measuring the effect of translation.

A means of indirectly assessing the value of exercises is to examine the type of discourse engendered in the L2 classroom. Recordings of lessons in the T and NoT groups were made as part of this project and analysis is underway. Moreover, through analysing the results of the pre-tests and post-tests of this study (which include a larger number of test items), we will be able to find out whether the remarkable NoT students continue to outperform the other students, and whether they do so in translation as well as in a written retelling directly in English.

Finally, this small-scale empirical undertaking has generated three hypotheses, ready for further testing: firstly, in initial stages of learning, gap exercises in L2 involving difficult grammatical structures of a binary kind are more conducive to learning than are translation exercises which require learners to translate full sentences from L1 to L2. Secondly, L2 learners with a combination of certain characteristics (high motivation, and good aptitude?) can learn difficult L2 grammatical structures well using any kind of form-focused production exercise. Thirdly, with regard to tests of difficult L2 structures, learners are more successful at completing gap tests in L2 than tests involving the translation of full sentences from L1 to L2.

## Acknowledgements

I am deeply grateful to all students who very readily and willingly agreed to participate as subjects in this study. In addition, I wish to thank the following colleagues who helped me make this study possible: Mats Johansson at Lund University, Ursula Wallin of Halmstad University and Ulla Ahlqvist at Per Brahe Upper Secondary School in Jönköping, Sweden.

## Notes

1. A more recent study is Biçer (2002), but as it compares two different ways of using translation for L2 proficiency enhancement ('process translation' versus 'translation used the traditional way') it is not immediately relevant here.

2. This is indeed the traditional way of teaching L2 grammar and proficiency, still adhered to at many European universities, and therefore referred to as the "academic style" by Cook

(2001). Questionnaires sent in 1999 to all 24 Swedish universities and colleges where English was taught revealed that *all* taught English grammar in this way.

**3.** In the gap test, there are six gaps. However, only three of them constitute test items (viz. *unemployment, people,* and *Swedish society*). The reason for excluding the other three was that for these, there are no differences between Swedish and English with regard to the use of the definite article (and students may be successful at these because of positive transfer rather than as a sign of learning).

**4.** Swedish and English differ markedly with regard to this structure. In English, NPs such as *British industry* and *food prices* are typically used with the zero article (e.g. *It is absurd not to give them the chance, and help* **British industry** *and world science* (British National Corpus B7C 2058, bold added), and *Food subsidies are reduced or thrown out altogether and* **food prices** *may double or triple overnight* (British National Corpus HH3 5803, bold added). In Swedish, on the other hand, the translation equivalents of *British industry* and *food prices* require the use of the definite article ('**den** brittiska industri**n**' and 'matpriser**na**'). In the case of *British industry*, where an adjective modifies the head noun, Swedish has redundancy in that both the definite article ('den') and a suffix ('-n') signalling definiteness are necessary.

**5.** A mean of 5.0 would have meant that *all* learners had circled 5 on a scale ranging from 1 to 5 for motivation, where 5 indicated the highest possible level of motivation.

**6.** The mean scores for work effort were calculated in the same way as for motivation, i.e. an average of 5.0 would have meant *all* students selecting 5 on a scale ranging from 1 to 5 for work effort, where 5 was the highest possible level of work effort.

**7.** This figure was arrived at by adding the learning scores (Table 3, column 4) for each student: 3+2+0+0+1 = 6.

**8.** This figure was arrived at by multiplying 3.0 (= the maximum score on the translation interval test) by 5 (= the number of students in the group), which is 15. Then 2 (for T6's pre-test score) was subtracted from 15, which gives us 13.

**9.** This is indeed the view expressed in several publications discussing the appropriate place of translation in L2 instruction (see, for example, Duff 1989; Munro 1992; Owen 2003; Rivera-Mills & Gantt 1999; Ross 2000; Stern 1992; Tudor 1987). However, none of these publications is based on empirical data; rather they are all based on the author's experience and intuition.

# References

Barbosa, H. G. & Neiva, A. M. S. (2003). "Using think-aloud protocols to investigate the translation process of foreign language learners and experienced translators". In F. Alves (Ed.), *Triangulating Translation*. Amsterdam and Philadelphia: John Benjamins.

Berggren, I. (1972). "Does the use of translation exercises have negative effects on the learning of a second language?" *Rapport 14*. Department of English, Gothenburg University, Sweden.

Biçer, A. (2002). Teaching Translation at English Language Teaching Departments: Process Approach vs. Traditional Approach. Unpublished PhD dissertation, Çukorova University, Turkey. British National Corpus: http://www.natcorp.ox.ac.uk

Cook, V. (2001). *Second Language Learning and Language Teaching: Third Edition*. London: Edward Arnold.

Duff, A. (1989). *Translation*. Oxford: Oxford University Press.

Enkvist, I. (1994). "Hur gör universitetsstuderande när de översätter? En studie i hur svenska studenter översätter till spanska" ["What do university undergraduates do when they translate? A study of Swedish students translating into Spanish"]. In M. Linnarud (Ed.), *Språk-Utvärdering-Test*. [Rapport från ASLA:s höstsymposium, Karlstad, 10–12 November 1994.]

Fraser, J. (1995). "Professional versus Student Behaviour". In C. Dollerup & V. Appel (Eds.), *Teaching Translation and Interpreting 3: New Horizons: Papers from the third language international conference, Elsinore, Denmark, 9–11 June 1995*. Amsterdam and Philadelphia: John Benjamins.

Fraser, J. (1996). "'I understand the French, But I Don't Know How to Put It Into English': Developing Undergraduates' Awareness of and Confidence in the Translation Process". In P. Sewell & I. Higgins (Eds.), *Teaching Translation in Universities: Present and Future Perspectives*. London: CILT.

Hummel, K. (1995). "Translation and Second Language Learning". *The Canadian Modern Language Review, 51*, 444–455.

Krings, H. P. (1987). "The Use of Introspective Data in Translation". In C. Færch & G. Kasper (Eds.), *Introspection in Second Language Acquisition*. Clevedon: Multilingual Matters.

Lörscher, W. (1993). "Translation Process Analysis". In Y. Gambier & J. Tommola (Eds.), *Translation & Knowledge. Scandinavian Symposium on Translation Theory* (pp. 195–212). University of Turku, Centre for Translation and Interpreting.

Malmkjær, K. (1994). "Translation in Language Teaching". *Working Papers in English and Applied Linguistics, 1*, 123–126.

Malmkjær, K. (1998). "Introduction: Translation and Language Teaching". In K. Malmkjær (Ed.), *Translation and Language Teaching: Language Teaching and Translation*. Manchester: St. Jerome.

Munro, S. R. (1992). "Translation: A tool or a goal?" *JCLTA, 1* (2), 45–53.

Omura, Y. (1996). Role of Translation in Second Language Acquisition: Do Learners Automatically Translate? Unpublished PhD dissertation. The University of Texas at Austin.

Owen, D. (2003 January). "Where's the treason in translation?" *Humanising Language Teaching Magazine*.

Rivera-Mills, S. V. & Gantt, B. N. (1999). "From Linguistic Analysis to Cultural Awareness: A Translation Framework for the Spanish Language Classroom". *JOLIB, 10* (2), 1–13.

Ross, N. J. (2000). "Interference and intervention: using translation in the EFL classroom". *Modern English Teacher, 9* (3), 61–66.

Slavikova, H. (1990). Translating and the Acquisition of Italian as a Second Language. Unpublished PhD dissertation. University of Toronto.

Stern, H. H. (1992). *Issues and Options in Language Teaching*. Oxford: OUP.

Tudor, I. (1987). "A framework for the translational analysis of texts". *The Linguist, 26* (2), 80–82.

Uzawa, K. (1994). Translating and Writing Processes of Adult Second Language Learners. Unpublished PhD dissertation. University of British Columbia.

Uzawa, K. (1996). "Second Language Learners' Processes of L1 Writing, L2 Writing, and Translation from L1 into L2". *Journal of Second Language Writing, 5,* 271–194.

## Appendix 1: Interval test: Translation

*Var god översätt följande text till engelska* [*Please translate the following into English*]:

De här nyheterna om arbetslösheten gör att folket inte litar på politikerna. Det finns inga bevis för att analyserna är rätt gjorda. Ett råd jag skulle vilja ge är att allmänheten måste tränas i att bli mer kritisk till tidningarna. Det svenska samhället behöver bli mer kritiskt till pressen, faktiskt.

_____

_____

_____

_____

_____

_____

_____

_____

_____

_____

Förnamn [Your first name] _____

## Appendix 2: Gap test

*Fyll i den bestämda artikeln (the) i de luckor där den behövs [Please insert the definite article where necessary]*:

This news about _____ unemployment causes _____ people not to trust _____ politicians. There is no evidence that the analyses have been carried out correctly. One piece of advice I would like to offer is that _____ public ought to be taught to become more critical of _____ newspapers. _____ Swedish society needs to be more critical of _____ press, actually.

**Förnamn [Your first name]** _____

# Do English-speakers really need other languages?*

Stephen Barbour

In this paper I shall discuss the crisis perceived by many in the unwillingness of speakers of English in Britain to learn other languages to a high level of proficiency (see particularly Nuffield 2000). My remarks apply in differing degrees to other English-speaking countries; I think, for instance, that the crisis is more severe in the United States, much less severe in Ireland, and circumstances are quite different in Canada, the last two being in any case officially bilingual states. In Britain today there can be no doubt that the learning and teaching of modern languages is in something of a crisis. This is perhaps most evident in higher education, where numbers of students reading for degrees in languages are in general slow decline compared to numbers in many other subject areas (see Nuffield 2000: 50–56).

In this paper I shall address the following questions:

1. Why has the crisis arisen?
2. Is it a significant crisis? Does a lack of knowledge of other languages bring disadvantages to individuals or to the community?
3. If it does matter, how can the situation be remedied? How can we persuade larger numbers of students to take advantage of the excellent courses that are provided by our Universities?

There are, I think, many reasons for the crisis. One is, I believe, a fundamental shift in the nature of higher education. Until about the 1960s our Universities, as distinct from some other institutions such as Technical Colleges or Teacher Training Colleges, catered generally for the relatively privileged. In such institutions some subjects, such as medicine and engineering, were studied for utilitarian reasons, but others, such as history and languages, were often studied simply for their intrinsic interest. People who studied them often moved on gaining their degrees into jobs that had no obvious connection with the subject of study; employers regarded degrees as a kind of proof that their new employee was reasonably intelligent, and that, by attending a University, particularly a prestigious one, a young person had acquired the social self confidence needed for (say) a managerial role.

Since that time much has changed. Although higher education still does not attract a true cross-section of the population, there are now many more students from beyond the white middle class. Many such students see little point in higher education that does not directly and obviously improve their job prospects. Additionally higher education has become steadily more expensive for students themselves and for their families, a development that encourages applications for courses that lead in a fairly straightforward way to well-paid employment. Languages degrees are often seen as leading in this obvious sense only to teaching, a profession in which pay and working conditions had, until recently, steadily worsened in relative terms. Actually many employers see things differently and value the skill that linguists can offer. Many simply need people with a knowledge of other languages and are having to recruit speakers of other languages abroad, while British universities continue to recruit, to degree courses in languages, chiefly middle-class students (see Footitt 2000).

Another reason for rather low numbers taking other languages may be that they are seen as 'difficult'. The cause of this may lie in general changes to school syllabuses. In the 1950s a high proportion of potential students of modern languages had also encountered Latin, even Classical Greek, whose structure, and cultural background, are much less familiar to the modern English-speaker, than those of French or German. In contrast these modern languages seemed relatively easy. Classical languages are now very rare in our school system.

There have been bold attempts to make modern languages attractive to a larger and more diverse student body. Britain did indeed for a while lead the world in vocationally oriented language studies, and university courses recruited well that combined modern languages and some more obviously vocationally oriented subject such as law or economics or business studies, pioneered particularly in the technological universities and the former polytechnics, but also elsewhere. The central premise of such courses is that knowledge of a language, or of a language and the associated culture, is a useful professional asset, as well as perhaps having intrinsic interest. I myself taught German on such courses for many years, and what we, in effect, said to our potential applicants was "You need to know German well in order to communicate with

German-speakers in a professional context". They believed us, and for a number of years such courses recruited strongly. Now, however, many of them are in difficulties.

Why do even vocationally oriented courses often now have recruitment difficulties? I think that xenophobia cannot be discounted. However, I think a major reason, which is surprisingly little discussed in Britain, is simply that English is the foremost language of international communication. English-speakers who have travelled are most likely to have visited major cities and tourist resorts, and in such places they will have discovered that they can get by in English.[1] Those who are not very interested in other languages, or not very confident linguistically, will hence not be motivated to learn them, as they may appear unnecessary for their purposes. Those who are interested may be demotivated by the experience, quite often reported to me, of working hard to construct an utterance in another language, only to receive an instant reply in English. I am convinced that the proficiency of English-speakers in other languages, even of quite well motivated students, is adversely affected by the knowledge that, if the going gets tough, they can switch to English. Even more demotivating is the experience of not a few of my students in Germany, who have been asked "Why are you learning German? We all speak English."

Is this a crisis of any great significance? Does it have any importance beyond the fact that it is threatening the viability of languages departments in our Universities? I think it does. Firstly, it means that a very high proportion of English-speakers in Britain and elsewhere are monolingual, a much higher proportion than is the case for speakers of most other languages. I now want to challenge what is, I believe, a very common popular assumption not only among English-speakers, but also among speakers of a number of other national languages with millions of speakers; it is that monolingualism, the ability to function effectively only in one language, or even only in one narrow range of varieties of one language, is the normal human condition. The corollary of this assumption is that the individual who can function effectively in more than one language is unusual, gifted, special. This is, in my view, simply mistaken. Monolingualism can in fact be seen as a product of modern conditions, where, in certain key areas, chiefly in western Europe, the growth of large, powerful nation-states led in all sorts of spheres to internal uniformity and external demarcation. In language this led to pressure inside states for greater use of the standard variety of the 'national' language, and to encouragement to use the national languages of other states only when this was necessary for trade or diplomacy (see Barbour & Carmichael 2000: passim). In many parts of the world monolingualism has simply not developed; a high proportion of the world's population uses at least two languages: a local or ethnically specific language and a language of wider communication; I include here cases where people use two or more varieties which are conventionally labelled 'dialects' of the same language, but where these dialects show major divergences from each other in structure and vocabulary – such cases are represented by Arabic and Chinese where varieties of the language may be as different from each other as are many distinct languages elsewhere in the world. An example of a multilingual state, not too untypical, is Tanzania, where everyone speaks a local or ethnically specific language, where a high proportion is fluent Kiswahili, which is the everyday language of only one relatively small ethnic group, and where a minority, but a highly significant minority, is fluent in English (see Mazrui & Mazrui 1998: 125–191).

Bilingualism or multilingualism are, then, not abnormal human conditions, but monolingualism may well be. But an abnormal condition does not need to be detrimental to the individual's well-being. I do, however, believe that monolingualism is detrimental, particularly if combined with monoculturalism. The two need not go together; it is perfectly possible to have culturally varied experience within one language, or, indeed, to express a narrow range of cultural experience in two languages. However, in practice they often do go together.

The disadvantages of monolingualism are many. There is, for example, considerable research evidence that monolinguals over the age of puberty are usually much poorer at language learning than are others. If an adult hence finds that he or she suddenly should learn another language for personal or career reasons, then this may be an enormously difficult task for a monolingual; a bilingual is much more likely to cope, all other things being equal (see Singleton 1989). People with wide linguistic and cultural experience are also likely to be better communicators in their first language; they are more likely to be aware of what is linguistically and culturally marked in their own experience, and to avoid it in communicating with people of different linguistic and cultural backgrounds. The speaker of British English who talks about a 'sticky wicket', or who uses sentences with temporal expressions as subjects, such as 'last year saw an increase in drug related crime' is not communicating well in English if the interlocutors come from a cultural and linguistic background beyond the English-speaking countries.

Much more seriously, for a monolingual, communication with speakers of other languages is dependent on the ability and willingness of the others to translate. My own specialism is German, and I shall now give examples of how communication in the widest sense between monoglot English-speakers and speakers of German can be problematic if the English-speakers rely entirely on the German-speakers to speak and write English. Communication between German-speakers and English-speakers is merely an example here; similar problems will arise if speakers of other languages are involved.

The first problem is that a very great deal is simply not translated. This might be written texts the English-speaker might want to read to be informed about the cultural and political background against which German-speakers operate, or simply fascinating literary texts which are good to read. Or it might be asides in business negotiations, which one side might prefer the other side not to understand, but which might be important.

What is translated would, in one kind of ideal world, always benefit from the input of a competent professional translator or interpreter, but in practice this is often not the case. It is rarely the case in informal or spontaneous texts, written or spoken, and, in any case, through lack of awareness of linguistic issues, through lack of resources or time, or through confidence in their command of the language, many users of English would simply not contemplate employing professionals. The result, in the case of German-speakers, is a variety or varieties of English which shows varying degrees of German influence, and which can sometimes be misleading or incomprehensible for English-speakers. In my own recent experience of what I shall term "German English", I have encountered the following problems. In grammar the frequent absence of the aspect distinctions is confusing. Consider the following exchange: At work, my question "Is Karl here?" elicited a response from a German-speaking colleague "I didn't see him". My reaction was puzzlement, since I thought it highly likely that he was there, and I expected the answer "I haven't seen him", which leaves open the possibility that he might be around somewhere. The answer "I didn't see him" more or less excludes this possibility, it suggests "He was here earlier, but I did not see him, and now he has gone." As in similar translated varieties, English that is (essentially) translated from German has unfamiliar usage of prepositions and other grammatical elements. In a journal article written in English by a German-speaker I recently had to struggle to understand the phrase "in the countries without former Soviet domination"; it could have meant either "in those countries which used to be under Soviet domination" or "in those countries which never experienced Soviet domination". Only after several instances of the phrase was I able to deduce from other evidence that the former meaning was intended.

In speaking English, German-speakers use many words that resemble German words closely in form. These may then, however, be used with the meanings of the similar German word, and this may differ markedly from the meaning which the word usually has in English. In most large German shops the place where you pay is called the "Kasse", a single noun, which is usually translated into the related single noun "Cash" in German English. This is seriously misleading for a speaker of British English, since it suggests that the only method of payment is in banknotes and coins, that customers have to go somewhere else to use a credit card, or even that the shop does not accept credit cards (in fact, in my experience, they usually do accept credit cards). The British equivalent, of course, is the phrase "Please pay here". In conversations, misunderstandings of this kind can be overcome by questions, but this is not possible in written texts, and difficult in formal lectures. In a recent lecture a respected German linguist discussed at some length the language use of 'academics'. As an academic, a university lecturer, I think this is an interesting topic, but academics are relatively a very small group, so a study of their language use is of limited applicability. Only gradually did it become clear that he meant graduates, a much larger group, who are termed *Akademiker* in German.

One way of describing what is happening here, is to say that a German variety of English is developing, or we could say that a range of German varieties of English or a range of European varieties is developing. I would regard this development as almost inevitable. No language, at least no language spoken by millions of speakers, is uniform; divergence and diversity is the norm. However, there are often forces creating some degree of uniformity or standardisation; if there are not, then a situation arises where a single language develops into more than one mutually unintelligible language, as happened to Latin after the collapse of the Roman Empire, when it gave rise to Spanish, French, Italian, Romanian and others. Standardising forces are communication between speakers of the language across the entire territory in which it is used, and across ethnic, national and social barriers, and the teaching of a common standardised variety. But there are forces working against standardisation; even in the era of electronic communication, there is certainly not thorough-going linguistic interaction between speakers of English from all of the groups that use the language. People communicate overwhelmingly within their own regions, nations, ethnic groups, professions and other interest groups. Even where English is the only widespread language in a state, as it is in Britain, the USA or Australia, or where it is an important language of wider communication within a state, as in India or Nigeria, there is very great variety, particularly in speech, and standards used in teaching vary quite noticeably between the states. The British social and educational elite, who had, and still do have, a key role in determining standards, are remarkably non-prescriptive, compared to other elites, such as the French, and this works against uniformity. This is sometimes seen as a facet of liberalism and tolerance, in contrast to French authoritarianism, but this is not the whole story; a lack of desire to instil standard British English in colonial peoples also arose from a feeling that this was an absurd exercise, since an African, for example, could never be an English gentleman, and so should not aspire to sound like one (see Anderman 1999). Within Britain, standard British English grammar and lexicon have, of course, been vigorously taught, but the teaching of a standard pronunciation is found chiefly in elite independent schools, scarcely elsewhere, in contrast to a universal teaching of a standard pronunciation in some other European countries, at least in earlier times.

At the present time, English-speaking linguistic tolerance is thoroughly espoused by linguists, and can, I believe, be seen as a highly positive attitude – telling people that their English is wrong, when they use English always, or frequently, and when it may be an important element of their individual or group identity, can be insulting and damaging.

However, our liberalism is not shared by all. In the linguistic market place, the standard varieties of the generally monoglot English-speaking countries, such as Britain and the USA, are more widely understood, and more highly valued, than other varieties (see Quirk 1985). Users of other varieties sadly find that they do have to shift towards these prestige norms in certain circumstances, for example if working as professional translators.

In states where English has no long local tradition of widespread use, and in states which were never colonised by English-speakers, the situation used to be different. There was an overt orientation towards the norm of (usually) either Britain or the USA, and deviations from those norms, if detected, were labelled as 'errors' in a quite uncomplicated way. This is, however, changing, as monoglot speakers of English form an ever-declining proportion of the total of users of the language. The 'decline of the native speaker' as it has been called (see Graddol 1999), has many symptoms; one of them is that some materials for teaching English in other European countries have for some time now departed, as does the course *Contacts* (Piepho & Bredella 1976), from the assumption that learners are acquiring the language in order to communicate with British or American people, and correctly work on the assumption that Germans, for example, now learn English to communicate not only with Britons or Indians, but also Chinese, Italians and even the French (see Berns 1995).

Two changes can be detected. There is firstly often a great confidence among users of English for whom it is a language learned at school or later.

Given the relatively weak tradition of prescriptivity among English-speakers, and also given certain norms of politeness and tolerance that they may observe, they may be reluctant to correct the English of other users. This seems very varied. I recently read that researchers in applied linguistics whose normal medium is a relatively lesser-used language, are deterred from publishing, because they have to publish in English, and because of the costs of having their work corrected by native-speakers (Candlin 2000). German-speaking writers who publish in English in the British Journal *German Politics* have no such problem, their work is published in uncorrected German English. Given that their English is imparted through education, and given that, in many European countries, the education system enjoys high status, there can even arise a view that a European variety is somehow more correct than British varieties. This view is reinforced by relatively weak prescriptivity of Britain; although German is arguably a much more diverse language than English, educated speakers of the language are (or were) more prepared to move to a narrowly defined prestige norm in formal contexts than are speakers of English, who (for example) are usually very reluctant indeed to shift their pronunciation to the prestige norm RP. This can lead German-speakers to believe that British people are using a non-standard dialect, when the user of British English may perceive their own speech as standard, but with a regional accent. For example one of my former students, who spoke standard Scottish English, easily comprehensible in England and also socially quite prestigious, was amazed to be told by the German-speaking English teacher in the school where he worked during his year abroad that he must abandon his dialect in the classroom (see also Durrell 1995).

Does any of this matter? Perhaps constant interaction between users of the language, whatever their linguistic background, will ensure that mutual comprehensibility will not be lost, and that users of English will increasingly be aware of those facets of their own usage which are only (say) Greek English or German English, and those which are international. They will hence parallel the behaviour of many Indian speakers of English, who are aware of Indianisms, which they should avoid when speaking to non-Indians. I think this may happen, but modifications due to a pressure to be comprehensible may not readily occur in texts in which there is only very slow feedback from addressees, if any at all, such as written texts and public announcements. I usually cope well with German English because I also know German, but I sometimes have serious problems with Greek English – my knowledge of Greek being very limited. On a recent visit to Greece the departure of our return aircraft was delayed because none of the passengers (apparently all resident in Britain) understood the instruction over the public address system for us to proceed to the 'Extra-Senggen departure area'. As far as I know, no term for 'special departure area for those holding passports of EU states which are not parties to the Schengen agreement' exists in English; and in any case, the Greek rendering of 'Schengen' sounded like 'Senggen'.

It is difficult to assess the import of comprehension problems of this type. Are they amusing curiosities, are they difficulties which the mobile section of the world's population will have to learn to live with, or are they symptoms of possible communication breakdown? In any case it seems to me that it would be beneficial to have a body of informed people who are aware of what is happening, and can understand and explain it. Translators, or, more exactly, well trained translators, or other people with translator awareness, would constitute such a body of informed individuals. There is, then, a clear need for more training of, and more use of professional translators, but also for the creation of a larger group with translator awareness.

How do we achieve this? One of the most successful translation classes I have taught was an undergraduate module at Middlesex University devised by Sue Myles. It was concerned very much with translator education, but was also designed as a first step in translator training. It focussed on translation from German into English. The members of the class came from a variety of linguistic and cultural backgrounds; not only were there speakers of British English and of German, there were also speakers of other languages, studying a range of other subjects, who wished to extend their knowledge of German (almost by definition they were also concerned to extend their knowledge of English). I remember teaching students who had come to Britain from Italy, Spain, Greece, the Caribbean and Somalia. The module's great virtue was that it was highly student-centred. Every class started from what the students knew about the language and about the subject matter of the text. The subject matter was discussed first, which often highlighted differences between the cultural and political background in the German-speaking countries and in Britain, and elsewhere, interesting in itself, but also highly relevant to translation. Students then prepared translations, from which they took turns to read in a following class. This highlighted the problems they encountered of a more linguistic nature. Time and time again students wrote or spoke English which other members of the group, from other backgrounds, found problematic. In other words, the module amounted to a very helpful exercise in examining the problems of cross-linguistic and cross-cultural communication. A sobering outcome was that some students, who had considered themselves translators before they took the module, came to realise that they had probably been producing seriously misleading texts.

Communication in the world today cannot rely exclusively on speakers of other languages learning English. Unless there is an input from speakers of English who have also learnt other languages, texts will be, to say the least, inefficient. It is perhaps unrealistic to expect sufficient speakers of English to learn languages with a relatively limited area of use, but then we need to make sure that (say) Greek-speaking translators from Greek into English have a very good knowledge indeed of widespread English varieties. Within the European Union, much is possible. Someone who wants to translate into a language learnt only at school has the opportunity to study translation in an environment where that language dominates. This could mean that Schools of Translation or specialist degrees in translation could, wherever their location, become truly international institutions or courses, to the enormous benefit of all concerned. Thanks to teachers like Sue Myles, the courses from which all could benefit are already partly in place.

I asked earlier in the paper how to overcome English-speakers' reluctance to learn other languages. There is no easy answer to this and I think it has now sadly become quite ingrained in the culture. One strategy is to make people aware of the disadvantages of monolingualism. Another is making our translation schools and departments into places of attractive international encounter, offering courses of the kind I have described. As well as translation classes we can often use existing expertise to impart knowledge of the institutions and culture of the area where the language is spoken.

To return to my title; "Do speakers of English really need other languages?". Speakers of English can perhaps get by without other languages, but, trapped within English, they will not only miss a great deal, they might even find themselves isolated in a pocket of monoglot-style English in a multilingual world, totally dependent on others to interpret that world for them in a whole range of perhaps diverging and only partly comprehensible new varieties of English.

## Notes

* I am grateful to Sheila Barbour for useful comments on an earlier version of this paper

1. Had they ventured further afield, or spoken to a broad social cross-section, their experience might have been rather different – see, for example, de Laine (1999) for a report

on inadequacies in the command of English among the Danes, a group who seem, on first impression, to have almost universal excellent knowledge of the language.

# References

Anderman, G. (1999). "European literature in translation: A price to pay". In D. Graddol & U. H. Meinhof (Eds.), *English in a Changing World* (pp. 69–78). Oxford: Catchline/AILA.

Barbour, S. & Carmichael, C. (Eds.). (2000). *Language and Nationalism in Europe*. Oxford: Oxford University Press.

Berns, M. (1995). "English in Europe: Whose language, which culture?" *International Journal of Applied Linguistics, 5*, 21–32.

Candlin, C. (2000). "Opinion". *AILA News, 4* (1).

de Laine, M. (1999). "Danes lost for words on the net". *The Times Higher Education Supplement,* 24th September 1999.

Durrell, M. (1995). "Sprachliche Variation als Kommunikationsbarriere". In H. Popp (Ed.), *Deutsch als Fremdsprache. An den Quellen eines Faches* (pp. 417–428). Munich: Iudicium.

Footitt, H. (2000). "Elite corps". *The Guardian,* 24th October, 2000.

Graddol, D. (1999). "The decline of the native speaker". In D. Graddol & U. H. Meinhof (Eds.), *English in a Changing World* (pp. 57–68). Oxford: Catchline/AILA.

Mazrui, A. Al. & Mazrui, A. M. (1998). *The Power of Babel: Language and Governance in the African Experience*. Chicago: University of Chicago Press.

Nuffield (2000). *Languages: The Next Generation. The Final Report and Recommendations of the Nuffield Languages Inquiry.* London: The Nuffield Foundation.

Piepho, H.-E. & Bredella, L. (1976). *Contacts: Integriertes Englischlehrwerk für Klassen 5–10*. Bochum: Kamp.

Quirk, R. (1985). "The English language in a global context". In R. Quirk & H. G. Widdowson (Eds.), *English in the World* (pp. 1–6). Cambridge: Cambridge University Press.

Singleton, D. (1989). *Language Acquisition: the Age Factor*. Clevedon, Philadelphia: Multilingual Matters.

# Index

In the series *Benjamins Translation Library* the following titles have been published thus far or are scheduled for publication:

35  SOMERS, Harold (ed.): Computers and Translation. A translator's guide. 2003. xvi, 351 pp.

36  SCHMID, Monika S.: Translating the Elusive. Marked word order and subjectivity in English-German translation. 1999. xii, 174 pp.

37  TIRKKONEN-CONDIT, Sonja and Riitta JÄÄSKELÄINEN (eds.): Tapping and Mapping the Processes of Translation and Interpreting. Outlooks on empirical research. 2000. x, 176 pp.

38  SCHÄFFNER, Christina and Beverly ADAB (eds.): Developing Translation Competence. 2000. xvi, 244 pp.

39  CHESTERMAN, Andrew, Natividad GALLARDO SAN SALVADOR and Yves GAMBIER (eds.): Translation in Context. Selected papers from the EST Congress, Granada 1998. 2000. x, 393 pp.

40  ENGLUND DIMITROVA, Birgitta and Kenneth HYLTENSTAM (eds.): Language Processing and Simultaneous Interpreting. Interdisciplinary perspectives. 2000. xvi, 164 pp.

41  NIDA, Eugene A.: Contexts in Translating. 2002. x, 127 pp.

42  HUNG, Eva (ed.): Teaching Translation and Interpreting 4. Building bridges. 2002. xii, 243 pp.

43  GARZONE, Giuliana and Maurizio VIEZZI (eds.): Interpreting in the 21st Century. Challenges and opportunities. 2002. x, 337 pp.

44  SINGERMAN, Robert: Jewish Translation History. A bibliography of bibliographies and studies. With an introductory essay by Gideon Toury. 2002. xxxvi, 420 pp.

45  ALVES, Fabio (ed.): Triangulating Translation. Perspectives in process oriented research. 2003. x, 165 pp.

46  BRUNETTE, Louise, Georges BASTIN, Isabelle HEMLIN and Heather CLARKE (eds.): The Critical Link 3. Interpreters in the Community. Selected papers from the Third International Conference on Interpreting in Legal, Health and Social Service Settings, Montréal, Quebec, Canada 22–26 May 2001. 2003. xii, 359 pp.

47  SAWYER, David B.: Fundamental Aspects of Interpreter Education. Curriculum and Assessment. 2004. xviii, 312 pp.

48  MAURANEN, Anna and Pekka KUJAMÄKI (eds.): Translation Universals. Do they exist? 2004. vi, 224 pp.

49  PYM, Anthony: The Moving Text. Localization, translation, and distribution. 2004. xviii, 223 pp.

50  HANSEN, Gyde, Kirsten MALMKJÆR and Daniel GILE (eds.): Claims, Changes and Challenges in Translation Studies. Selected contributions from the EST Congress, Copenhagen 2001. 2004. xiv, 320 pp. [EST Subseries 1]

51  CHAN, Leo Tak-hung: Twentieth-Century Chinese Translation Theory. Modes, issues and  debates. 2004. xvi, 277 pp.

52  HALE, Sandra Beatriz: The Discourse of Court Interpreting. Discourse practices of the law, the witness and the interpreter. 2004. xviii, 267 pp.

53  DIRIKER, Ebru: De-/Re-Contextualizing Conference Interpreting. Interpreters in the Ivory Tower? 2004. x, 223 pp.

54  GONZÁLEZ DAVIES, Maria: Multiple Voices in the Translation Classroom. Activities, tasks and projects. 2004. x, 262 pp.

55  ANGELELLI, Claudia V.: Revisiting the Interpreter's Role. A study of conference, court, and medical interpreters in Canada, Mexico, and the United States. 2004. xvi, 127 pp.

56  ORERO, Pilar (ed.): Topics in Audiovisual Translation. 2004. xiv, 227 pp.

57  CHERNOV, Ghelly V.: Inference and Anticipation in Simultaneous Interpreting. A probability-prediction model. Edited with a critical foreword by Robin Setton and Adelina Hild. 2004. xxx, 266 pp. [EST Subseries 2]

58  BRANCHADELL, Albert and Lovell Margaret WEST (eds.): Less Translated Languages. vii, 389 pp. + index. *Expected Winter 04-05*

59  MALMKJÆR, Kirsten (ed.): Translation in Undergraduate Degree Programmes. 2004. vi, 202 pp.

60  TENNENT, Martha (ed.): Training for the New Millennium. Pedagogies for translation and interpreting. xxv, 265 pp. + index. *Expected Spring 2005*

61  HUNG, Eva (ed.): Translation and Cultural Change. Studies in history, norms and image-projection. xvi, 188 pp. + index. *Expected Spring 2005*